MATH SAT 800:
How to Master the Toughest Problems

By:

Daniel Eiblum, M.S.Ed. Editor-in-Chief
Michael Forman, M.S., Editor
Nargess Memarsadeghi, Ph.D.
Kimberly Noonan, M.S.
Matthew Konicki, M.A.
Elnatan Reisner
Hunter Brooks
Asa Pally
Andrew Newens

D1511854

ISBN: 1-4392-0006-8
ISBN-13: 978-1439200063

Visit www.booksurge.com to order additional copies.

Booksurge Publishing
Charleston, SC

CONTENTS

INTRODUCTION

Math SAT 800: How to Master the Toughest Problems contains 425 math SAT problems suited for students who have already taken the SAT or PSAT (or at least a practice SAT test). This book is most appropriate for students who scored 550 or above out of a maximum possible score of 800 on the math portion of the SAT. The chapters in this book will provide students with ample opportunity to practice only the most difficult problems found on the SAT, rated a 4 or a 5 out of 5 on the ETS scale of difficulty. The goal of this book is to maximize your score by zeroing in on only the most difficult problems that appear on the math section of the SAT exam.

How to Use this Book

To begin, we strongly recommend that you take the practice SAT test in chapter 1. Your practice test results will not reflect your potential score, as the problems included in chapter 1 are rated difficult on the SAT, meaning a level 4 or 5 out of 5 on the ETS scale. Your potential score will be significantly higher than your score on this first test, so don't be discouraged if you can solve only a few problems initially. This book will give you the opportunity to practice and solve the most difficult problems. After you have completed most or all of the problems throughout this book, take the second test at the end of the book. You will be amazed at how many more difficult problems you will be able to answer correctly.

As a result of solving the problems in this book, you will be prepared for the more difficult problems on the actual SAT. Our ultimate goal in writing this book is to provide students with enough practice to enter the exam and tackle even the most challenging of questions with confidence.

Some Problem Solving Techniques

This book will provide you with different strategies for mastering the math portion of the SAT. The book will also walk you through solving some of the difficult questions from past SAT exams. Before you get started, we have some general advice that is crucial to mastering the SAT.

- **Practice :** Practice, practice, practice! It can not be stressed enough how important practice is for mastering anything, especially the SAT. Just as you can't learn how to play baseball, play the piano, or become a black belt in karate by reading a book and not actually practicing it, nor will you be able to master the SAT without practice. This book will give you valuable strategies for dealing with all sorts of questions that the SAT will throw at you but these strategies are worthless in a vacuum. If you don't practice, then you will not actually learn how to apply the strategies you learn. Practice also leads us into the next important item to master the SAT.

- **Time management :** The SAT is as much about how you manage your time as much as it is about what you know. For the math sections of the test, you have, on average, a little over one minute per problem. Don't let this amount of time scare you since the easy questions will take less time and leave you more time for the more difficult questions. This leads us to the next item.

- **Learn to skip :** While the questions on the test generally move from easy to hard, it is not a rule. You can find easy problems right after much harder problems. This is especially true on section with the free response questions. The last two or three multiple choice questions before the free response tend to be difficult questions but the first couple of free response questions are easy. Learn to skip the hard ones and come back to them later. **Every single question on the SAT is worth the same number of points!** So answer the ones you can do easily first and come back to the harder ones later. You will have a much easier time if you come back to hard ones than if you spend a lot of time on a hard one only to have to rush through the rest of the section. Also note that since the re-centering happened over ten years ago, it is possible to get an 800 without getting every question right. You can typically skip one or two questions and still get a perfect score. What do you do once you have answered all the easy ones and have to tackle the hard ones? The first you thing you can try is...

- **Use the answers :** For every question, except the ten free response questions, you already have the correct answer on the page. You just have to find it. You can often find it without actually solving the problem. Consider for example the following question :

Josh has 14 coins made up of nickels and dimes. The change adds up to $1.25. How many dimes does he have?

A. 5   B. 7   C. 9   D. 11   E. 13

The algebraic solution would consist of setting up a system on linear equations and solving. Let N be the number of nickels and D be the number of dimes. Then we have that $N + D = 14$ and $0.05N + 0.1D = 1.25$. You could then solve using your favorite method of handling a system of equations. While this will get you the answer, it takes up time that you could use to tackle other questions. Instead of solving, use the answers. Suppose that Josh had 7 dimes. Then he also has 7 nickels. So he has a total of $0.70 + 0.35 = 1.05$ dollars. That answer is too small so the correct choice has to be either 11 or 13. Pick either and check if it works. If it does, you have the answer. If it doesn't, the remaining option is the answer. Note that since the answer choices are almost always in ascending or descending order, by starting with the middle choice, you can often eliminate two of the other choices at the same time. This saves a little bit of time versus trying every single answer choice in order. But what do you do about the ones where the answers are not just numbers but contain variables?

- **Eliminate the variables :** Many of the harder math questions are difficult because they contain very few numbers. So make-up some numbers and put them in place of the variables and try the problem again. Almost every single question like this becomes very easy with numbers. They also become a lot easier to understand if you know what is being asked. What makes this trick extra useful is that you can use those same numbers in place of the same variables in the answers. Once you have solved the problem with your numbers and you know what the answer is, check the given answers with your numbers to see which one matches. Very often only the correct answer will work. But even if more than one works, you will have eliminated some incorrect choices. For example, consider the following question :

Tonya and Steve collected p pounds of newspaper to recycle. If Tonya collected t pounds, which of the following shows the number of pounds collected by Steve?

A. $p + t$ B. $p - t$ C. $p \div t$ D. $t - p$ E. $t \cdot p$

Let's make this easier by setting $p = 25$ and $t = 10$. Then, clearly Steve collected $25 - 10 = 15$ pounds. So the correct answer is B) $p - t$. But even if you can't translate from the numbers back to the variables, you could plug the numbers into every answer choice and see what you get. Then the choice become :

A. 35   B. 15   C. $\frac{25}{10} = \frac{5}{2} = 2.5$ D. -15 E. 250

Only one of these matches what we calculated with our numbers so it must be the correct answer.

Most problems on the math SAT are multiple choice. For these problems you can choose to apply one of the following methods:

- Solve the problem and check to see if your answer appears as one of the answer choices. If it does, you probably reached the correct answer, although the other answer choices are created by ETS with the intention that they could conceivably result from a careless error or incorrect assumption.

- Sometimes, particularly for more visual learners, it is immensely helpful to draw a diagram. For example, if the problem discusses a cylinder that is half full of water that drains over a period of time at a particular rate, by all means, draw the cylinder! This is useful for most people because otherwise you are using part of your brain to visualize something, leaving you with less brain power to solve the problem.

Some More Miscellaneous Problem Solving Methods:

- Read the problem at a rate of speed that would be just right for you to accurately grasp what the content and context are.

- Then read the problem again, and determine what is given and what is being asked. Some problems are written in a way that may seem ambiguous.

- Number the problem of the test on your sheet of paper. This will avoid confusion when copying your answer into the answer grid.

- Jot down what is given, what is needed to solve the problem, and what is the unknown that you need to solve for.

- Decide whether you need to solve or substitute. If you are solving, think about what steps you would need to take and utilize the given information correctly.

- Determine if the givens are sufficient to solve the problem. Usually they are, except sometimes one or more of the units of the data might need to be converted to be consistent with the other/s, such as in a time problem, when some inputs are in hours while others in minutes.

- Solve the problem and check to see if your answer matches one of the answer choices. If not, you may have misread the problem, so start again at step 2.

- Another process useful in solving geometric problems is to write down all the information on a figure that can be derived from the given information before trying to answer the question.

The steps given above collectively represent a general approach. But you must apply specific knowledge to the problem in question. Try to apply the general process to the specific problem. When you work on the problems in this (or any other book), try to understand the process required to solve a problem as opposed to the specific knowledge needed. Hopefully, these tips will get you in the right frame of mind for the rest of the book and for mastering the math SAT.

ABOUT THE AUTHORS

Daniel Eiblum, M.S.Ed., Editor-in-Chief received a BA in Geophysical Sciences from the University of Chicago in 1988, and then earned his Master of Education degree from Johns Hopkins University in 2000. He has over ten years of tutoring experience in mathematics ranging from Algebra I through Calculus, in addition to Math SAT preparation. He founded a tutoring agency in 2000 called, Ivy League Tutoring Connection, that serves the Washington DC - Baltimore Metropolitan area. Currently he resides in Bethesda, MD

Michael Forman, M.S., Editor has both a Bachelor of Science degree (1963) and a Master of Science degree (1965) in Physics and Applied Math from the University of Massachusetts at Lowell. He was a professional mathematician and physicist at NASA for 40 years and has published in several scientific journals. He began tutoring math and physics in January 2005. Math courses include pre-Algebra through Calculus and Math SAT preparation. Currently he resides in Conway, SC.

Nargess Memarsadeghi, Ph.D., has a Ph.D. in Computer Science from the University of Maryland at College Park (2007). She also received her M.S. (2004) and B.S. (2001) in Computer Science from the same school. She has been working as a computer engineer and researcher at NASA Goddard Space Flight Center in Greenbelt, MD since July 2001. She worked as a teaching assistant for the Computer Science Department of the University of Maryland (Fall 2002- Spring 2003) and tutored for the Math Learning Center of Montgomery College at Germantown, MD (1998-2000). Currently she resides in Silver Spring, MD.

Kimberly Noonan, M.S. has a Bachelor of Science degree in Mathematics from the University of Richmond (1996), and both a Master of Science in Mathematics and a Master of Science in Computer Science from the University of North Carolina at Chapel Hill (2002, 2004). Professionally, she works as an Operations Research Analyst on National Airspace Modeling projects for the Federal Aviation Administration. She taught College Algebra through Multivariable Calculus at the University of North Carolina as a teaching assistant, and tutored at Chapel Hill High School in Algebra I through Calculus from 1996-2003. She has also tutored various mathematical subjects for Ivy League Tutoring Connection, in Washington DC. Currently she resides in Washington DC

Matthew Konicki, M.A. has a Bachelor of Science degree in Mathematics from Mary Washington University (1999) and a Master of Arts in Mathematics (2004) from The University of Maryland at College Park. He has been a mathematics instructor at the University of Maryland since 2004, teaching various math courses including statistics and calculus. He has also been a mathematics instructor at Georgetown University, The University of Delaware, American University, and Catholic University. He is a member of the Mathematical Association of America.

Elnatan Reisner, has a BS in Computer Science and Mathematics from Brandeis University (2005) and is currently pursuing a Ph.D. in Computer Science at the University of Maryland/College Park. He worked as an applied research mathematician at the Department of Defense in 2003, and a researcher at the Center for Computing Sciences in Bowie, MD in 2004. He earned a Computer Science Prize for Outstanding Achievement in 2005 at Brandeis University. Currently he resides in Silver Spring, MD.

Hunter Brooks, has a BA in Mathematics and Linguistics from Dartmouth College and is pursuing a Ph.D. from the University of Maryland. He was a teaching assistant for the mathematics department at Dartmouth College from 2004 through 2006, where he taught four-hour classes to twenty rising juniors and seniors. He tutored at the Academic Skills Center at Dartmouth College and was an independent math tutor from 2001-2006. Currently he resides in College Park, MD.

Asa Palley has a BA in mathematics from Bowdoin College. She tutored Calculus for the Mathematics Department at Bowdoin College and also taught AP Calculus at Lisbon High School in Brunswick, Maine from 2005-2006. She was the co-captain of St. Albans School High School Math Team in Washington DC. Currently she resides in Chevy Chase, MD.

Andrew Newens has a BS in Mechanical and Aerospace Engineering from Princeton University and a Master of Arts in Christian Counseling from Capital Bible Seminary. He tutored SAT preparation (math and verbal) as well as high school math and science at C2 Education Centers. Currently he resides in Arlington, VA.

CHAPTER 1

ASSESSMENT EXAM

1. A small square is removed from a large square, reducing the area of the large square by 4%. How many times longer is the side of the large square than the side of the small square?

   A. $\frac{2\sqrt{6}}{5}$

   B. $\sqrt{5}$

   C. 3

   D. 5

   E. $5\sqrt{2}$

2. A triangle in the xy-plane has corners $(-3,0)$, $(0,3)$, and $(3,0)$. The line $y = \frac{1}{3}x + 1$ separates the triangle into two pieces. What is the area of the piece lying below the line?

   A. 3

   B. $\frac{10}{3}$

   C. $\frac{7}{2}$

   D. $\frac{9}{2}$

   E. 4

3. A bowling ball with a radius of 6 inches is rolled forward in a straight line and comes to a stop after traveling 32 feet. How many *full* revolutions did the bowling ball make? (Ignore any incomplete revolutions it made.)

   A. 9

   B. 10

   C. 11

   D. 12

   E. 13

4. A car salesman wants to display 5 cars in a line in front of the showroom window. He has two SUVs, two sedans, and one sports car. The only stipulation is that he does NOT want to put the SUVs on either end of the line. How many possible arrangements of cars will he have?

   A. 48

   B. 36

C. 24

D. 12

E. 9

5. Jack says he has two coins in his hand, each of a different value (out of either pennies, nickels, dimes, or quarters). Lisa says, "So do I." What is the probability that, putting their money together, they can afford a pack of gum for 50 cents?

A. $\frac{11}{36}$

B. $\frac{5}{18}$

C. $\frac{1}{4}$

D. $\frac{4}{18}$

E. $\frac{7}{36}$

6. Nine contestants are entered into a competition. The top four contestants with the most points will win first place, second place, third place, and fourth place, respectively. How many ways can the four winning contestants be ordered?

A. 6561

B. 3024

C. 1024

D. 361

E. 36

7. An ice cream store has 12 different ice cream flavors and 5 different toppings to choose from. If a child has a choice of any two flavors of ice cream and any one topping, how many possible combinations are available to her, assuming that she will choose two different flavors of ice cream?

A. 60

B. 120

C. 330

D. 660

E. 720

8. What is the remainder of dividing 23425 by 18?

A. 4

B. 7

C. 10

D. 13

E. 16

9. A number whose units digit is 7 is raised to some positive integer power. Which of the following is definitely FALSE?

   A. The units digit of the result is 1
   B. The units digit of the result is 3
   C. The units digit of the result is 6
   D. The units digit of the result is 7
   E. The units digit of the result is 9

10. A medical solution for cold contains s grams of salt for each w grams of water. If one wants to use r less grams of water, how much less salt should be added to the solution so that the correct ratio of salt to water in mass be preserved?

   A. $\frac{sr}{w}$
   B. $\frac{rw}{s}$
   C. $\frac{s}{rw}$
   D. $\frac{w}{rs}$
   E. $\frac{ws}{r}$

11. The ratio of the area of circle A with radius r to the circumference of circle B with radius r' is c. What is the ratio of the area of circle A to that of circle B?

   A. $\frac{c}{2r'}$
   B. $\frac{2c}{r'}$
   C. $\frac{2r'}{c}$
   D. $\frac{r'}{2c}$
   E. $\frac{c}{r'}$

12. x is a 2-digit positive integer. When its digits are reversed, the result is a 2-digit positive number equal to $2x + 2$. What is the product of the digits of x?

   A. 10
   B. 52
   C. 54
   D. 63
   E. 72

13. The following multiplication is performed; which is a possible value for the digit N?

   $$\begin{array}{r} J\ K\ L\ M \\ \times\quad 4\ 2 \\ \hline 4\ 0\ 3\ N \end{array}$$

3

A. 0

B. 2

C. 4

D. 6

E. All of the above

14. The diagram below depicts a large rectangle whose perimeter is being covered by alternating circles and small rectangles. The circles each have radius 2 and the small rectangles are each 2×4. When the large rectangle's perimeter is completely covered, what will be the total area of the shaded regions—the areas inside the small shapes that are also inside the large rectangle?

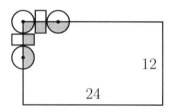

Note: Figure not drawn to scale.

A. $48 + 20\pi$

B. $12 + 20\pi$

C. 44π

D. $18 + 10\pi$

E. $36 + 10\pi$

15. If you can buy A apples for C cents, how many dollars does it cost to buy X apples?

A. $\frac{CX}{100A}$

B. ACX

C. $\frac{CA}{X}$

D. $\frac{100CA}{X}$

E. $\frac{AX}{100C}$

16. A crew of 20 people takes 200 days to build 2 houses. How long will it take a crew of 10 people to build 3 houses? Assume any person on the crew can do any job, that they all work at the same speed, and that all materials are on hand when needed.

A. 200 days

B. 300 days

C. 600 days

D. 750 days

E. 1200 days

17. A semicircle sits inside a trapezoid as shown. What proportion of the trapezoid's area is occupied by the semicircle?

A. $\frac{\pi}{4}$
B. $\frac{3\pi}{16}$
C. $\frac{\pi}{8}$
D. $\frac{\pi}{6}$
E. $\frac{2\pi}{9}$

18. The area of the square is 36. All four semicircles are the same size and all four intersect at the center of the square. What is the area of the shaded region?

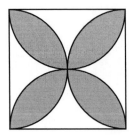

A. $72 - 18\pi$
B. 3π
C. 9π
D. $36 - 9\pi$
E. $18\pi - 36$

19. The cube below is made up of 27 smaller cubes. The shaded black represents holes; the innermost column of three cubes and the innermost row of three cubes is missing. What is the surface area of the cube if the surface area of the cube without the missing portions is 216?

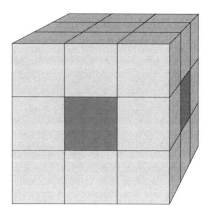

A. 244
B. 272
C. 316
D. 318
E. 328

20. Which of the following shows the graph of $y = (\sqrt{x})^2$?

A.

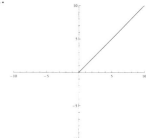

B.

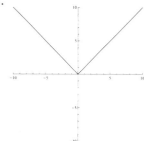

C.

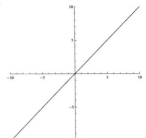

E.

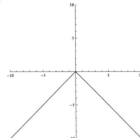

D.

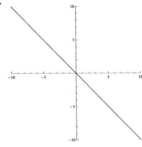

ASSESSMENT EXAM SOLUTIONS

1. **D.** We first label the side of the large square x and the side of the small square y. Since removing the small square reduces the area by 4%, we have

$$
\begin{aligned}
x^2 - y^2 &= .96x^2 \\
.04x^2 &= y^2 \\
.2x &= y \\
x &= 5y.
\end{aligned}
$$

Thus, the side of the large square is five times longer.

2. **D.** The x-intercept of the line $y = \frac{1}{3}x + 1$ is $(-3, 0)$ and so the line intersects the triangle at one of its corners and another point, splitting the triangle into two other triangles. The unknown point is the intersection of the line $y = \frac{1}{3}x + 1$ with the line passing through the points $(3, 0)$ and $(0, 3)$, which is $y = -x + 3$. Setting these lines equal to each other and solving gives the point of intersection:

$$
\begin{aligned}
\frac{1}{3}x + 1 &= -x + 3 \\
\frac{4}{3}x &= 2 \\
x &= \frac{3}{2} \\
y &= -\frac{3}{2} + 3 = \frac{3}{2}.
\end{aligned}
$$

Thus, the area of the triangle under the line is $\frac{1}{2} \times 6 \times \frac{3}{2} = \frac{9}{2}$.

3. **B.** The bowling ball travels a distance equal to its circumference every time it makes one full revolution. The radius is 6 inches, which is $\frac{1}{2}$ a foot, making its circumference π feet. That is, the bowling ball travels π feet for each revolution. Since it came to a stop after 32 feet, it made exactly $\frac{32}{\pi} = 10.1859\ldots$ revolutions, and so made 10 full revolutions.

4. **B.** There are 5 positions to fill and 5 cars to place, with limitations. On one end position, he can place any of the three cars that are not SUVs. After having done that, on the other end position he can place either of the two remaining cars that are not SUVs. The result would look like this: $\underline{3}\ \_\ \_\ \_\ \underline{2}$. In the three middle positions, he can place the three remaining cars, including the SUVs, in any of the positions. Therefore, the number of possible car arrangements would be: $3 \times 3 \times 2 \times 1 \times 2 = 36$.

5. **A.** With two coins, and four choices of coin type (p, n, d, q), there are 6 possible unique combinations of two different coins that each could have: {pn, pd, nd, nq, qp, qd}, and their corresponding sums are {6, 11, 15, 30, 26, and 35} cents. It follows that the total possible number of combinations between what Jack has and what Lisa has, since they are independent events, is $6 \times 6 = 36$.

Only certain combinations will ensure that the sum of both Jack's and Lisa's money is ≥ 50 cents: four of these can happen in two ways {15+35, 26+30, 26+35, 30+35} by reversing their order, while three of them can happen in only one way {26+26, 30+30, 35+35} because they are the same number repeated. This means that there are $(4 \times 2) + 3 = 11$ possible combinations which ensure that the sum of both of their money is ≥ 50 cents.

Therefore, the probability that together they can afford a 50 cent pack of gum is $\frac{11}{36}$.

6. **B.** There are 4 winning positions to be filled. Starting with first place, there are 9 possibilities to fill that position. After first place is determined, there are 8 possibilities to fill second place. After that, there are 7 possibilities to fill third place. And after that, there are 6 possibilities to fill fourth place. Therefore, the number of ways the four winning contestants could be ordered is $9 \times 8 \times 7 \times 6 = 3024$.

7. **C.** First, only consider the ice cream: her first choice of ice cream has 12 possibilities, and her second choice of ice cream, if it is different from the first, has 11 possibilities. Multiplying them together, she will have $12 \times 11 = 132$ possible permutations. But since the order of the ice cream scoops doesn't matter ("chocolate and vanilla" versus "vanilla and chocolate"), we are therefore solving for combinations, not permutations. We must divide by the number of positions factorial, which is $2! = 2 \times 1 = 2$. So, the number of combinations is $132 \div 2 = 66$. Then, in order to take the choice of toppings into account, we just multiply 66 by the number of toppings available, which is 5 toppings: $66 \times 5 = 330$.

8. **B.** The remainder is the difference between 23425 and the greatest integer less than 23425 that is divisible by 18. This integer must be even since 18 is even, and its sum of digits must be divisible by 9, since 18 is divisible by 9. First we treat this problem as division by 9. Subtract 7 from 23425 to get 23418, which is the greatest integer less than 23425 that is divisible by 9. This happens to be an even number, so we're done, and the answer is $23425 - 23418 = 7$. If the number were odd, we would subtract another 9 to make it even.

Alternatively, one can solve this using a calculator. Note that $23425/18 = 1301.38888\ldots$. The remainder of the division is the decimal part of the quotient, $0.38888\ldots$ multiplied by the divisor, 18. So, $18 * 0.38888\ldots = 7$.

9. **C.** If one recalls that an odd number raised to an integral power is odd, we can immediately note the units digit can not be 6. Thus, the correct answer is C. More specifically, we can solve this problem by raising 7 to positive integer powers until the pattern emerges.

$$7^1 = 7, \quad 7^2 = 49, \quad 7^3 = 343, \quad 7^4 = 2401, \quad 7^5 = 16807$$

Thus, the only unit digits we can get are 1, 3, 7, and 9.

10. **A.** We know that the solution contains $\frac{s}{w}$ grams of salt for each gram of water. Therefore, the amount of salt needed for r grams of water to maintain this ratio is $\frac{s}{w} \times r = \frac{sr}{w}$. The longer approach to this problem is that we are looking for x grams of salt such that

$$
\begin{aligned}
\frac{s}{w} &= \frac{s - x}{w - r} \\
ws - sr &= ws - wx \\
sr &= wx \\
x &= \frac{sr}{w}.
\end{aligned}
$$

11. **B.** Based on the problem description we have

$$
\begin{aligned}
\frac{\pi r^2}{2\pi r'} &= c \\
\frac{r^2}{2r'} &= c \\
r^2 &= 2r'c.
\end{aligned}
$$

The question is asking for

$$\frac{\pi r^2}{\pi r'^2} = \frac{r^2}{r'^2} = \frac{2r'c}{r'^2} = \frac{2c}{r'}. \quad \text{(using the above result)}$$

12. **A.** Let T be the 10's digit and U be the units (1's) digit. Then $TU = x$ and $UT = y$. So:

$$
\begin{aligned}
10U + T &= 2(10T + U) + 2 \\
8U &= 19T + 2
\end{aligned}
$$

$19T + 2$ must be even since it is divisible by 8. Therefore T is even. Since U is an integer less than 9, $19T + 2$ must be equal to 64. So we can eliminate 4,6,8 for T. 0 doesn't work either because $\frac{2}{8} = \frac{1}{4}$, so T must be 2. Solving $8U = 19 * 2 + 2$ gives $U = 5$, so the product is 10.

13. **B.** This is actually a question about divisibility rules; see the chapter on number theory for more information. The final answer must be divisible by 42 and hence must be divisible by 3. So the digits in the final answer should sum to a multiple of 3. Thus $4 + 0 + 3 + N = 7 + N$ must be divisible by 3. The only choice for which this works is when $N = 2$.

14. **A.** If we finish placing the circles and small rectangles around the perimeter, we get the following situation:

With this picture, we see that there are 12 small rectangles in total around the perimeter. Each extends into the large rectangle as a 2×2 square, which has area 4, so the total area due to the rectangles is $12 \times 4 = 48$.

We can also see that there are 8 circles which have semicircles in the large rectangle, and there are 4 which have only one quarter in the rectangle. 8 semicircles and 4 quarter-circles is the equivalent of $8 \times \frac{1}{2} + 4 \times \frac{1}{4} = 4 + 1 = 5$ full circles. Since each circle has area $\pi \times 2^2 = 4\pi$, the total shaded area in the circles is 5 times this, or 20π.

Adding these two pieces gives the $48 + 20\pi$.

15. **A.** If we can buy A apples for C cents, then each apple costs $\frac{C}{A}$ cents. So it costs $\frac{CX}{A}$ cents to buy X apples. Convert cents to dollars by dividing by 100, yielding an answer of $\frac{CX}{100A}$ dollars. Double check this by putting in real numbers: If I can buy $A = 10$ apples for $C = 50$ cents (5 cents per apple), and I want to buy $X = 25$ apples, it should cost me 125 cents, or $1.25 = \frac{CX}{100A}$ dollars.

16. **C.** If 20 people take 200 days to build 2 houses, it would take 20 people 100 days to build 1 house, meaning it should take 1 person 2000 days to build a house. So a crew of 10 people could build 1 house in 200 days. So building 3 houses will take 600 days.

17. **D.** The height of the trapezoid is the radius of the semicircle, so the area of the trapezoid is

$$r \times \frac{2r + 4r}{2} = 3r^2.$$

Thus, the ratio of the area of the semicircle to the area of the trapezoid is

$$\frac{\frac{1}{2}\pi r^2}{3r^2} = \frac{\pi}{6}.$$

18. **E.** To obtain the shaded area we take the area of the square and subtract the non-shaded area. The non-shaded area is in four identical pieces, and it is easiest to calculate half of the non-shaded area and double it. To calculate, say, the area of the left and right pieces we subtract the area of the top and bottom semicircles from the area of the square. Since the area of the square is 36, the side of the square is 6 and so the radius of the semicircle is 3. Thus, $36 - 9\pi$ is the area of the non-shaded left and right pieces. Doubling this gives the total non-shaded area, and we subtract that from 36 to obtain the area of the shaded region: $36 - (72 - 18\pi) = 18\pi - 36$.

19. **B.** If the surface area is 216 then $6s^2 = 216$, so $s = 6$. This means that each small square is 2 by 2. To find the total surface area, we have four sides that contain 8 squares of $2x2$ and two sides that contain 9 squares of $2x2$. That gives us $4*8*2*2+2*9*2*2 = 200$ for the outside surface of the cube. If we look at the surface area produced by one missing row, we have four faces times 3 squares each that have as dimensions 2 by 2. That's $4*3*2*2 = 48$ additional square units. Similarly the 2nd missing row adds 48 additional square units. But oops, we double counted the very middle cube, which has six faces of $2*2$. Therefore we need to subtract that from the total. So we have $200 + 48 + 48 - 6*2*2 = 272$.

20. **A.** The function $y = (\sqrt{x})^2$ has the same values as $y = x$ since they are inverse functions. However, the domain of the function is $(0, \infty)$ since one cannot insert a negative number into the square root sign and get a real number. The line $y = x$ is a function you should know. It originates at the origin and slopes upwards with a slope of 1. Therefore, A is correct.

How to Interpret Your Score

The better you perform on the assessment test, the more promise you have were you to take the real SAT today. However, this doesn't mean that you don't have strong promise to do well on future exams, as long as you continue to study this book from cover to cover. Practice is the name of the game.

If you answered few questions correctly, don't worry - you still have the ability to learn the material and score high. A score of seven or above out of 20 demonstrates considerable promise. If you scored higher than fifteen out of twenty, congratulations – you can easily score well over 700, perhaps even achieve a score of 800. The reason for this is that those tough level 4 and 5 problems appear less frequently on an actual SAT exam. Therefore, it is not expected that at this stage of the game you will score very high on the assessment test.

This book is a compilation of problems to reinforce skills needed to do well on the SAT math portion, and it is assumed that this is not your first SAT book. We would recommend taking (an) SAT test(s) from your other SAT book/s or take the actual SAT test before and after working with our material and compare those results.

If your scores are not what you aim for right away, don't despair. Compare the score you receive on the final assessment test at the end of the book to the score you obtained on the assessment test, and see how far you've come.

One item you should pay attention to right now is to notice what kinds of problems stump you. Are they mostly geometry problems? (in which case you should spend more time on the geometry chapters), or are they word problems? (in which case the word problem chapters are especially important that you work on).

Working through the entire book will almost guarantee a much higher score on the real SAT. If you can master the techniques used to solve these problems, you are ready for an 800!

CHAPTER 2

NUMBER THEORY

Arithmetic and number theory problems test your knowledge of the real line, arithmetic and geometric sequences, elementary algebraic identities, divisibility rules, special properties of integers and prime numbers, as well as the relationship between integers, rational numbers, and real numbers.

Integers, Rational Numbers and Real Numbers

The set of positive integers, $1, 2, 3, \ldots$, also called **natural numbers** is contained in the set of integers. The set of integers is contained in the set of rational numbers. The set of rational numbers, each of which can be expressed as a quotient of integers $\frac{p}{q}$ where $q \neq 0$, is contained in the set of real numbers. The real numbers consist of the rational numbers and the irrational numbers, which cannot be expressed as a quotient of integers. Some examples of irrational numbers are π, e, and $\sqrt{2}$.

1. Which of the following statements is true?

I. The sum of any two positive integers is a positive integer.
II. The ratio of any two nonzero integers is an integer.
III. Any rational number raised to a nonzero, rational number power is a rational number.

A. I only
B. II only
C. III only
D. I and II
E. I and III

ANSWER: A.

I. This is true, since the set of positive integers is closed under addition. That is, let n and m be any two positive integers, then $n + m$ is also a positive integer.

II. False: Let $n = 3$ and $m = 4$, then the ratio $\frac{n}{m} = \frac{3}{4}$ is a rational number not an integer.

III. False: Raising the rational number 2 to the positive, rational power $\frac{1}{2}$ gives $(2)^{\frac{1}{2}} = \sqrt{2}$, an irrational number.

2. Let x be a rational real number. Which of the following expressions MAY equal zero?

A. $x^2 + 1$
B. $-|x^3 + 1| + 1$
C. $\sqrt{x^2 + 25}$
D. $|x^3 + 2|$
E. $\frac{3x^3 + 18}{x^2}$

ANSWER: B. Quick answer: Let $x = 0$. Then B. $= -|x^3 + 1| + 1 = -|0 + 1| + 1 = -1 + 1 = 0$.

Longer, more complete answer: Make each expression into an equation where the right hand side is zero, and try to solve for x:

A. $x^2 + 1 = 0 \iff x^2 = -1$

This equation has no solution in the real numbers.

B. $-|x^3 + 1| + 1 = 0 \iff |x^3 + 1| = 1 \iff x^3 + 1 = 1$ or $x^3 + 1 = -1 \iff$
$x^3 = 0$ or $x^3 = -2 \iff x = 0$ or $x = -\sqrt[3]{2}$

One of the solutions we found, $x = 0$, is rational, so this must be the correct answer and we can stop here, but we will continue to show why the other answer choices are wrong.

C. $\sqrt{x^2 + 25} = 0 \iff x^2 + 25 = 0 \iff x^2 = -25$

This equation has no solution in the real numbers.

D. $|x^3 + 2| = 0 \iff x^3 + 2 = 0 \iff x = -\sqrt[3]{2}$

The only solution of this equation, $-\sqrt[3]{2}$, is not a rational number.

E. $\frac{3x^2 + 18}{x^2} = 0 \iff 3x^2 + 18 = 0 \iff 3x^2 = -18 \iff x^2 = -6$

This equation has no solution in the real numbers.

The Real Line

Recall that the intervals on the real line can be open, closed, or both. There are several notations used to represent intervals. Consider the following,

Interval	Double inequality	Absolute value inequality
$[a,b]$	$a \leq x \leq b$	$\left|x - \frac{a+b}{2}\right| \leq \frac{b-a}{2}$
(a,b)	$a < x < b$	$\left|x - \frac{a+b}{2}\right| < \frac{b-a}{2}$
$[a,b)$	$a \leq x < b$	not applicable
$(a,b]$	$a < x \leq b$	not applicable

3. The inequality $25 \leq x \leq 75$ is equivalent to

A. $|x + 35| \leq 20$
B. $|x + 40| \leq 20$
C. $|x + 45| \leq 25$
D. $|x - 50| \leq 25$
E. $|x - 55| \leq 30$

ANSWER: D. The length of this closed interval is $75 - 25 = 50$. Thus, the "radius" is $r = \frac{50}{2} = 25$, and the "center" is $a = 25 + \frac{50}{2} = 25 + 25 = 50$. Using the fact that an inequality such as $a - r \leq x \leq a + r$ is equivalent to $|x - a| \leq r$ we can see that the answer is choice **D**.

Arithmetic and Geometric Sequences

An arithmetic sequence is a sequence of numbers such that the difference between every two consecutive numbers is constant. Given that the first number in the sequence is a_1 and the fixed difference is d, the corresponding arithmetic sequence is $a_1, a_1 + d, a_1 + 2d, a_1 + 3d, \ldots$ Using the above notation, given a finite arithmetic sequence of n terms, the last term is given by $a_n = a_1 + (n - 1)d$, and the sum of all n terms is $\frac{(a_1 + a_n)n}{2}$.

Typical problems involving arithmetic sequences ask one of the following:

1. Given the first few terms and the last term of the sequence, $a_1, a_2, a_3, \ldots, a_n$, determine the number of terms in the sequence, and the sum of all the terms. Since $d = a_2 - a_1$ and the number of terms is $n = \frac{a_n - a_1}{d} + 1 = \frac{a_n - a_1}{a_2 - a_1} + 1$.

2. Given the first few terms $a_1, a_2, a_3, \ldots$ and the number of terms n in the finite sequence, determine the last term and the sum of all terms. As defined above, we use the following $d = a_2 - a_1$ and $a_n = a_1 + (n - 1)d$.

A geometric sequence is a sequence of numbers such that the ratio between every two consecutive numbers is constant. Given that the first number in the sequence is a_1 and the fixed ratio is q, the corresponding geometric sequence is $a_1, a_1 q, a_1 q^2, \ldots$ Using the above notation, given a finite geometric sequence of n terms, its' last term is $a_1 q^{n-1}$, and the sum of all n terms is $a_1 \frac{q^n-1}{q-1}$. If the geometric sequence is infinite and $|q| < 1$ then the sum of this infinite sequence is $\frac{a_1}{q-1}$.

4. Consider the arithmetic sequence, $3, 7, 11, \ldots$. What is the 301st term?

A. 1203

B. 1204

C. 1205

D. 1206

E. 1207

ANSWER: A. Consider the following:

$$
\begin{array}{l|l}
\text{1st term} & 3 = 3 + 4 \cdot 0 \\
\text{2nd term} & 7 = 3 + 4 \cdot 1 \\
\text{3rd term} & 11 = 3 + 4 \cdot 2 \\
\text{4th term} & 15 = 3 + 4 \cdot 3 \\
\ \vdots & \\
\text{301st term} & ? = 3 + 4 \cdot 300
\end{array}
$$

Thus, the 301st number in the sequence is $3 + 4 \cdot 300 = 1203$.

5. Consider the geometric sequence, $3, 6, 12, 24, \ldots$. What is the sum of the first 10 terms?

A. 1536

B. 1023

C. 1024

D. 3069

E. 3072

ANSWER: D. Note that

$$
\begin{array}{l|l}
\text{1st term} & 3 = 3 \cdot 2^0 \\
\text{2nd term} & 6 = 3 \cdot 2^1 \\
\text{3rd term} & 12 = 3 \cdot 2^2 \\
\text{4th term} & 24 = 3 \cdot 2^3 \\
\ \vdots & \\
\text{10th term} & ? = 3 \cdot 2^1 0
\end{array}
$$

The sum of the first 10 terms $= 3 * \frac{2^{10}-1}{2-1} = 3069$

Elementary Algebraic Identities

$$(a+b)^2 = a^2 + 2ab + b^2$$
$$(a-b)^2 = a^2 - 2ab + b^2$$

6. Let a and b be positive integers and suppose $a^2 - b^2 = p$ where p is a prime number. What is the value of a in terms of p?

A. p
B. $p - 1$
C. $\frac{p-1}{2}$
D. $\frac{p+1}{2}$
E. $2p$

ANSWER: D. First note that $a > b$, since prime numbers are positive integers. Now factor $a^2 - b^2$ using the identity $a^2 - b^2 = (a-b)(a+b)$. So, $p = (a-b)(a+b)$. Since p is prime, the only factors of p are 1 and itself. Thus, $a + b = p$ and $a - b = 1$. The second equality yields $b = a - 1$. Substituting that into the first equality gives $p = a + b = a + a - 1 = 2a - 1$. Thus, $a = \frac{p+1}{2}$.

Divisibility Rules

A number is divisible by 2 if it is even or equivalently if its units digit is $0, 2, 4, 6,$ or 8. A number is divisible by 3 if the sum of its digits is divisible by 3. A number is divisible by 4 if the number formed by its tens and units digits is divisible by 4. A number is divisible by 5 if its units digit is 0 or 5. A number is divisible by 6 if it is even and the sum of its digits is divisible by 3. A number is divisible by 8 if the number formed by its hundreds, tens, and units digits is divisible by 8. A number is divisible by 9 if the sum of its digits is divisible by 9. A number is divisible by 15 if its units digit is 0 or 5 and sum of its digits is divisible by 3.

7. Suppose x is a positive integer such that the remainder of x divided by 3 is 1, while the remainder of x divided by 5 is 3. What is the smallest possible value for x?

A. 10
B. 13
C. 18
D. 23
E. 28

ANSWER: B. Consider the integers (in order) that satisfy each condition:

1st condition	7		10	13	16		19	22		25	28
2nd condition		8		13		18			23		28

We could have stopped at 13, the first match and our answer. Note that the first row in the table is an arithmetic sequence with a difference of 3, and the second row is an arithmetic sequence with a difference of 5.

8. A number whose units digit is 3 is raised to a positive integer power. Which of the following is definitely FALSE?

A. The units digit of the result is 1
B. The units digit of the result is 3
C. The units digit of the result is 6
D. The units digit of the result is 7
E. The units digit of the result is 9

ANSWER: C. For any integers n and m, $(2m + 1)^n$ for $m \geq 0$ is always odd since the number inside the parentheses is always odd and an odd number raised to any power is odd. Specifically, note that $3^1 = 3$, $3^2 = 9$, $3^3 = 27$, $3^4 = 81$, and $3^5 = 243$.

So, the units digit can be $3, 9, 7,$ or 1, but not 6.

Practice Problems

1. How many ways are there to express 24 as a sum of two prime numbers?

   A. 0
   B. 1
   C. 2
   D. 3
   E. 4

2. If $-1 < x < 0$, which of the following statements MUST be true?

   A. $x^5 < x^6 < x^7$
   B. $x^5 < x^7 < x^6$
   C. $x^7 < x^5 < x^6$
   D. $x^7 < x^6 < x^5$
   E. $x^6 < x^7 < x^5$

3. Choose the correct containment of sets:

   A. prime numbers $\subset$ integers $\subset$ real numbers $\subset$ rational numbers
   B. rational numbers $\subset$ integers $\subset$ real numbers $\subset$ prime numbers
   C. prime numbers $\subset$ integers $\subset$ rational numbers $\subset$ real numbers
   D. integers $\subset$ real numbers $\subset$ prime numbers $\subset$ rational numbers
   E. prime numbers $\subset$ odd integers $\subset$ integers $\subset$ rational numbers

4. A magician possesses three magical miniature sand hourglasses labeled A, B, and C, which can contain 8, 10, and 12 minutes worth of sand, respectively. At 8:00AM, the magician claps his hands and all three sand hourglasses start start at exactly the same time. Whenever any of the hourglasses runs out of sand, it magically and instantaneously flips itself and its sand starts running again. At what time of day will all three sand hourglasses run out of sand simultaneously for the first time since the magician clapped his hands?

   A. 8:45AM
   B. 9:20AM
   C. 10:00AM
   D. 11:40AM
   E. 12:15PM

5. Let S be the sum of n consecutive integers, where n is an odd positive integer. What is the median of the n numbers?

   A. $\dfrac{n}{2}$

   B. $\dfrac{S}{2}$

   C. $\dfrac{S-n}{2}$

   D. $\dfrac{S^2}{2n}$

   E. $\dfrac{S}{n}$

6. If $\frac{|x+5|}{2} = 4$ and $3|y+2| = 9$, then $|x+y|$ could equal each of the following EXCEPT

   A. 2

   B. 4

   C. 6

   D. 12

   E. 18

7. If you divide 123454321 by 6, what remainder will you get?

   A. 1

   B. 2

   C. 3

   D. 4

   E. 5

8. What is the remainder when you divide by 9 the number $111\ldots1$ consisting of 55 digits, each of which is 1?

   A. 0

   B. 1

   C. 2

   D. 3

   E. 4

9. Find a pair of two positive integers x and y such that dividing $3x + 5y$ by 7 gives a remainder of 4 and the sum of $x + y$ is minimal.

   A. 1

   B. 2

   C. 3

D. 4

E. 5

10. 243 people, numbered 1 through 243 counterclockwise, are standing in a large circle. Person 1 holds a pack of 243 tickets that are to be distributed among the 243 people. He takes one ticket, and passes the remaining pack of 242 tickets to person 4; person 4 takes a ticket and passes the pack of remaining 241 tickets to person 7, and so on. In general, each person who receives the pack of tickets takes one ticket, even if he or she already has one or more tickets, and passes the pack of remaining tickets to the person that is 3 positions to his right. When all 243 tickets have been distributed, how many people in the circle received at least one ticket?

    A. 27

    B. 81

    C. 121

    D. 162

    E. 243

11. What is the sum of the first 10 prime numbers?

    A. 126

    B. 129

    C. 131

    D. 132

    E. 135

12. Let x be a real number not equal to zero. Which of the following expressions MUST be equal to a number smaller than zero but greater than -1?

    A. $-\dfrac{x^2 + 2x}{x^2 + 3x}$

    B. $\dfrac{-2x + 3}{3x - 5}$

    C. $-\dfrac{|x + 1|}{x + 2}$

    D. $-\dfrac{x^3}{x^4}$

    E. $-\dfrac{2(x^2 + 1)}{3x^2 + 3}$

13. The repeating decimal representation of $\frac{1}{7}$ is $0.142857142857\ldots$ What is the 99th digit to the right of the decimal point?

   A. 1
   B. 4
   C. 2
   D. 8
   E. 5

14. Let S be the smallest set of integers containing such that 3 is in S and the product of any two numbers in the set is also in the set. How many elements must S have?

   A. 1
   B. 3
   C. 9
   D. 81
   E. infinitely many

15. Let S be the smallest, nonempty set of integers such that the product of any two elements in the set is also in the set. How many elements must S contain?

   A. 0
   B. 1
   C. 2
   D. 3
   E. infinitely many

16. Suppose p is a prime number, a and b are integers, and the product ab is divisible by p. Which of the following MUST be true?

   A. a and b are both divisible by p
   B. a is divisible by p, but b is not divisible by p
   C. b is divisible by p, but a is not divisible by p
   D. a or b or both are divisible by p
   E. Neither a nor b is divisible by p

17. Let n be a number whose unit digit is 4.

   I. n^{1051} has units digit 4
   II. n^{2402} has units digit 8
   III. n^{984} has units digit 6

   A. I only
   B. I and II
   C. I and III

D. II and III

E. I, II, and III

18. A sculptor requires a slab of marble that weighs at least 10 lbs and at most 30 lbs. If x represents the weight of a slab of marble that does NOT meet the sculptor's criteria, which of the following inequalities represents all possible values of x?

A. $|x + 20| > 30$

B. $|x + 10| > 20$

C. $|x - 10| > 20$

D. $|x - 10| > 10$

E. $|x - 20| > 10$

19. Given that x is nonzero and $-1 < x < 1$, which of the following is NECESSARILY true?

   I. $x^3 > x^4$

  II. $x^2 - 1 < 0$

 III. $\sqrt{|x|} < \frac{1}{|x|}$

A. I only

B. II only

C. I and III

D. II and III

E. I, II, and III

20. What is the remainder of dividing 13424 by 18?

A. 4

B. 6

C. 10

D. 13

E. 16

21. Let a and b be two positive integers such that $a^4 - b^4 = 15$. What is the value of a ?

A. 1

B. 2

C. 3

D. 4

E. 5

22. What is the smallest positive integer m such that the equation $x^2 + mx + 6 = 0$ has two distinct solutions?

   A. 1
   B. 2
   C. 3
   D. 4
   E. 5

23. If a and b are nonzero integers and $2a^4 - 3ab = 0$ then b is divisible AT LEAST by

   A. 2
   B. 3
   C. 6
   D. 9
   E. 18

24. If a, b and c are positive integers such that $ab = 4c^2$ and such that a and b have no prime factor in common, then which of the following MUST be true?

   I.   Either a or b is divisible by 4
   II. b is the square of an integer
   III. $a - b$ is odd

   A. I only
   B. II only
   C. III only
   D. I and II
   E. I, II and III

25. Let A be the set of all rational numbers (fractions) of the form $\frac{a}{b}$ reduced to lowest terms such that a and b have no prime factors in common, and the denominator b is odd. For example, A contains $\frac{4}{1}$, $\frac{2}{5}$, $\frac{13}{9}$ and $\frac{-15}{7}$, but A doesn't contain $\frac{3}{8}$. Which of the following statements MUST be true?

   I.   the sum of every two fractions in A is also in A
   II. the product of every two fractions in A is also in A
   III. the reciprocal of every nonzero fraction in A is also in A

   A. I only
   B. II only
   C. III only
   D. I and II
   E. I, II and III

26. Let A be the set of all rational numbers (fractions) of the form $\frac{a}{b}$ reduced to lowest terms such that a and b have no prime factors in common, and the denominator b is the square of a positive integer. For example, A contains $\frac{4}{1}$, $\frac{2}{25}$, $\frac{13}{9}$ and $\frac{-15}{49}$, but A doesn't contain $\frac{3}{8}$. Which of the following statements MUST be true?

    I.   the sum of every two fractions in A is also in A

    II.   the product of every two fractions in A is also in A

    III. A contains the fractions $\frac{1}{2^{n!}}$ for all positive integers $n \geq 5$

  A. I only

  B. II only

  C. III only

  D. I and II

  E. I, II and III

27. If a and b are two positive integers greater than 1 that have no prime factors in common, and their geometric mean equals 10, what could a equal?

  A. 2

  B. 4

  C. 6

  D. 8

  E. 10

28. The Fibonacci sequence is defined as follows: The first term is 1, the second term is 1, and every term after these two equals the sum of the two terms that immediately precede it. So, for example, the first few terms in the sequence are

$$1, 1, 2, 3, 5, \ldots$$

since $3 = 1 + 2$, $5 = 2 + 3$, etc. How many terms in this sequence that are less than 100 are prime numbers?

  A. 2

  B. 3

  C. 4

  D. 5

  E. 6

29. Let a be the sum of 25 consecutive integers whose median is m, and let b be the sum of 15 consecutive integers whose median is n. What does $\dfrac{a}{b}$ equal?

  A. $\dfrac{2m}{3n}$

B. $\dfrac{3m}{5n}$

C. $\dfrac{5m}{3n}$

D. $\dfrac{m}{3n}$

E. $\dfrac{5m}{n}$

30. Let A be the set of all integers that give a remainder of 3 when divided by 5. Which of the following must be true for any two integers x and y in the set A

    I. $x + y$ is in A
    II. $x - y + 3$ is in A
    III. $xy - 1$ is in A

A. I only
B. II only
C. III only
D. II and III
E. I, II and III

31. Let M be the set of integers that can be written as $n^2 - 1$ for positive integers n. How many integers less than 100 in set M can be written as a product of exactly TWO prime numbers?

A. 1
B. 2
C. 3
D. 4
E. 5

32. How many pairs of prime numbers exist such that each pair's sum equals 22?

A. 1
B. 2
C. 3
D. 4
E. 5

33. Let M be the set of integers that can be written as $n^2 - 1$ for positive integers n. How many integers less than 100 in set M can be written as a product of exactly THREE prime numbers, not necessarily distinct?

A. 1
B. 2
C. 3
D. 4
E. 5

34. If $x < 0 < 2y$, then of the following values which is the least?

   A. $-x$
   B. $-2y$
   C. 0
   D. $-(2y + x)$
   E. $-(2y - x)$

35. If $x^2 + y^2 = 40$ and $xy = -12$, what is the value of $(x - y)^2$?

   A. 16
   B. 26
   C. 40
   D. 52
   E. 64

36. Consider the following system of equations:

$$x - 2y = 10$$
$$3x - wy = 30$$

For what value of w will the system have no solution?

   A. 6
   B. 2
   C. 0
   D. -2
   E. -6

37. The greatest integer in a sum of consecutive odd integers is 37. If the sum, in absolute value, is 80, how many integers are in the sum?

   A. 39
   B. 40
   C. 41
   D. 78
   E. 80

38. Let r and q be any positive integers where $r > q$. Define the operation $\&$ by $r\&q = \dfrac{2^{2r+q}}{2^{r-q}}$. For how many positive integers r is $r\&1 = 4$?

    A. 0
    B. 1
    C. 2
    D. 4
    E. infinitely many

39. Let x be any positive integer. Define y, z, and t according to the following set of rules:

    a. $y = x + 2$
    b.   if y is odd, $z = y + 2$
         if y is even, $z = y - 1$
    c. $t = \left(\frac{z+1}{2}\right)$

    Which of the following statements must be true?

    I. $t > 0$
    II. z is odd
    III. t is even

    A. I only
    B. II only
    C. I and II only
    D. II and III only
    E. I, II and III

40. What is the least positive integer a, such that $16a$ is the cube of an integer?

    A. 1
    B. 2
    C. 4
    D. 8
    E. 10

41. Suppose the set S contains all odd positive integers between 1 and 50 inclusive. That is, $S = \{1, 2, 3, 5, \ldots, 50\}$ The ratio of primes to non-primes in S is

    A. $12 : 13$
    B. $13 : 12$
    C. $14 : 11$
    D. $15 : 10$
    E. $16 : 9$

42. How many distinct prime factors of 132 are not distinct prime factors of 24?

    A. 0
    B. 1
    C. 2
    D. 3
    E. 4

Answers to Practice Problems

1. **D.** Starting with the first prime number, 2, we have $2 + 22 = 24$, but 22 is not prime. Similarly, $3 + 21 = 24$, but 21 is not prime. Next, for 5, we have $5 + 19 = 24$, and 19 is prime. Continuing in this way, we get $24 = 5 + 19 = 7 + 17 = 11 + 13$. Thus, there are 3 pairs.

2. **B.** First, note that x^6 is positive for any $x \neq 0$ whereas x^5 and x^7 are negative for any $x < 0$. Therefore, in the given interval, x^6 is greater than both x^5 and x^7. Thus, we can eliminate answer choices **A**, **D**, and **E**. Next, note that if x is a POSITIVE fraction less than 1, i.e. $0 < x < 1$, then $x^7 < x^5$. If x is a NEGATIVE such fraction, i.e. $-1 < x < 0$, then the previous inequality becomes $x^5 < x^7$. Thus, the answer is $x^5 < x^7 < x^6$.

3. **C.** The correct containment is

$$\text{prime numbers} \subset \text{integers} \subset \text{rational numbers} \subset \text{real numbers}$$

   Prime numbers are special integers. Integers are fractions (rational numbers) in which the denominator is 1. Finally, rational numbers are real numbers that can be expressed as fractions. Answer choice **E** is incorrect because the existence of the even prime number 2 precludes the set of prime numbers from being contained in the set of odd integers.

4. **C.** We need to find the smallest number that is divisible by 8, 10, and 12. Such a number is called the least common multiple, and it is computed by taking the product of the highest powers of the prime factors of each of the three numbers. In our case the least common multiple of 8, 10, and 12 is $2^3 \cdot 5 \cdot 3 = 120$. Add 120 minutes, or 2 hours, to 8:00AM to get 10:00AM.

5. **E.** Let's consider a concrete example first. Suppose $n = 11$, and denote the median (middle number) by m. Then there are 5 numbers to the "left" of m and 5 numbers to the "right" of m (recall that n is odd). The smallest integer is $m - 5$, and the largest is $m + 5$. The entire sequence looks like

$$(m - 5) + (m - 4) + \cdots + m + \cdots + (m + 4) + (m + 5)$$

   As you can see, the sequence is symmetric in the sense that when we take the sum, -5 and 5 cancel, -4 and 4 cancel, and so on. We are left with $11m$. Thus, $S = 11m$, so $m = S/11$. Since the symmetry of the sequence doesn't depend on n, the number of integers, we get the general result $m = S/n$.

6. **B.** Solve both equations.

$$\frac{|x+5|}{2} = 4 \qquad\qquad\qquad 3|y+2| = 9$$
$$|x+5| = 8 \qquad\qquad\qquad |y+2| = 3$$
$$x+5 = 8 \text{ or } x+5 = -8 \qquad y+2 = 3 \text{ or } y+2 = -3$$
$$x = 3 \text{ or } x = -13 \qquad\qquad y = 1 \text{ or } y = -5$$

Thus we have four possibilities:

$$|3+1| = 4$$
$$|3-5| = 2$$
$$|-13+1| = 12$$
$$|-13-5| = 18$$

Hence, we can eliminate the answer choices that correspond to 2, 4, 12, and 18, and we end up with answer choice **B** which corresponds to 6.

7. **A.** First note that 123454321 is not divisible by 2. The sum of digits of 123454321 is $2 \cdot (1 + 2 + 3 + 4) + 5 = 2 \cdot 10 + 5 = 25$. Thus 123454321 is not divisible by 3 either. So we are looking for the greatest integer less than 123454321 that IS divisible by 6, and the difference between the two will be the remainder we're looking for. If we subtract 1 from 123454321, the units digit changes from 1 to 0, we get an even number, and the sum of digits becomes $25 - 1 = 24$ divisible by 3. Thus the new number is divisible by 6, and since it is 1 less than 123454321, the remainder of dividing 123454321 by 6 is 1.

   Alternatively, one can solve this using a calculator. Note that $123454321/6 = 20575720.1666$ The remainder of the division is the decimal part of the quotient, $0.1666\ldots$ multiplied by the divisor, 6. So, $6 * 0.1666\ldots = 1$.

8. **B.** A number is divisible by 9 if the sum of its digits is divisible by 9. Since each of the given number's digits is 1, the sum of its digits is just the number of digits, i.e. 55. What is the greatest integer divisible by 9 that is less than or equal to the given number? By simply changing the units digit from 1 to 0 we get a new number divisible by 9 (since its sum of digits is 54), which is 1 less than the given number. Thus, the remainder we get from dividing the given number by 9 is 1.

9. **C.** Note that the first few numbers that give remainder 4 when divided by 7 are:

$$11, 18, 25$$

Now, starting with the smallest number in the list, 11, we look for x and y such that $(3 * x + y) = 11$. To do this, we subtract successive multiples of 3 from 11 until we obtain a multiple of 5. If necessary, subtract successive multiples of 5 until we obtain a multiple of 3.

$11 - 3 = 8$ is not divisible by 5, but $11 - 3 \cdot 2 = 5$ is divisible by 5, so we found our first pair: $x = 2, y = 1$. This pair sums to 3. A quick check shows that the pair $x = 1, y = 1$ doesn't work, so we conclude that the sum of the pair $x = 2, y = 1$ is minimal.

10. **B.** The sum of the digits of 243 is 9, so 243 is divisible by 9. A quick factoring shows $243 = 3^5 = 3 \cdot 81$, so the circle of 243 people can be divided into 81 consecutive nonoverlapping "arcs" where each arc consists of 3 people standing next to each other. Starting from any relative position (1, 2, or 3) in any arc, by adding 3 to this position we land in the SAME relative position in the "next" arc. Thus, the only people who participate in the distribution of tickets are those who have the same relative position in each arc, specifically, the position that gives a remainder of 1 when divided by 3. Since we divided the circle into 81 arcs, and only one person per arc participates in the distribution of tickets, when all tickets are distributed only 81 people will have at least one ticket. Furthermore, each of these 81 people will have exactly 3 tickets.

11. **B.** The first 10 prime numbers are 2, 3, 5, 7, 11, 13, 17, 19, 23, 29. You find them by writing down 2, and then mentally going over the list of odd numbers starting from 3, and writing down each odd number that cannot be factored. For example, we do not include 27 in our list of primes since $27 = 3^2$.

Note that our list does not contain 1. That's because 1 is not a prime number! The two most common mistakes made by students are (a) to consider 1 to be a prime number, and (2) to forget entirely about the special prime number 2, which is the only even prime number.

There is a neat way to find quickly the sum of our list of 10 prime numbers without using a calculator (the same "trick" can be applied to any list of numbers you wish to add). Look for pairs or triples, not necessarily adjacent, that sum up to multiples of 10. For example:

2	3	5							10
			7				23		30
				11		19			30
					13	17			30
								29	29

We get a shorter list of intermediate sums, most of which are multiples of 10, hence easy to sum. Thus, the total sum is $10 + 30 + 30 + 30 + 29 = 129$.

12. **E.** The keyword here is MUST, which is why it is emphasized. For each answer choice, we will try to simplify it and determine whether the expression is in the required range for ALL nonzero x's. As part of our simplification, we are allowed to divide by x since the problem states that $x \neq 0$. A quick way to eliminate wrong answers is to try to find an x that makes an expression zero. If such an x is found, the expression does not meet the requirements of the problem.

   A. $-\frac{x^2+2x}{x^2+3x} = -\frac{x(x+2)}{x(x+3)} = -\frac{x+2}{x+4}$
      If you let $x = -2$ then this expression equals zero.

   B. $\frac{-2x+3}{3x-5} = -\frac{2x-3}{3x-5} = -\frac{2\left(x-\frac{3}{2}\right)}{3\left(x-\frac{5}{3}\right)}$
      If you let $x = \frac{3}{2}$ then this expression equals zero.

   C. $-\frac{|x+1|}{x+2}$
      If you let $x = -1$ then this expression equals zero.

   D. $-\frac{x^3}{x^4} = -\frac{1}{x}$
      For any $x < 0$ the expression is positive, whereas we are looking for the expression that must be negative for any nonzero x.

   E. $-\frac{2(x^2+1)}{3x^2+3} = -\frac{2(x^2+1)}{3(x^2+1)} = -\frac{2}{3}$
      This expression's value is the constant $-\frac{2}{3}$, which is within the required range $(-1, 0)$ for any x, so answer choice **E** must be the correct answer.

13. **C.** We need to skip "groupings" of 142857 until we reach the group that contains the 99th digit. The greatest multiple of 6 that is less than or equal to 99 is $96 = 6 \cdot 16$. So, the 96th decimal place completes the 16th group of 142857 and the 97th, 98th, and 99th decimal place are given by 1, 4, and 2 respectively. Thus, the answer is 2.

14. **E.** Since the set contains 3, it must also contain the product $3 \cdot 3 = 9$. But then, since 3 and 9 are in the set, it must also contain the product $3 \cdot 9 = 27$, and so on for all powers of 3.

15. **B.** The answer is very simple: it is the singleton set that consists only of the integer 1, since $1 \cdot 1 = 1$. The problem says "two numbers," not "two different numbers," so this solution is correct.

16. **D.** Prime numbers form the basic building blocks of the integers, in the sense that each integer can be uniquely decomposed into a product of prime numbers. Therefore, when we are told that p divides the product ab, we infer that a or b or both must contribute p to the product. Hence, the correct answer choice is **D**. In fact, this result can be

used as the definition of a prime number, which is equivalent to the usual definition (p is prime if and only if the only integers that divide it are 1 and p). To see why it is not necessarily true if p is not prime, let $p = 4$, $a = 6$ and $b = 10$. The product $ab = 60$ is divisible by 4, but neither a nor b is divisible by 4.

17. **C.** If the units digit of n is 4, then the units digit of any positive integer power of n is either 4 or 6. Note that $4 \cdot 4 = 16$ and $4 \cdot 6 = 24$. So, n^2 has units digit equal to 6 and n^3 has units digit equal to 4. Continuing in this way, we see that raising n to a positive EVEN integer results in a number whose units digit is 6 and raising n to a positive ODD integer results in a number whose units digit is 4. Hence, I and III are true.

18. **E.** The sculptor's requirement can be expressed as the double inequality $10 \le x \le 30$ which is also equivalent to the interval $[10, 30]$ on the real line. Recall that $|x - a| \le b$ represents an interval of length $2b$ centered at a. The points that do not satisfy this inequality are all the points outside the interval, i.e. $|x - a| > b$. In our case, the closed interval $[10, 30]$ has length $20 = 2 \cdot 10$ and is centered at $(10 + 20)/2 = 20$, therefore it is represented by $|x - 20| \le 10$. Thus, the answer is $|x - 20| > 10$.

19. **D.** First note that the condition imposed on x in the problem is equivalent to $0 < |x| < 1$. Now, I is false since $\left(\frac{-1}{2}\right)^3 = \frac{-1}{8} < \frac{1}{16} = \left(\frac{-1}{2}\right)^4$. II is true since $|x| < 1$ implies that $|x|^2 = x^2 < 1$. III is true. To see why, note that the inequality $\sqrt{|x|} < \frac{1}{|x|}$ subject to the conditions of the problem is equivalent to $\sqrt{x} < \frac{1}{x}$ subject to the condition $0 < x < 1$. Since in this new equality x is positive, we are allowed to divide and multiply both sides by x without having to worry about changing the sign of the inequality.

$$\sqrt{x} < \frac{1}{x} \qquad \text{(given inequality)}$$
$$x\sqrt{x} < 1 \qquad \text{(multiply by } x\text{)}$$
$$x^2 x < 1 \qquad \text{(square both sides)}$$
$$x^3 < 1 \qquad \text{(simplify)}$$
$$x < 1 \qquad \text{(take cubic root)}$$

the last step is equivalent to the condition $0 < x < 1$, so the proof is complete. But there is a simpler explanation: If $0 < x < 1$ then $\frac{1}{x} > 1$ (can you see why?), but $\sqrt{x} < 1$. Thus, $\sqrt{x} < 1 < \frac{1}{x}$.

20. **B.** One can solve this using a calculator. Note that $23424/18 = 1301.333\ldots$. The remainder of the division is the decimal part of the quotient, $0.333\ldots$ multiplied by the divisor, 18. So, $18 * 0.333\ldots = 6$.

21. **B.** We apply the algebraic identity $a^2 - b^2 = (a+b)(a-b)$ to the given expression.

$$a^4 - b^4 = (a^2 + b^2)(a^2 - b^2) = (a^2 + b^2)(a+b)(a-b) = 15 = 3 \cdot 5$$

Since a and b are both positive integers, it follows that $a > b$, and since 3 and 5 are both prime numbers, it follows that $a^2 + b^2 = 5$ and $(a+b)(a-b) = 3$. This, in turn, implies that $a + b = 3$ and $a - b = 1$. Add the two preceding equations to solve for a: $2a = 4 \Rightarrow a = 2$.

Alternatively, one can solve this problem by noting $b^4 = a^4 - 15$. Since $b^4 > 0$, a can not be 1. If $a = 2$, then $b = 1$, which is feasible. All the other choices yield irrational values for b. Thus, B is the answer.

22. **E.** A quadratic equation $ax^2 + bx + c = 0$ has two distinct solutions when the discriminant is positive, that is $\Delta = b^2 - 4ac > 0$. In our case, $a = 1$ and $c = 6$ so $\Delta = m^2 - 4 \cdot 1 \cdot 6 > 0$ which is equivalent to $m^2 > 24$. The smallest positive integer m that satisfies this inequality is $m = 5$.

23. **E.** Rearrange the equation as $2a^4 = 3ab$, and divide both sides by a (we are allowed to do this because a and b are nonzero integers) to get $2a^3 = 3b$. Since a and b are nonzero integers, it follows that $3b$ is divisible at least by 2, hence b is divisible at least by 2. Similarly, $2a^3$ is divisible at least by 3, hence a is divisible at least by 3. But this implies that a^3 is divisible at least by 27, and therefore $3b$ is divisible at least by $2 \cdot 27 = 54$. Thus, b is divisible at least by $\frac{54}{3} = 18$.

24. **E.** Since a and b share no prime factor in common, and since $ab = (2c)^2$ is the square of an integer, a and b each must be the square of an integer. Thus, statement II must be true. Also, since the product ab is divisible by 4, statement I must be true. Statement III is also true, because only one of a or b is divisible by 2, and since they share no factor in common, the other one is odd. Hence, $a - b$ is odd, since even $\pm$ odd = odd.

25. **D.** Statement I is true, since the common denominator of two fractions with odd denominators must also be odd. Statement II is also true since the product of two fractions with odd denominators must also have an odd denominator. Statement III is false. For example, the reciprocal of $\frac{2}{3}$ is $\frac{3}{2}$, which doesn't have an odd denominator.

26. **C.** Statement I is false, since the denominator of $\frac{1}{4} + \frac{2}{25} = \frac{25+8}{100} = \frac{33}{100}$ is not a square of an integer. Statement II is false, since the denominator of $\frac{2}{9} \cdot \frac{3}{4} = \frac{1}{6}$ is not a square of an integer. Statement III is true since $n!$ is even for all $n \geq 5$, so $n!$ can be written as $2k$ for some positive integer k. Then the denominator of $\frac{1}{2^{n!}} = \frac{1}{2^{2k}} = \frac{1}{(2^k)^2}$ is the square of the integer 2^k.

27. **B.** By definition, the geometric mean of a and b equals $\sqrt{ab}$. Given $\sqrt{ab} = 10$, then $ab = 100 = 2^2 \cdot 5^2$. Since a and b have no prime factors in common, a must be either 4 or 25. Only 4 is listed as an answer choice, so the correct answer is **B**.

28. **D.** We must first write out the Fibonacci sequence up to 100,

$$1, 1, 2, 3, 5, 8, 13, 21, 34, 55, 89$$

and determine which terms are prime numbers. 1 is not a prime number. 2, 3, 5, and 13 are prime numbers. $21 = 3 \cdot 7$, $34 = 2 \cdot 17$, and $55 = 5 \cdot 11$ are not prime numbers. It remains to check whether 89 is prime. You can use your calculator to check if there are any primes $< \sqrt{89} < 10$ that divide evenly 89. Or you can see that it is not divisible by 2 since it is odd, it is not divisible by 3 since its sum of digits is not divisible by 3, and it is not divisible by 5 since its last digit is neither 0 nor 5. The only prime left to check is 7. Note that 77 is evenly divisible by 7, and so for 89 to be evenly divisible by 7, the difference $89 - 77 = 12$ must also be divisible by 7, which it isn't. Therefore, 89 must be prime. Thus, we counted a total of 5 primes: 2, 3, 5, 13, 89.

29. **C.** The series whose sum is a can be expressed as

$$(m - 12) + (m - 11) + \cdots + (m - 1) + m + (m + 1) + \cdots + (m + 11) + (m + 12)$$

and similarly, the series whose sum is b can be expressed as

$$(m - 7) + (m - 6) + \cdots + (m - 1) + m + (m + 1) + \cdots + (m + 6) + (m + 7)$$

Both series are symmetric, in the sense that in the first, all numbers cancel and we're left with 25 m's, whereas in the second we are left with 15 n's. Thus, $a = 25m$, $b = 15n$, and $\frac{a}{b} = \frac{25m}{15n} = \frac{5m}{3n}$.

30. **D.** Since x and y belong to the set A, they each give a remainder 3 when divided by 5. Thus, $x = 5n + 3$ and $y = 5m + 3$ for some integers n and m.

Statement I is false since $x + y = 5n + 3 + 5m + 3 = 5(n + m) + 6 = 5(n + m + 1) + 1$ gives a remainder of 1 when divided by 5, hence does not belong to the set A;

Statement II is true since $x - y + 3 = 5n + 3 - 5m - 3 + 3 = 5(n - m) + 3$ gives a remainder of 3 when divided by 5, hence belongs to A;

Statement III is true since $xy - 1 = (5n + 3)(5m + 3) - 1 = 5(5mn + 3n + 3m) + 9 - 1 = 5(5mn + 3n + 3m + 1) + 3$ gives a remainder of 3 when divided by 5, so belongs to A.

31. **B.** $n^2 - 1 = (n + 1)(n - 1)$ implies that we need to examine the following products to determine which ones are the products of exactly two primes:

$$1 \cdot 3 \quad \text{no (1 is not a prime number)}$$
$$2 \cdot 4 \quad \text{no}$$
$$\boxed{3 \cdot 5} \quad \text{YES}$$
$$4 \cdot 6 \quad \text{no}$$
$$\boxed{5 \cdot 7} \quad \text{YES}$$
$$6 \cdot 8 \quad \text{no}$$
$$7 \cdot 9 \quad \text{no}$$
$$8 \cdot 10 \quad \text{no}$$
$$9 \cdot 11 \quad \text{no}$$

Thus, only the two integers $15 = 3 \cdot 5 = 4^2 - 1$ and $35 = 5 \cdot 7 = 6^2 - 1$ in M are less than 100 and can be written as the product of exactly two primes.

32. **C.** Since 22 is prime, and 2 is the only prime number, we can immediately eliminate the pair $(2, 20)$ from our count, and consider only odd numbers starting from 3, since 1 is not a prime number. We need to examine only five pairs:

$$3 + 19 \quad \text{YES}$$
$$5 + 17 \quad \text{YES}$$
$$7 + 15 \quad \text{no}$$
$$9 + 13 \quad \text{no}$$
$$11 + 11 \quad \text{YES}$$

Thus, there are only three such pairs.

33. **C.** $n^2 - 1 = (n+1)(n-1)$ implies that we need to examine the following products to determine which ones are the products of exactly three primes, not necessarily distinct:

$$1 \cdot 3 \quad \text{no}$$
$$\boxed{2 \cdot 4} \quad \text{YES } (2 \cdot 2 \cdot 2)$$
$$3 \cdot 5 \quad \text{no}$$
$$4 \cdot 6 \quad \text{no}$$
$$5 \cdot 7 \quad \text{no}$$
$$6 \cdot 8 \quad \text{no}$$
$$\boxed{7 \cdot 9} \quad \text{YES } (7 \cdot 3 \cdot 3)$$
$$8 \cdot 10 \quad \text{no}$$
$$\boxed{9 \cdot 11} \quad \text{YES } (3 \cdot 3 \cdot 11)$$

Thus, only the three integers $8 = 2 \cdot 2 \cdot 2 = 3^2 - 1$, $63 = 7 \cdot 3 \cdot 3 = 8^2 - 1$, and $99 = 3 \cdot 3 \cdot 11 = 10^2 - 1$ in M are less than 100 and can be written as the product of exactly three primes.

34. **E.** Given $x < 0 < 2y$, multiplying by -1 shows $-2y < 0 < -x$. Thus, answer A and answer C may be eliminated. Since x is negative, $-x$ is positive, and the value of answer D, $-(2y+x) = -2y-x$ is bigger than $-2y$. So, answer D may be eliminated. Similarly, the value of answer E, $-(2y - x) = -2y + x$, must be less than $-2y$. Therefore, the least value is answer E.

35. **E.** Apply the FOIL method and substitute the given values as follows

$$
\begin{aligned}
(x-y)^2 \ &= (x-y)(x-y) \\
&= x^2 - 2xy + y^2 \\
&= (x^2 + y^2) - 2xy \\
&= 40 - 2*(-12) \\
&= 64
\end{aligned}
$$

36. **A.** The equations given represent two lines in the xy-coordinate plane. A solution to the set of equations corresponds to a point (x, y) that lies on both lines. So, two equations have no common solution if the lines they represent are parallel. Lines are parallel if their equations differ by a multiple. For example, for any real numbers a, b, and c, the lines represented by $ax+by = c$ and $2ax+2by = 2c$ are parallel. So, multiply the first equation by 3 to obtain

$$
\begin{aligned}
3x - 6y &= 30 \\
3x - wy &= 30
\end{aligned}
$$

If $w = 6$, then the lines are parallel.

37. **B.** Since 37 is the largest integer, one must consider the sum of consecutive integers less than 37. Note that $37 + 35 = 72$ and $37 + 35 + 33 = 105$. Continuing in this way only yields larger numbers. So, in order to bring the sum back to 78, the consecutive integers must include some negative numbers. Consider the sum $-37 - 35 - 33 \ldots - 1 + 1 + 3 \ldots + 33 + 35 + 37 = 0$. And, $-41 - 39 = -80$. So, the consecutive odd integers are $-41, -39, \ldots, 35, 37$, for a total of 40 numbers.

38. **A.** Recall properties of exponents, to simplify the fraction as follows

$$
\begin{aligned}
r \& q &= \frac{2^{2r+q}}{2^{r-q}} \\
&= 2^{(2r+q)}2^{-(r-q)} \\
&= 2^{(2r+q)-(r-q)} \\
&= 2^{2r+q-r+q} \\
&= 2^{r+2q}
\end{aligned}
$$

Given that $4 = r\&1$, $4 = 2^{r+2}$ yields only one solution, $r = 0$.

39. **E.** Given $x > 0$, choose a few values for x and follow the rules. First consider $x = 1$, so $y = 3$ and y is odd. So, $z = y + 2 = 5$. So, $t = \frac{z+1}{2} = \frac{6}{2} = 3$. Next consider $x = 2$, so $y = 4$ and y is even. So, $z = y - 1 = 3$. So, $t = \frac{z+1}{2} = \frac{4}{2} = 2$. For any other value of $x > 2$, z will always be positive and hence $t > 0$. Thus, I is always true. Following the rules, if y is odd, the value of $z = y + 2$ will always be odd and thus the numerator of t, $z + 1$, will always be even and t will be even. If y is even, subtracting 1 will always yield an odd number, so similarly the value of $z = y - 1$ will always be odd and thus the numerator of z will be even and t will be even. So, II and III is always true. Therefore, the correct answer is E.

40. **E.** Consider the cubes of the consecutive integers and find the first one divisible by 16. $1^3 = 1, 2^3 = 8, 3^3 = 27$, and $4^3 = 64$. Note that $64 = 4 * 16$. So, the correct answer is 4.

41. **C.** The odd primes contained in S are

$$3, 5, 7, 11, 13, 17, 19, 23, 29, 31, 37, 41, 43, 47$$

i.e. S contains 14 odd prime numbers. Since S contains $50/2 = 25$ odd integers, the number of odd non-primes in S is $25 - 14 = 11$. Thus, the ratio of odd primes to odd non-primes in S is $14 : 11$.

42. **B.** $132 = 2 \cdot 66 = 2 \cdot 2 \cdot 33 = 2 \cdot 2 \cdot 3 \cdot 11$. So, 132 has three distinct prime factors: 2, 3, and 11. The distinct prime factors of $24 = 2^3 \cdot 3$ are 2 and 3, so 11 relatively prime to 24. Thus, the answer is 1.

CHAPTER 3

ADVANCED ALGEBRA

Advanced algebra problems involving functions are very common on the SAT. You should be familiar with the various aspects of functions and their graphs, including translations, compositions, domain, range, and the evaluation of functions. Polynomials appear in many problems on the SAT, sometimes in conjunction with functions. You should be able to factor, add, subtract, multiply and evaluate polynomials, and to solve polynomial equations. You are also expected to manipulate and solve systems of equations, direct and inverse variation problems, and absolute value equations.

When a variable raised to a power is compared to the same variable raised to a different power, you should pick numbers to plug into the variable. Specifically, you should pick a number less than -1, between -1 and 0, between 0 and one, and finally a number greater than 1.

1. $x^4 \leq x^2$ for which of the following:

I. $0 \leq x \leq 1$
II. $-1 \leq x \leq 0$
III $x \leq -1$

A. I only
B. II only
C. I and II only
D. II and III only
E. I, II, and III

ANSWER: C. We should consider a negative integer less than one, a negative number between zero and one, and a number between zero and one. If we choose -2, we have $x^4 = (-2)^4 = 16$, and $x^2 = (-2)^2 = 4$. Therefore x^4 is greater than x^2, and the inequality in III fails. We now try $-.5$. $x^4 = \frac{1}{16}$, while $x^2 = \frac{1}{4}$. Therefore the inequality in II holds. If we choose $.5$, $x^4 = \frac{1}{16}$, while $x^2 = \frac{1}{2}$. Therefore x^4 is smaller than x^2, and I holds. Therefore the answer is I and II only.

When a problem is given involving numbers to plug in, try to at first simplify the expression. Be careful about the order of operations.

2. If $x = 4$ and $y = \frac{1}{2}$, $(x^3 - \sqrt{x})^{\frac{\sqrt{2x}}{\sqrt{4xy}}} =$

   A. 48
   B. 62
   C. 64
   D. 72
   E. 84

   ANSWER: B. We could first get rid of the x term: $\frac{\sqrt{2x}}{\sqrt{4xy}} = \sqrt{\frac{1}{y}}$. If $x = 4$ and $y = \frac{1}{2}$, $(x^3 - \sqrt{x})^{\frac{\sqrt{1}}{\sqrt{2y}}} = 62^{\frac{1}{1}} = 62^1 = 62$

When an expression is compared to another expression, try canceling like terms first.

3. $x^2 y^2 = 16y$ If x is an integer smaller than 5 and greater than 0, what are ALL values of y that would validate the above equation?

   A. $(-\infty, \infty)$
   B. $(0, \infty)$
   C $(1, 4, \frac{4}{9})$
   D. $(0, 1, 4, \frac{16}{9})$
   E. $(1, 4, \frac{16}{9}, 16)$

   ANSWER: E. We know y must be positive because if y were negative $16y$ would be negative, but $x^2 y^2$ must be positive. A negative couldn't equal a positive. We can simplify: $x^2 y = 16 \Rightarrow x^2 = \frac{16}{y}$. Since x is an integer smaller than five, $x^2 = 0, 1, 4, 9, 16$. Therefore $y = 1, 4, \frac{16}{9}, 16$.

Problems involving three variables when only two equations are given call for canceling a variable that appears in both equations, then solving in terms of the other two variables. Look for a term whose coefficient is identical.

4. What is $3b + 3c$ equal to if $4a + 3b = c + 17$ and $3a - 2b + c = b + 4$?

A. $5a + 1$
B. $5b - 3$
C. $3b - 2c$
D. $4c + 5$
E. $-4c - 6$

ANSWER: D.

$$4a + 3b - c = 17$$
$$+3a - 3b + c = 4$$
$$7a = 21$$
$$a = 3$$

Substitute a into the 1st equation:

$$4 * 3 + 3b - c = 17$$
$$3b = c + 5$$

Adding $3c$ to both sides:

$$3b + 3c = (c + 5) + 3c$$
$$3b + 3c = 4c + 5$$

Two functions $f(x)$ and $g(x)$ are inverse if $f(g(x)) = g(f(x)) = x$. The domain, though, does not have to be the same.

5. $f(x) = \sqrt{x}$, $g(x) = x^2$. Which of these statements are true?

I The two functions, $f(x)$ and $g(x)$ are inverses.
II. $g(f(x)) = f(g(x))$
III The domain for $g(f(x)) = $ the domain for $f(g(x))$.

A. I only
B. II only

C. I and II only
D. I and III only
E. I, II, and III

ANSWER: C. The functions are inverses since $f(g(x)) = x$, $(\sqrt{x^2})$ and $g(f(x)) = x$, $(\sqrt{x}^2)$. By definition of inverse functions $g(f(x)) = f(g(x))$. But the domain for $g(x)$ is $(-\infty, \infty)$ and the domain for $f(x)$ is $(0,\infty)$. Therefore the domain for $f(g(x)) = (-\infty,\infty)$, and since the value of x in $(f(x))$ must be either zero or positive, the domain of $g(f(x))$ is $(0,\infty)$. Therefore the two domains are not equal.

In problems involving absolute value functions, one must take two possibilities into account: 1. ignore the absolute value sign, and 2. take the negative of the expression within the absolute value.

6. Given $|x - y| + 8 \le 16$, which of the following statements are true:

A. $-x + 2 \le y \le x - 3$
B. $x - 8 \le y \le x + 8$
C. $3 \le y \le 8 - x$
D. $y \ge 8 - x$ or $y \le -8 + x$
E. $y \ge x - 8$ or $y \le 3 + x$

ANSWER: B. $|x - y| + 8 \le 16 \Rightarrow |x - y| \le 8$. This statement is equivalent to the following statement: The distance between x and y is smaller or equal to 8, which implies that $x - y$ lies between -8 and 8.

$$-8 \le x - y \le 8$$
$$x - y \le 8$$
$$\Rightarrow y \ge x - 8$$
$$or :$$
$$x \ge y - 8$$
$$\Rightarrow x + 8 \ge y$$
$$Therefore :$$
$$x - 8 \le y \le x + 8$$

Some problems appear hard to tackle, but all that is needed is substituting one variable for another.

7. Let $y^2 + 5y + x = 6$ for constant x, and let $y = (1 - x)$ be one solution to the equation. What are the values of x?

    A. $(-5, 6)$
    B. $(\sqrt{5}, 7)$
    C. $(16, -4)$
    D. $(\sqrt{17} - 423, -\sqrt{17} - 423)$
    E. $(0, 6)$

ANSWER: E. Substitute $(1 - x)$ for y:

$$(1 - x)^2 + 5(1 - x) + x = 6$$
$$x^2 - 2x + 1 + 5 - 5x + x = 6$$
$$x^2 - 6x = 0$$
$$x(x - 6) = 0$$
$$x = 0, 6$$

A common denominator must be chosen when a variable or variables are in the denominator.

8. $\frac{1}{x} + \frac{1}{2x} + \frac{1}{3x} = ?$

    A. $x^2 + \frac{3x}{2} + 1$
    B. $3x^2 + 2x + 1$
    C. $\frac{11}{6x}$
    D. $\frac{5}{3x}$
    E. $\frac{3x^2 + 2x + 1}{3x^2}$

ANSWER: C. If we choose $6x$ to be the common denominator of the three terms, we have:

$$\frac{6}{6x} + \frac{3}{6x} + \frac{2}{6x} = \frac{11}{6x}$$

Two important rules about exponents:
1. $x^a * x^b = x^{a+b}$
2. $(x^a)^b = x^{a*b}$

9. If x and y are positive integers, which of the following is equivalent to $(9x^2)^{4y} - (3x)^y$?

    A. $(27x)^{3y}$
    B. $(3x)^{7y}$
    C. $3^y(x^8 - x^y)$
    D. $(3x)^y[(3x)^{7y} - 1]$
    E. $(3x)^y[(3x)^{7y} - (3x)]$

ANSWER: D. Since the terms that are being subtracted have different bases, the first step is to factor the first term to have the same base as the second:

$$(9x^2)^{4y} - (3x)^y =$$
$$(3^2x^2)^{4y} - (3x)^y =$$
$$[(3x)^2]^{4y} - (3x)^y$$
$$(3x)^{8y} - (3x)^y$$

The terms still have different exponents, so we can't subtract them. We can factor out the term $(3x)^y$ and get $(3x)^y[(3x)^{7y} - 1]$.

Problems involving domains of square root expressions call for determining for which values the expression within the square root sign are positive.

10. For what values of x would the below expression be real?

$$\frac{\sqrt{-3x-2}-\sqrt{4x-1}}{-2x+1}$$

A. $x > \frac{2}{3}$

B. $x \leq \frac{-2}{3}$, $x \neq \frac{1}{2}$

C. $\frac{-1}{4} < x < \frac{2}{3}$, $x \neq \frac{1}{2}$

D. $x \neq \frac{1}{2}$

E. $\frac{-2}{3} < x < \frac{1}{4}$

ANSWER: B. Because of the first square root expression, x must be smaller than or equal to $\frac{-2}{3}$, while because of the second square root expression, x must be greater than or equal to $\frac{1}{4}$. But the first restriction won't allow x to be greater than or equal to $\frac{1}{4}$. The denominator would be zero if x was equal to $\frac{1}{2}$.

Practice Problems

1. If $x \neq 0$ and x and y are integers, which of the following is always true?

   I. $x^{2y} > 0$
   II. $x^y * y^x \geq 0$
   III. $x^{2y} * y^{2x} \geq 0$

   A. I only
   B. I and II only
   C. II and III only
   D. I and III only
   E. I,II, and III

2. The expression $\frac{3\sqrt{x}+2\sqrt{y}}{\sqrt{x}-\sqrt{y}}$ is equal to:

   A. $\frac{3x+6\sqrt{xy}+2y}{x-y}$
   B. $\frac{3x+6\sqrt{xy}+2y}{x-y}$
   C. $\frac{3x+5\sqrt{xy}+2y}{x+y}$
   D. $\frac{3x+5\sqrt{xy}+2y}{x-y}$
   E. $\frac{2x+3y}{x+y}$

3. If $3x + 5y = z + 5$ and $12x + z = -25 - 10y$, then what is the average of x and y?

   A. $\frac{-2}{3}$
   B. $\frac{1}{3}$
   C. $\frac{-5}{2}$
   D. $\frac{15}{2}$
   E. $\frac{16}{5}$

4. For all positive real numbers x, let $f(x) = \frac{x^2-1}{7}$. If $f(x) = 24$, what is the value of $f(2x - 15)$?

   A. $\frac{13}{2}$
   B. $\frac{33}{2}$

C. $\frac{120}{7}$

D. $\frac{442}{3}$

E. $\frac{678}{5}$

5. If $x^2 - 4x > 21$, which of the following is true?

A. $x < -7$ or $x > 3$

B. $-3 < x < 7$

C. $x < -3$ or $x > 7$

D. $-7 < x < 3$

E. $3 < x < 7$

6. Let x be an integer and $x^5 > x^3$ and $y^2 \geq y$. Which of the following is true?

I. $x^4 > x^2$

II. $2y$ can equal 0 and 2

III. $x^6 > 3x^5$

A. I only

B. II only

C. I and II only

D. I and III only

E I, II, and III

7. $z = (y^4 + y^2)^{\frac{\sqrt{x}}{2x+1}}$. What is the range of the function if the expression is a real number and x and y are integers?

A. $z > 0$

B. $\frac{1}{2} > z \leq \frac{3}{4}$

C. $z > 1$

D. $z \geq 1$

E. $1 \leq z \leq 16$

8. $g(x) = \sqrt{x}$, $f(x) = x^2$, $h(x) = g(x + 1)$ What is h(g(f(x)))?

A. $f(x^2 + 1)$

B. $g(x + 1)$

C. x

D. $x^2 + 1$

E. $f(x - 1)$

9. Given $y = -x^2 + 2x + 2$, which of the following equals y?

A. $-(x - 1)^2 + 3$

B. $-(x + 2)^2 + 2$

C. $-(2x - 1)^2 - 1$

D. $(x + 1)^2 + 4$

E. $(x + 2)^2 - 2$

10. Given $x = \sqrt{y + z}$, $z = (x - 1)^2$, what is y in terms of x only?

A. $-x + 1$

B. $-2x + 1$

C. $2x - 1$

D. $3x + 3$

E. $-3x + 4$

11. $3x^2 = 2y$ and $2z^2 = \sqrt{x + 1}$, what is y in terms of z only?

A. $5z^8 - 13\sqrt{z} + 1$

B. $16z^4 + 3z^2 + z + 1$

C. $24z^8 - 12z^4 + \frac{3}{2}$

D. $z^2 - 13z$

E. $\frac{1}{4}z^8 - 6z^4 + \frac{2}{3}$

12. All of the following expressions are real numbers. Which of the following expressions must be greater than zero?

I. $(x^2 + 1)(\sqrt{x} - 2)$

II. $(-2)^{2y} + y^{-2x}$

III. $(3y - 2x)^{2y - 3x}$ if $y > x$

A. I only
B. II only
C. I and II only
D. II and III only
E. I, II, and III

13. What is the domain of $(x+2)^{\frac{x+2}{x+1}}$?

A. $x \neq -1$
B. $x \neq 0, -1$
C. All real numbers
D. $x \neq 0, -2$
E. $x \neq -1, -2$

14. Given $y^2 = \sqrt{x-1}$, which of the following could be true?

I. $2x - 2 = 2y^4$
II. $(x-1)^2 + 1 = 0$
III. $y^2 = 2x$

A. I only
B. II only
C. I and II only
D. II and III only
E. I, II, and III

15. If $a^{-2}b^3 = \sqrt{cd^{-1}}$ and $d = x + 1$, what is x equal to in terms of a,b,c,and d?

A. $\frac{ca^4}{b^6} - 1$
B. $\frac{ca^2}{b^3} + 1$
C. $\frac{b^3}{a^2c}$
D. $\frac{b^{\frac{3}{2}}}{a^2c}$
E. $\frac{c^{\frac{1}{2}}a^2}{b^3}$

16. What is x in terms of a,b, and c, if: $\frac{x^{\frac{1}{3}}}{a} - x^{\frac{1}{3}} = bc$?

    A. $\frac{1}{bc} + x^{\frac{1}{3}}$

    B. $\frac{1}{bc} + x^{\frac{-1}{3}}$

    C. $\frac{a^3 b^3 c^3}{(1-a)^3}$

    D. $\frac{x^{\frac{1}{3}}}{bc + x(\frac{1}{3})}$

    E. $\frac{b^2 + \frac{1}{c}}{x}$

17. $\sqrt{xy} = 16y$. If y is an integer, what can x equal?

    A. $(0, \infty)$
    B. $(0, 16)$
    C. $(0, 16, 256)$
    D. $(16n, n \in \text{integer})$
    E. $(256n, n \in \text{integer} > 0)$

Answers to Practice Problems

1. **D.** x^{2y} is always greater than zero if y is an integer because $2y =$ an even integer, and any number raised to an even power is greater than or equal to zero. If $y = 0$, $x^0 = 1$, which is greater than zero. Therefore I is always true. III is true: x^{2y} is always positive (even power, $x \neq 0$) and y^{2x} is either zero (if y is zero) or positive. A positive number times a positive number is positive. II is false because x could be negative and y can be positive or vice versa.

2. **D.** Multiply the numerator and the denominator by $\sqrt{x} + \sqrt{y}$

$$\frac{3\sqrt{x}+2\sqrt{y}}{\sqrt{x}-\sqrt{y}} * \frac{\sqrt{x}+\sqrt{y}}{\sqrt{x}+\sqrt{y}} = \frac{3x+3\sqrt{xy}+2\sqrt{xy}+2y}{x-y-\sqrt{xy}+\sqrt{xy}} = \frac{3x+5\sqrt{xy}+2y}{x-y}$$

3. **A.** Because there are two equations and three unknowns, it seems as if we can't solve for each variable. However, if we rearrange the terms in the equations and line up like terms in an addition problem, we see that the z terms cancel out:

$$3x + 5y - z = 5$$
$$12x + 10y + z = -25$$

Adding the two equations:

$$15x + 15y = -20$$
$$x + y = \frac{-4}{3}$$

To find the average of x and y, we divide the sum by 2:

$$\frac{x+y}{2} = \frac{\frac{-4}{3}}{2} = \frac{-4}{6} = \frac{-2}{3}$$

So, the average of x and y is $\frac{-2}{3}$

4. **C.** We are attempting to find x such that $f(x) = 24$. So, we substitute 24 for $f(x)$ to get: $24 = \frac{x^2 - 1}{7}$.

We can cross multiply to solve for x:

$x^2 - 1 = 168$, or $x^2 = 169 \Rightarrow x = 13$.

We now want to find f($2x - 15$), which is:

$$f(2(13) - 15) = f(11)$$
$$= \frac{11^2 - 1}{7}$$
$$= \frac{121 - 1}{7} = \frac{120}{7}.$$

5. **C.** If we subtract 21 from both sides of the inequality, we get $x^2 - 4x - 21 > 0$. We can factor and set equal to 0, and then determine for which values it is positive or greater than 0.

$$x^2 - 4x - 21 > 0$$
$$(x - 7)(x + 3) > 0$$

Now set each factor equal to zero and solve:

$$x - 7 = 0, x = 7$$
$$x + 3, x = -3$$

The zeros are where the sign of the values of the equation change from negative to positive, and vice versa. We'll use the factored form of the equation $0 = (x - 7)(x + 3)$ for efficiency.

For the interval $x < -3$, pick -4 as a test point. Substituting -4 into $(x - 7)(x + 3)$ yields the product of two negatives so the that the result is positive or greater than zero. Therefore, one interval is $x < -3$.

For the interval $-3 < x < 7$, pick 0 as a test point. Substituting 0 into $(x - 7)(x + 3)$ yields the product of a negative and a positive, so the result is negative.

For the interval $x > 7$, pick 8 as a test point. Substituting 8 into $(x - 7)(x + 3)$ yields the product of two positives, so the result is positive. So one interval is $x > 7$.

6. **C.** I is true. If x^5 is greater than x^3, then x must be greater than 1. If x is greater than 1, x^4 must be greater than x^2. Consider $y^2 \geq y$. The equation holds true if y equals 0 and 1 (not the only solutions). Therefore in that case $2y = 0$ or 2. Therefore II is true. Comparing x^6 with $3x^5$. Since x is an integer and $x^5 > x^3$, x must be greater than one, or an integer greater than or equal to 2. If we consider the value of x^6 if x is two, x^6 is 64. For $3x^5$, when x is equal to 2, $3x^5 = 96$. Therefore $3x^5$ is greater than x^6, so the statement is false. Therefore the only true statements are I and II.

7. **D.** x must be greater or equal to zero since we can only take the square root of zero or a positive number if the expression is real, as stated. Therefore $\frac{\sqrt{x}}{2x+1}$ is also greater or equal to zero since 2 times a positive number plus 1 is positive and $2 * 0 + 1$ is positive. $y^4 + y^2$ is positive if $y \neq 0$. It is stated that y is an integer greater than zero, so we don't have to worry about this case. Therefore we have a positive number greater than or equal to two, raised to the zero or positive integer greater than or equal to one. The minimum number is $2^0 = 1$, and therefore the expression is greater than or equal to 1.

8. **B.** $h(g(f(x))) = h(g(x^2)) = h(\sqrt{x^2}) = h(x) = g(x + 1)$.

9. **A.** There are two ways to solve this problem. The long way is to complete the square:

$$-x^2 + 2x + 2 =$$
$$-(x^2 - 2x - 2) =$$
$$-[(x^2 - 2x + 1) - 1 - 2] =$$
$$-[(x^2 - 2x + 1) - 3] =$$
$$-[(x - 1)^2 - 3] =$$
$$-(x - 1)^2 + 3$$

However, this is a timed test. Therefore, it is better to eliminate answer choices. Choice B will have a $4x$ term, choice C will have a $4x^2$ term, Choice D will have a constant of 5, and choice E will have a $4x$ term. That leaves A as the only possible answer.

10. **C.** If $z = (x - 1)^2$, $z = x^2 - 2x + 1$

If $x = \sqrt{y + z}$, $x^2 = y + z$

Substitute $x^2 - 2x + 1$ for z in $x^2 = y + z$:

$$x^2 = y + x^2 - 2x + 1$$
$$y = 2x - 1$$

11. **C.** Solution: Square both sides of the equation: $2z^2 = \sqrt{x + 1}$

$$4z^4 = x + 1$$
$$4z^4 - 1 = x$$
$$(4z^4 - 1)^2 = x^2$$
$$16z^8 - 8z^2 + 1 = x^2$$

Using the equation: $2y = 3x^2$:

$$2y = 3(16z^8 - 8z^4 + 1)$$
$$y = \frac{3}{2}(16z^8 - 8z^4 + 1)$$
$$y = 24z^8 - 12z^4 + \frac{3}{2}$$

12. **D.** If $\sqrt{x-2}$ is real as stated in the question x must be greater than or equal to two. If $x = 2$, I is equal to zero. The problem asked which expressions are greater than zero. Therefore, I is false. Since x must be greater than or equal to two, $x^2 + 1$ must be greater than or equal to 5 ($2^2 + 1$), and hence positive. II must be true: Any number raised to an even power must be positive. If $y = 0$, we have $(-2)^0 + 0^{-2x} = 1$, which is greater than zero. III must be true: If $y > x$, $3y - 2x$ must be positive. A positive number raised to any power is always positive. The exponent being specifically $2x - 3y$ is irrelevant.

13. **E.** $x + 1$ cannot equal zero since the denominator cannot equal 0. Therefore x cannot equal -1. x cannot equal -2 because we would have $0^{\frac{0}{x+1}} = 0^0$. 0^0 is undefined.

14. **A.** Solution:

I is true:

$$y^4 = x - 1$$
$$2y^4 = 2(x - 1)$$

II is false since:

$$(x-1)^2 + 1 = 0$$
$$x^2 - 2x + 1 + 1 = 0$$
$$x^2 - 2x + 2 = 0$$

Using the quadratic formula, the discriminant $\sqrt{b^2 - 4ac} = \sqrt{4 - 4*2*1} = -4$ which is not real. Note that the equation: $y^2 = \sqrt{x-1}$ is not relevant. III is false, since:

Check to see whether: $2x = y^2$

$$2x = \sqrt{x-1}$$
$$4x^2 = x - 1$$
$$4x^2 - x + 1 = 0$$

The determinant $\sqrt{1 - 4*4*1} = \sqrt{-17}$ is not real.

15 **A.** We have $\frac{b^3}{a^2} = \sqrt{\frac{c}{d}}$. Substituting $x+1$ for d:

$$\frac{b^3}{a^2} = \sqrt{\frac{c}{d}}$$
$$\frac{b^3}{a^2} = \sqrt{\frac{c}{x+1}}$$

Squaring both sides:

$$\frac{b^6}{a^4} = \frac{c}{x+1}$$
$$b^6(x+1) = ca^4$$
$$x + 1 = \frac{ca^4}{b^6}$$
$$x = \frac{ca^4}{b^6} - 1$$

16. **C.** We have:

$$\frac{x^{\frac{1}{3}} - ax^{\frac{1}{3}}}{a} = bc$$

$$x^{\frac{1}{3}} - ax^{\frac{1}{3}} = abc$$

$$(x^{\frac{1}{3}})(1 - a) = abc$$

$$x^{\frac{1}{3}} = \frac{abc}{1 - a}$$

$$x = \frac{a^3 b^3 c^3}{(1 - a)^3}$$

17. **E.** If $\sqrt{xy} = 16y, xy = 256y^2, x = 256y.$ y must be positive since if it were negative we would have $\sqrt{xy} = $ a negative number. Therefore x must be a multiple of 256. $256n$ is a positive multiple of 256 if n is positive.

CHAPTER 4

RATES, RATIOS, AND PERCENTAGES

Rates

Rates measure how a quantity changes with respect to another quantity. Rates are often calculated in terms of a unit of time (e.g. minutes, seconds, etc.). For example, speed is a rate because it measures the change in distance over time: speed = distance/time. The same relationship applies to calculating other rates except that the quantities can be different from distance and time. Usually you are asked to calculate a new rate after one of the quantities involved has changed (e.g. speed or time in the example above). You may also be asked to calculate the original quantities after you are given some initial information about a rate.

1. Edwin and Jacob read a book for their assignment in English class. Edwin read it at the rate of 30 pages per minute while Jacob read the same book at the rate of 15 pages per minute. If the total time they both spent to read the book was an hour, how many pages did the book have?

   A. 100
   B. 200
   C. 300
   D. 600
   E. 150

   ANSWER: D. Let t_1 represent the number of minutes that it took Edwin to read the book. Then, $(60 - t_1)$ equals Jacob's time in minutes. We know that

$$\begin{aligned}
30t_1 &= 15(60 - t_1) \\
2t_1 &= 60 - t_1 \\
3t_1 &= 60 \\
t_1 &= 20
\end{aligned}$$

   The total number of pages read by Edwin equals the product of the time he spent reading and his reading rate. Therefore, the total number of pages is $20 \times 30 = 600$.

This is the recommended way of solving the problem for a timed test such as the SAT. A complete description of the solution is as follows.

Let t_1, r_1, and p_1 represent the time it took Edwin to read the book, his reading speed, and total number of pages he read respectively. Similarly, let t_2, r_2, and p_2 represent these quantities for Jacob. Then, we have:

$$
\begin{aligned}
r_1 &= \frac{p_1}{t_1} \implies t_1 = \frac{p_1}{r_1} \\
r_2 &= \frac{p_2}{t_2} \implies t_2 = \frac{p_2}{r_2} \\
t_1 + t_2 &= 60 \\
\frac{p_1}{r_1} + \frac{p_2}{r_2} &= 60
\end{aligned}
$$

Notice that $p_1 = p_2$ since they are both reading the same book. Then, the last equation results in the following:

$$
\frac{p_1}{15} + \frac{p_1}{30} = 60
$$

We then multiply both sides by 30 (the common denominator of the two fractions):

$$
\begin{aligned}
2p_1 + p_1 &= 30 \times 60 \\
3p_1 &= 30 \times 60 \\
p_1 &= 600
\end{aligned}
$$

2. A pool has a drain, which can remove water from the pool at the rate of 100 liters per minute, and several pipes, each of which can pump water into the pool at the rate of 50 liters per minute. How many pipes are needed to pump water into the pool while the drain is open, so that the pool is filled twice as fast as when the drain is closed and one third as many pipes are allowed to pump water into the pool?

A. 3
B. 4
C. 5
D. 6
E. 7

ANSWER: D. When the drain is open and n pipes pump water into the pool, the pool is filled at the rate of $50n - 100$ liters per minute. When the drain is closed and

$\frac{n}{3}$ pipes pump water into the pool, the pool is filled at the rate of $50 \times \frac{n}{3}$ liters per minute. This gives rise to the equations:

$$\frac{50n - 100}{50 \times \frac{n}{3}} = \frac{2}{1}$$

$$50n - 100 = 2\left(50 \times \frac{n}{3}\right)$$

$$150n - 300 = 100n$$

$$50n = 300$$

$$n = 6$$

Ratios

Ratios represent the relationship or proportion of two quantities with respect to each other. Ratio of a quantity a with respect to another quantity b can be presented either as a fraction $\frac{a}{b}$ or by the notion $a : b$. Sometimes you are given two ratios and you are asked to calculate a third ratio. You should keep in mind that the ratio of two fractions can be converted to a multiplication equation. That is, dividing a fraction $\frac{a}{b}$ by another fraction $\frac{c}{d}$ is the same as multiplying the first fraction by the inverse of the second fraction.

$$\frac{a}{b} \div \frac{c}{d} = \frac{\frac{a}{b}}{\frac{c}{d}} = \frac{a}{b} \times \frac{d}{c}$$

3. The sum of two numbers is $\frac{7}{5}$ of the second number. What is the ratio of the sum of these numbers to their difference (first number minus the second number)?

A. $\frac{2}{5}$
B. $\frac{5}{2}$
C. $\frac{-5}{2}$
D. $\frac{-7}{3}$
E. $\frac{-3}{7}$

ANSWER: D. Let x and y represent the first and the second number respectively.

Then we have:

$$x + y = \frac{7}{5}y$$

$$x = \frac{7}{5}y - y = \frac{7}{5}y - \frac{5}{5}y = \frac{2}{5}y$$

$$\frac{x+y}{x-y} = \frac{\frac{7}{5}y}{\frac{2}{5}y - y} = \frac{\frac{7}{5}y}{\frac{2}{5}y - \frac{5}{5}y} = \frac{\frac{7}{5}y}{\frac{-3}{5}y} = \frac{7}{5} \times \frac{5}{-3} = \frac{-7}{3}$$

In other problems, you may be given a ratio and some information indicating how the quantity in the numerator or the quantity in the denominator, or both, have changed. Then, you are asked to calculate the new ratio after these changes occur.

Some problems require you to know the geometric relationship between different lengths and areas of shapes in order to calculate a desired ratio.

4. What is the ratio of the circumference of a circle with radius r to the perimeter of a square whose sides are $\frac{\pi}{5}$ of the circle's radius?

A. $\frac{1}{2}$
B. $\frac{1}{5}$
C. $\frac{2}{5}$
D. $\frac{1}{10}$
E. 2.5

ANSWER: E. The circumference of a circle with radius r is $2\pi r$ and the perimeter of a square with sides equal to s is $4s$. Thus, the desired ratio is:

$$\frac{2\pi r}{4s} = \frac{2\pi r}{4 \times \frac{\pi}{5}r} = \frac{2\pi}{\times 4\pi} \frac{5}{} = \frac{5}{2} = 2.5$$

5. The cost of gas is d dollars to fill an empty tank of a car which has capacity for 12 gallons. Each gallon lasts for m miles on a highway. What is the cost to drive one mile in this car?

A. $\frac{12m}{d}$
B. $\frac{12}{md}$

C. $\frac{m}{12d}$

D. $\frac{d}{12m}$

E. $\frac{12d}{m}$

ANSWER: D. Since the cost of 12 gallons of gas is $\$d$ dollars, the cost of one gallon is $\frac{d}{12}$. This amount can buy one gallon, which can last for m miles. Therefore, the cost for driving one mile is $\frac{d}{12} \div m = \frac{d}{12} \times \frac{1}{m} = \frac{d}{12m}$.

Percentages

Percentages are a special case of ratios where you represent ratio of a quantity x with respect to 100 units of the quantity y. There are different equivalent ways of representing percentages. For example, twenty percent can be written as a fraction $(\frac{20}{100})$, as a number derived by simplifying the fraction (0.2), or by the common percentage notion (20%). You need to carefully read questions and distinguish among cases where a quantity decreases or increases in percentage.

For example, if a number x increases by 20% its new value is $x + 0.2x = 1.2x$, and if it decreases by 20% the new value would be $x - 0.2x = 0.8x$. Watch out for problems where a value changes in percentage several times successively; you cannot add and subtract the percentage changes to get the final overall change in percentage of the original value.

You may also be given a ratio, where one of its components (numerator, denominator, or the ratio itself), decreases or increases by some percentage of its original value. Then, you are asked to calculate how another component's value is affected as a result of this change.

6. Nancy paid $1000 for a round trip plane ticket to India. If the air fare for this trip increases 4% per year, how much would the same trip cost her in three years?

A. 1125

B. 1120

C. 1160

D. 1080

E. 1040

ANSWER: A. This problem can be solved in one step using the compound interest formula. That is, x amount of the initial money, after p periods of time, with interest

i, will amount to t, where $t = x(1 + i)^p$. For this problem, $t = 1000 \times (1.04)^3 = 1000 \times 1.04 \times 1.04 \times 1.04 = (10.4)^3 = 1124.864$. If we round the answer to the first digit, choice A. is the closest answer. The step by step solution to this problem is as follows.

Air fare after the 1st year: $1000 + 0.04 \times 1000 = 1000 + 40 = 1040$
Air fare after the 2nd year: $1040 + 0.04 \times 1040 = 1040 + 41.6 = 1081.6$
Air fare after the 3rd year: $1081.6 + 0.04 \times 1081.6 = 1081.6 + 43.264 = 1124.864$

Mixed Problems

It is often the case that you need to use different concepts to solve one problem that may involve fractions or ratios, increase or decrease of values in percentages, or geometric properties mixed together.

7. A fraction's numerator decreased by 10% and its denominator increased by $\frac{1}{5}$ of its original value. What is the ratio of the new fraction to the old one?

   A. $\frac{3}{2}$
   B. $\frac{3}{4}$
   C. $\frac{27}{25}$
   D. $\frac{25}{27}$
   E. $\frac{6}{5}$

   ANSWER B. Let n and d represent the original fraction's numerator and denominator, and n' and d' represent the new fraction's numerator and denominator respectively. Then,

   $$\frac{n'}{d'} = \frac{n - 0.1n}{d + \frac{1}{5}d} = \frac{0.9n}{\frac{6}{5}d} = \frac{9}{10} \times \frac{5}{6} \times \frac{n}{d} = \frac{3}{4} \times \frac{n}{d}$$

   The question is asking for the following:

   $$\frac{\frac{n'}{d'}}{\frac{n}{d}} = \frac{\frac{3}{4} \times \frac{n}{d}}{\frac{n}{d}} = \frac{3}{4}$$

8. If a circle's circumference increases by a constant number c, how much will its radius increase by?

A. c

B. $2\pi c$

C. $\frac{2\pi}{c}$

D. $\frac{c}{2\pi}$

E. $\frac{1}{2\pi c}$

ANSWER D. Let r and $r + x$ be the radii of the original and the enlarged circles respectively. Then, the difference between their circumferences is c.

$$
\begin{aligned}
2\pi(r + x) - 2\pi r &= c \\
2\pi r + 2\pi x - 2\pi r &= c \\
2\pi x &= c \\
x &= \frac{c}{2\pi}
\end{aligned}
$$

Therefore, anytime a circle's circumference is increased by c it means that its radius has increased by $\frac{c}{2\pi}$. Remembering this relationship can help you answer similar questions for different values of c.

9. The angles of a triangle are in the ratio Kx:6x:4x. What is the smallest integer value of K for the triangle to be a right triangle?

A. -2

B. 1

C. 2

D. 4

E. 8

ANSWER C. For any right triangle, one angle is 90 degrees and the sum of the other two angles is also 90 degrees. Therefore, one of the following three cases are possible:

$$
\begin{aligned}
Kx &= 6x + 4x = 90 & (1) \\
Kx &= 10x = 90 \\
x &= 9, K = 10
\end{aligned}
$$

$$6x \ = \ Kx + 4x \ = \ 90 \tag{2}$$
$$6x \ = \ (K+4)x \ = \ 90$$
$$x \ = \ 15$$
$$K+4 \ = \ \frac{90}{15} \ = \ 6$$
$$K \ = \ 2$$

$$4x \ = \ Kx + 6x = 90 \tag{3}$$
$$4x \ = \ (K+6)x = 90$$
$$x \ = \ \frac{90}{4} = \frac{45}{2}$$
$$K+6 \ = \ \frac{90}{x} = \frac{90}{1} \times \frac{2}{45} = 4$$
$$K+6 \ = \ 4$$
$$K \ = \ -2$$

Although the third case gives the smallest integer, it is not an acceptable answer since a triangle's angle cannot be negative. Therefore, K = 2 is the correct answer.

10. For the function g, $g(x)$ is directly proportional to x, where $x > 0$. If $g(9) = 4$, then what is the value of $g(6)$?

A. $\frac{4}{9}$
B. 1
C. $\frac{8}{3}$
D. 6
E. $\frac{27}{2}$

ANSWER C. $g(x)$ being directly proportional to x means that $g(x) = kx$ for some constant k. Since $g(9) = 4$, $g(x)$ is equal to 4 when x is 9. We can substitute these values in the equation above and solve for k:

$$g(x) \ = \ kx$$
$$4 \ = \ k \times 9$$
$$k \ = \ \frac{4}{9}$$

Substituting the value of k into the original equation gives us $g(x) = \frac{4}{9}x$. We now substitute the 6 into this equation to find $g(6)$. Thus, $g(6) = \frac{4}{9} \times 6 = \frac{8}{3}$.

Practice Problems

1. Sara, Kathy, and Julie have $50. Peter, Sara, and Kathy have $\frac{8}{5}$ of that amount. If Peter has three times as much as Julie has, how much money does Julie have?

    A. $15
    B. $25
    C. $10
    D. $20
    E. $30

2. Sara spent $\frac{1}{3}$ of her grocery money on fruit. If she spent $\frac{2}{5}$ of this money on apples and the rest on oranges, what percentage of her total money was spent on oranges?

    A. 10%
    B. 15%
    C. 20%
    D. 25%
    E. 30%

3. Six apples, three oranges, and two pomegranates cost twenty dollars. If a pomegranate costs four times as much as an apple while an orange costs twice as much as an apple, how much does a pomegranate cost?

    A. $1
    B. $2
    C. $3
    D. $4
    E. $5

4. The length of a rectangle is 1.5 times the length of a square's side. If the width of the same rectangle is 25% less than the length of each side of the square, what is the ratio of the area of the square to that of the rectangle?

    A. $\frac{1}{3}$
    B. $\frac{8}{9}$
    C. $\frac{2}{1}$
    D. $\frac{3}{3}$
    E. $\frac{8}{3}$

5. In a city, 1% of high school seniors with an interest in science are likely to major in geology in college. Of those majoring in geology, the ratio of females to males is 3:1. If 20% of this city's high school seniors are interested in science, and if the number of females in this group who will major in geology in college is 21, what is the total number of high school seniors in this city?

   A. 2800
   B. 28000
   C. 1400
   D. 14000
   E. 6300

6. The conversion ratio of the U.S. dollar to China's yuan is 1:8. An American tourist spent 80% of his money in China. If he had 600 yuan left at the end of his trip, how much money did he have in dollars when he started his journey?

   A. 3000
   B. 1500
   C. 750
   D. 375
   E. 7500

7. If the width and length of a rectangle R, are 20 percent and 30 percent, respectively, less than the radius of a circle C, what is the ratio of the rectangle's area to the circle's area?

   A. $\frac{14}{25\pi}$
   B. $\frac{25\pi}{14}$
   C. $\frac{56}{\pi}$
   D. $\frac{\pi}{56}$
   E. $\frac{25}{\pi}$

8. If N pencils cost the same as M pens, and each pencil costs 25 cents, how many dollars does each pen cost?

   A. $\frac{M}{4N}$
   B. $\frac{N}{4M}$
   C. $\frac{4N}{M}$
   D. $\frac{4M}{N}$
   E. $\frac{25N}{M}$

9. A salad dressing is made by mixing olive oil and vinegar. In a 500ml bottle of dressing, the ratio of olive oil to vinegar is 3 to 1. In a 300ml bottle of the same dressing, the same ratio is 5 to 1. If we mix these two bottles of salad dressing in a bigger container, what ratio of the final mixture would be olive oil?

   A. 8:10
   B. 10:8
   C. 8:2
   D. 32:25
   E. 25:32

10. Twenty percent of a university's students represent half of those who majored in sciences. One third of the students majoring in arts are one sixth of the total students' population at this university. What is the ratio of the number of students who majored in sciences to those who majored in arts at this university?

   A. $\frac{4}{5}$
   B. $\frac{2}{5}$
   C. $\frac{5}{4}$
   D. $\frac{5}{2}$
   E. $\frac{1}{5}$

11. John drove from Baltimore to New York with an average speed of 60 miles per hour. If it took him four hours to get to NY, and he drove $\frac{1}{3}$ of the total distance with an average speed of 40 miles per hour, what was his average speed (in miles per hour) for the rest of his trip?

   A. 60
   B. 70
   C. 80
   D. 90
   E. 100

12. Digits of a three digit number add up to 18. The lowest position digit is half of the digit at the next higher position. The digit at the highest position is half of the sum of the other two digits. What number are we talking about?

   A. 486
   B. 684
   C. 846

D. 648

E. 963

13. In a city the gas price increased from \$2.4 per gallon to \$2.5 per gallon. John used to spend \$96.00 per month on gas. How much more does he now have to pay each month to get the same amount of gas as before?

A. \$9.6

B. \$0.1

C. \$0.4

D. \$4.0

E. \$9.6

14. Five percent of Ali's paycheck goes toward his health insurance and 30% of it is deducted for income tax. This year, his health insurance premium is three times more than last year. What is the ratio of his last year's income after deductions to this year's?

A. 3

B. $\frac{7}{9}$

C. $\frac{9}{7}$

D. $\frac{11}{13}$

E. $\frac{13}{11}$

15. Julie wants to buy a car that costs \$12,000. The dealer will give it to her for 5% less during a holiday sale. Julie also qualifies for a 3% new college graduate discount. The state requires that she pays 5% sales tax on the final sales price. What percentage of the original price will she end up not paying at the end?

A. 3.4

B. 4.3

C. 3

D. 8

E. 13

16. The area of a circle is 4 times larger than its circumference. What is the area of a circle whose radius is 25% less than the mentioned circle?

A. 9π

B. 36π

    C. π

    D. 16π

    E. 4π

17. A party of six paid \$18 in gratuity for their dinner at a restaurant. If they had paid 15% of their total bill for the tip, how much on average did each person pay?

    A. \$17

    B. \$20

    C. \$23

    D. \$25

    E. \$28

18. Jack bought a microwave at a 20% discount. Based on state laws he is required to pay 8% sales tax. What is the ratio of the total amount he would have had to pay before the sale to the total amount he actually paid?

    A. 0.8

    B. 1.25

    C. 1.2

    D. 1.28

    E. 0.72

19. If the value of a decreases by 25% and the value of b increases by 25%, how would the ratio of a to b change?

    A. increases by 25%

    B. decreases by 25%

    C. does not change.

    D. decreases by 50%.

    E. decreases by 40%.

20. A right circular cylinder has height h and a circular base with radius r. The volume of this cylinder is 6 times more than a sphere with radius r. What is the ratio of h to r?

    A. $\frac{4}{3}$

    B. 2

    C. 4

    D. 6

    E. 8

Solutions to Practice Problems

1. **A.** We present each person's money by their first name initial: s, k, j, and p. Let's translate the problem as we read it into equations:

$$
\begin{aligned}
s + k + j &= 50 \\
p + s + k &= \frac{8}{5}(50) = 8(10) = 80 \\
p &= 3j
\end{aligned}
$$

We are interested in j so we need to write equations in terms of j. Using the third equation, substitute p in terms of j in the second equation: $3j + s + k = 80$. We know something about $s + k + j$ from the second equation though. Putting these together we have:

$$
\begin{aligned}
3j + s + k &= 80 \\
2j + j + s + k &= 80 \\
2j + 50 &= 80 \\
2j &= 30 \\
j &= 15
\end{aligned}
$$

2. **C.** If Sara spent $\frac{2}{5}$ of the fruit money on apples, it means that she spent the remaining $\frac{3}{5}$ on oranges. Considering her total money, it means that she spent $\frac{1}{3} \times \frac{3}{5} = \frac{1}{5}$ of her total money on oranges.

$$
\begin{aligned}
\frac{1}{5} &= \frac{x}{100} \\
x &= \frac{100}{5} = 20
\end{aligned}
$$

3. **D.** Let's first translate the problem into equations as it reads, assuming that a, o, and p stand for prices of buying an apple, orange, and a pomegranate respectively.

$$
\begin{aligned}
6a + 3o + 2p &= 20 \\
p &= 4a \\
o &= 2a
\end{aligned}
$$

Substituting for p and o in the first equation gives us the following:

$$
\begin{aligned}
6a + 3(2a) + 2(4a) &= 20 \\
6a + 6a + 8a &= 20 \\
20a &= 20 \\
a &= 1 \\
p &= 4a = 4
\end{aligned}
$$

4. **B.** Let x present the length of each side of the square. Area of the square is then $A_1 = x^2$. Now the length of the rectangle is $1.5x = \frac{3}{2}x$, while its width is $x - 0.25x = 0.75x = \frac{3}{4}x$. Thus, the area of the rectangle is $A_2 = \frac{3}{4}x \times \frac{3}{2}x = \frac{9}{8}x^2$. The question is asking for $\frac{A_1}{A_2} = \frac{x^2}{\frac{9}{8}x^2} = \frac{8}{9}$.

5. **D.** We know that 21 females will major in geology. We also know that the ratio of females majoring in geology to the males is 3:1, which means $\frac{21}{3} = 7$ males have majored in geology. Therefore, $21 + 7 = 28$ high school seniors in this city have majored in geology. These students are 1% of the seniors with an interest in science. Thus, $28 \times 100 = 2800$ of the total seniors like science. We also know that 20% of senior students were interested in science. Let x present the total number of high school seniors in this city. Then, $\frac{20}{100} = \frac{2800}{x}$, and thus $x = \frac{2800 \times 100}{20} = 14000$.

6. **D.** Let x represent the total amount of money at the beginning of the journey in yuan. We know that $\frac{600}{x} = \frac{20}{100}$, since 80% of the money was spent already. Thus, $x = \frac{600 \times 100}{20} = 600 \times 5 = 3000$. Now we can convert the total initial money to dollars using the conversion rate. Let d represent the total initial money in dollars:

$$
\begin{aligned}
\frac{1}{d} &= \frac{8}{3000} \\
d &= \frac{3000}{8} = \frac{1500}{4} = \frac{750}{2} = 375
\end{aligned}
$$

7. **A.** Let r represent the circle's radius. The circle's area is πr^2. Let w and l, respectively, represent the width and length of the rectangle. We know that $w = r - 0.2r = 0.8r$ and that $l = r - 0.3r = 0.7r$. The area of the rectangle is then calculated as $w \times l = 0.8r.7r = 0.56r^2$. All that remains to calculate is the ratio of the area of the rectangle to that of the circle:

$$
\frac{0.56r^2}{\pi r^2} = \frac{0.56}{\pi} = \frac{56}{100\pi} = \frac{28}{50\pi} = \frac{14}{25\pi}
$$

Please note that $\frac{0.56}{\pi}$, $\frac{56}{100\pi}$, and $\frac{28}{50\pi}$ are all other forms of the same ratio, and thus are correct answers. However, only the most simplified version is among the choices.

8. **B.** Since we need the final answer in dollars we convert the price of each pencil to dollars first. Each pencil costs 25 cents or \$0.25. Therefore, N pencils cost \$0.25N, which is the same price as M pens. Calculating the price for one pen results in $\frac{0.25N}{M} = \frac{25N}{100M} = \frac{N}{4M}$.

9. **E.** The question is asking for the ratio of the olive oil to the total dressing. We know that the total dressing is 500ml + 300ml = 800ml. Now, we want to calculate what volume of this salad dressing is made of olive oil. To do so, we need the volume of the olive oil in each of the initial two bottles. Note that the problem has give the ratio of olive oil to vinegar, not olive oil to the total dressing volume. Therefore, the ratio by volume of olive oil to the total dressing is 3:4 and 5:6 for the 500ml and 300ml bottles, respectively. Let O_1 and O_2 represent volumes of the olive oil in the first and second bottle, respectively. We then have:

$$\frac{O_1}{500} = \frac{3}{4}$$
$$O_1 = \frac{3 \times 500}{4} = \frac{3 \times 250}{2} = 3 \times 125 = 375$$
$$\frac{O_2}{300} = \frac{5}{6}$$
$$O_2 = \frac{5 \times 300}{6} = 5 \times 50 = 250$$

Total volume of olive oil is $O_1 + O_2 = 375 + 250 = 625$ml. Thus, the ratio of the olive oil to the total dressing is $\frac{625}{800}$. We can easily simplify this fraction by recalling that $625 = 25 \times 25$. That is $\frac{625}{800} = \frac{25 \times 25}{8 \times 100} = \frac{25}{8 \times 4} = \frac{25}{32}$.

10. **A.** Let a and s represent the total number of students who majored in arts and sciences, respectively, and let t be the total number of students in the university. We have:

$$\frac{20}{100}t = \frac{1}{2}s$$
$$\frac{1}{5}t = \frac{1}{2}s$$
$$s = \frac{2}{5}t$$
$$\frac{1}{3}a = \frac{1}{6}t$$
$$a = \frac{3}{6}t = \frac{1}{2}t$$

Therefore,

$$\frac{s}{a} = \frac{\frac{2}{5}t}{\frac{1}{2}t} = \frac{2}{5} \times 2 = \frac{4}{5}$$

Note that 't's cancel, and division of a fraction by another fraction is equivalent to multiplying the first fraction by the reciprocal of the second fraction.

11. **C.** In order to figure out the average speed for the remaining $\frac{2}{3}$ of the traveled distance, we need to know both the distance traveled and the time it took to travel for this segment of the trip. We can calculate this distance by first calculating the total traveled distance $d = 60$ (miles/hour) $\times$ 4 (hours)$= 240$ miles. The part we are interested in involves traveling $\frac{2}{3} \times 240 = 2 \times 80 = 160$ miles. We also know that $\frac{1}{3} \times 240 = 80$ miles was traveled with the speed of 40 miles per hour, which means that it took 80 (miles) $\div 40$ (miles/hour) $= 2$ hours to travel $\frac{1}{3}$ of the total distance. Since the total trip took 4 hours, it means that the remaining 160 miles were also traveled in 2 hours. This implies that the average speed for the rest of the trip was $160 \div 2 = 80$ miles per hour.

12. **B.** The easiest approach for solving this problem is by eliminating the choices that do not meet the required conditions. First, the sum of the digits should add up to 18. For all choices this is true. Next, the digit at the lowest position should be half of the next digit. This means that the right most digit should be half of the middle digit. This is true only for choices B. and E.. Finally, the left most digit should be half of the sum of the other two digits. This is true only for choice B., where we have $6 = \frac{8+4}{2}$.

The second approach would be to solve for the answer. Suppose the three digit number is presented as xyz. Then, we know

$$\begin{aligned} x + y + z &= 18 \\ y &= 2z \\ x &= \frac{y+z}{2} \end{aligned}$$

Putting it all together in the first equation we have:

$$
\begin{aligned}
\frac{y+z}{2} + (2z) + z &= 18 \\
\frac{(2z+z)}{2} + 3z &= 18 \\
z + \frac{z}{2} + 3z &= 18 \\
\frac{9z}{2} &= 18 \\
\frac{z}{2} &= 2 \\
z &= 4
\end{aligned}
$$

Then, $y = 2z = 2 * 4 = 8$, and $x = \frac{8+4}{2} = 6$. The number we needed was presented by digits xyz, or 684.

13. **D.** We know that John has to spend $0.1 more per gallon. First, we calculate how many gallons of gas he was buying per month. That calculates as 96 (dollars) $\div 2.4$ (dollars/gallon). Therefore, 96 (dollars) $\div \frac{24}{10}$ (dollars/gallon) = 96 (dollars) $\times \frac{10}{24}$ = 96 (dollars) $\times \frac{5}{12}$ (gallon/dollars) = $8 \times 5 = 40$ (gallons).

So, John was buying 40 gallons of gas per month and now he has to pay $0.1 more per gallon, which is $40 \times 0.1 = 4.0$ dollars.

14. **E.** Let t represent Ali's total income before deductions. Last year his net income was $t - (0.05t + 0.3t) = t - 0.35t = 0.65t$. This year, his health insurance deductions are three times more than last year. This means that his health insurance is $3 \times 0.05t = 0.15t$. Therefore, this year his net income after deductions is $t - (0.15t + 0.3t) = t - 0.45t = 0.55t$. The ratio of Ali's last year net income to this year's after deductions is $\frac{0.65t}{0.55t} = \frac{65}{55} = \frac{13}{11}$.

15. **A.** Julie is getting a 5+3=8 percent discount on the original car price. This makes the new price for her: $12000 - 0.08 \times \$12000 = \$12000 - \$960 = \$11040$. In addition, she has to pay %5 of this price for sales tax. So, she will end up paying $\$11040 + (0.05 \times \$11040) = \$11040 + \$552 = \$11592$. This is $\$12000 - \$11592 = \$408$ less than the original car price. The question is asking for x, where $\frac{408}{12000} = \frac{x}{100}$. Finally, $x = \frac{408 \times 100}{12000} = \frac{408}{120} = \frac{102}{30} = 3.4$.

16. **B.** Let r represent the radius of the first circle. Then,

$$
\begin{aligned}
\pi r^2 &= 4(2\pi r) \\
r &= 8
\end{aligned}
$$

Let r' be the radius of the second circle. We know that $r' = r - \frac{1}{4}r = 8 - \frac{1}{4}8 = 8 - 2 = 6$. The area of the circle with radius r' is $\pi r'^2 = \pi(6)^2 = 36\pi$.

17. **C.** Each person pays their share of the total bill and tip. We know that each person's share of the tip is $\$18 \div 6 = \$3$. Let t be the total cost of the meals.

$$\frac{15}{100} = \frac{18}{t}$$
$$t = \frac{100 \times 18}{15} = \frac{100 \times 6}{5} = 20 \times 6$$

We do not need to simplify further, since the cost of each person's meal is $\frac{t}{6} = \frac{20 \times 6}{6} = 20$. Thus, each person had to pay $\$3 + \$20 = \$23$.

18. **B.** Let x represent the original price of the microwave. Then, Jack had to pay $x + 0.08x = 1.08x$ before the sale. Instead, he had paid $(x - 0.2x) + 0.08(x - 0.2x) = 0.8x + 0.08 * 0.8x = 0.8x + 0.064x = 0.864x$. The question is asking for the ratio of the cost before the sale to the actual cost:

$$\frac{1.08x}{0.864x} = \frac{1.08}{0.864} = \frac{1080}{864}$$

You can either do the division directly or keep simplifying the above fraction. Below is one way of simplifying the fraction by dividing both the numerator and denominator by 4, 3, 9, and finally by 2:

$$\frac{1080}{864} = \frac{270}{216} = \frac{90}{72} = \frac{10}{8} = \frac{5}{4} = 1.25$$

19. **E.** Let a' and b' represent the new values of a and b. We have $a' = a - 0.25a = 0.75a$ and $b' = b + 0.25b = 1.25b$. The question is asking for $\frac{a'}{b'} = \frac{0.75a}{1.25b} = \left(\frac{75}{125}\right)\frac{a}{b} = \left(\frac{3}{5}\right)\frac{a}{b}$. Therefore, $\frac{a'}{b'}$ is $\frac{3}{5} = \frac{6}{10} = 60\%$ of the original ratio $a : b$. That is, we have had a 40% decrease in ratio of $a : b$.

20. **D.** The volumes of the cylinder and the sphere in this problem are $\pi r^2 h$ and $\frac{4\pi r^3}{3}$.

$$\frac{\pi r^2 h}{\frac{4\pi r^3}{3}} = 6$$
$$\frac{3r^2 h}{4r^3} = 6$$
$$\frac{3h}{4r} = 6$$
$$\frac{h}{r} = \frac{6 \times 4}{3} = 8$$

CHAPTER 5

PATTERNS, SYMBOLS, AND DIGITS

This chapter deals with some important odds and ends of the SAT. In your high school math curriculum, you have probably never spent much time on patterns and sequences, on abstract symbolic operations, or on manipulating the digits of positive integers. The SAT recognizes this, so they don't ask questions that involve a deep knowledge of the underlying phenomena. Instead, they tend to sneak in creative 'tricks' from number theory or algebra, disguised as problems of some other form.

Many students get very frustrated with "trick" questions, since they seem to require some sort of supernatural insight that can't be learned. Actually, with these questions, the secret is not ingenuity, but practice. There are only so many sequences that fit reasonably into the high school math curriculum - arithmetic and geometric ones in particular - and these are the "tricks" that come up the most often. Familiarity with these types of problems will greatly enhance your chances of coming up with the right idea "out of nowhere" when the SAT throws one at you.

We will discuss the most common types of questions in these categories.

Finding Hidden Patterns

In patterns questions, the SAT might give you a pattern explicitly and ask you to manipulate it or extend it to compute later digits. On the SAT, you NEVER have to guess a pattern (For example, the SAT never includes questions such as: "What comes next in the sequence 2, 3, 5, 8, . . . ?"). You just have to answer questions about a pattern after they give you a rule which explains the pattern.

You might also see a number theory problem or a word problem where finding a pattern is the only way to get a solution in a quick period of time. These problems tend to involve what looks like an unreasonably complicated calculation at first, where noticing a pattern makes the calculation much simpler. In fact, if on the SAT, you stare at a problem and think you know how to find the answer, but know that it would take 5 or 6 minutes, it's a safe guess that the problem was designed for you to find a pattern. We'll do one example of this sort of problem before discussing the more specific patterns that often show up.

1. Leon tallies his days in prison on the wall, tallying each day with a vertical line for every first, second, third, and fourth days, and a diagonal line on every fifth day. (So after 7 days in prison, Leon had drawn four vertical lines, one diagonal line, and two more vertical lines). Leon has drawn a total of 4043 vertical lines; how many days has he been in prison?

   A. 4043
   B. 5053
   C. 5054
   D. 20514
   E. 20515

   ANSWER: B. The trick is figuring out the relationship between the number of vertical lines and the number of diagonal lines in a tally. What if Leon had drawn a total of 6 vertical lines? The first four would be associated with an extra diagonal line; the next two wouldn't have been. So what matters is the largest multiple of 4 which is less than the given number. In our case, of the 4043 vertical lines, 4040 of them are in clusters of four corresponding to a diagonal line; hence there are 1010 diagonal lines. So Leon has been in prison a total of 5053 days.

One particularly famous pattern shows up so often that it is worth knowing how to work with (and to practice with sequence notation):

2. The Fibonacci sequence starts with the numbers $F_1 = 1$ and $F_2 = 1$. After that, the term F_n is given by the sum $F_{n-2} + F_{n-1}$. Which of the following is equal to $F_{250} - F_{248}$?

   A. F_2
   B. $F_{247} + F_{248}$
   C. 1003
   D. 10003
   E. 100003

   ANSWER: B. The Fibonacci sequence is probably the most famous sequence of natural numbers. You aren't expected to memorize anything about it for the SAT, but you should be familiar with it by now. By the rule for calculating Fibonacci terms,

   $$F_{250} - F_{248} = F_{249}.$$

   Applying the rule once more,

   $$F_{249} = F_{247} + F_{248}.$$

By the way, answers C, D, and E are all way too small. The actual answer is over fifty digits long!

Arithmetic and Geometric Sequences and Series

Two types of patterns are vitally important on the SAT: the arithmetic and geometric sequences which you should know about from your high school algebra course. Don't forget to know the formula for the nth term in an arithmetic or geometric sequence and the sum of an arithmetic or geometric series. Even though you shouldn't have to memorize formulas for the SAT, knowing them greatly reduces the amount of thinking you'll have to do on a series or sequence problems. Here are the four formulas.

In an arithmetic sequence with first term a_1 and common difference d, the nth term is given by

$$a_n = a_1 + (n-1)d$$

Further, the sum S_n of the first n terms is given by the average of the first and last terms times the number of terms; in symbols,

$$S_n = n\frac{a_1 + a_n}{2}$$

In geometric sequences with first term a_1 and common ratio r, the nth term is given by

$$a_n = a_1 r^{n-1}$$

The sum S_n of the first n terms is given by

$$S_n = a_1 \frac{r^n - 1}{r - 1}$$

Here are arithmetic and geometric sequence and series questions:

3. What is the sum of the first 100 even positive integers?

   A. 505
   B. 5050
   C. 10000
   D. 10100

E. 20000

ANSWER: D. There are many ways to get this problem; we'll show two. First, you can use the formula for the sum of a general arithmetic series: $a_1 = 2$, $d = 2$, and $n = 100$; plug these in to get that $a_n = 200$ and hence that the sum is $(100)(101) = 10100$.

If you don't want to memorize this formula, you can also use the formula for the sum of the first n numbers, $\frac{n(n+1)}{2}$. The sum of the first 100 even positive integers is the same as twice the sum of the first 100 positive integers:

$$2 + 4 + \ldots + 200 = 2(1 + 2 + \ldots + 100).$$

Thus, the answer is $(100)(101) = 10100$.

4. A geometric series is written with first term 10 and common ratio 2. What is the sum of terms 10 through 17?

   A. 130048
   B. 131071
   C. 655360
   D. 1300480
   E. 1310710

   ANSWER: D. Again, there are several ways to do it. You could find the 10th term and make it the first term of a "new" geometric series with common ratio 2, of which you could then find the sum of the first 8 terms. You could also use the formula to find the sum of the first 17 terms, then subtract the sum of the first 9 terms.

Cyclic Patterns

A common type of pattern question, which may or may not explicitly involve sequences, is a question hinting at a cyclic pattern. These are patterns in which, after a certain number of actions occur, the system is back at its starting place. If a pattern is cyclic, you can figure out what will happen very late in the pattern by figuring out when the pattern begins to repeat itself. A bit of familiarity with remainder arithmetic goes a long way in breaking apart cyclic pattern problems; see the number theory chapter for help. Here is an example:

5. There is a round analog clock lying flat on a table. At 12 PM, the hour hand is facing due north. Whenever Marsha walks by the clock, she rotates it 120 degrees clockwise. At some time later in the day, the hour hand is facing due south. Which of the following might be this time?

A. 2 PM
B. 3 PM
C. 5 PM
D. 7 PM
E. 8 PM

ANSWER: A. Rotating a circle by an angle that's divisible by 360 is a cyclic pattern. After a certain number of rotations, the clock's position goes back to the original position. In this case, there are three possible positions of the clock: 12 can face north (if Marsha has walked by the clock three times, six times, etc.); 8 can face north (if Marsha has walked by one time, four times, etc.), or 4 can face north (if Marsha has walked by two times, five times, etc.). In the first case, 6 faces south; in the second, 2 faces south; in the third, 10 faces south. So of the given answer choices, only A can occur.

Symbols

Most SATs include 3 or 4 questions involving a new symbol defined within the questions themselves. This new symbol might be a binary operation (like the $+$ in $a + b$, which takes two numbers, a, and b, and returns a third number, their sum), a unary operation (like $|x|$, which takes one number, x, and returns one number, its absolute value), or a relationship (like $x < y$, which, depending on x and y is a true or false statement about x and y).

Very often, symbol questions on the SAT are simple, once you understand how to translate the symbol into mathematics. Since this book is aimed at improving your SAT reasoning skills, we have made several difficult symbol questions. The principle for the difficult and easy questions is exactly the same: break down every symbol the SAT introduces into simpler mathematical language.

The most common symbols problems introduce binary operations. That is, they tell you some strange way to combine two numbers and produce a third number; not addition, multiplication, subtraction, or division, but some new way altogether. These symbols can test your mathematical knowledge from a variety of areas:

6. If z and y are real numbers greater than zero, then $z \star y$ is the length of the leg of a right triangle whose hypotenuse has length z and whose other leg has length y. Suppose that $13 \star x = 3x \star 9$. What is the value of x?

   A. 2.5
   B. 3

C. 4

D. 5

E. 7

ANSWER: D.: Using the Pythagorean theorem, we can translate $13 \star x$ to $\sqrt{169 - x^2}$ and $3x \star 9$ to $\sqrt{9x^2 - 81}$. So our equation, after squaring both sides, becomes

$$169 - x^2 = 9x^2 - 81.$$

Solving this quadratic equation gives

$$x = \pm 5.$$

The solution -5 doesn't make sense in the context of this question (and isn't an answer choice), so the answer is 5. (Once you translated $\star$ into the normal mathematics, you could just plug in the five answer choices, of course).

Don't make the common mistake of assuming that these new symbols have the same properties as familiar ones. For example, just because many familiar operations are commutative:

$$x + y = y + x$$

doesn't mean a symbol will be. Instead of trying to work with the symbols, immediately translate them to a more familiar mathematical language where you are more familiar with the rules.

7. The symbol $b \bigtriangledown c$ is the number of distinct real number solutions to the equation $x^2 + bx + c = 0$. If $d \bigtriangledown 4 = 4 \bigtriangledown d$, which must be true of d?

A. $d = 4$

B. $d = 4$ or $d < -4$

C. $d \geq 4$

D. $d \leq -4$

E. $d \leq 0$

ANSWER: B. Recall that the number of real number solutions is related to the discriminant of the equation, the expression $b^2 - 4c$ For general quadratic equations

$$0 = ax^2 + bx + c,$$

84

the discriminant is

$$b^2 - 4ac.$$

If the discriminant is positive, there are two real number solutions; if it is zero, there is one; if it is negative, the solutions are complex numbers. So the claim in the problem is equivalent to the claim that the expressions $d^2 - 16$ and $16 - 4d$ have the same sign. If d is less than -4, both these expressions are positive. If d is exactly 4, both are 0. Otherwise, their signs are different.

DIGITS

Digit questions ask you to manipulate the digits of a number. The critical underlying phenomenon to understand here is place value, a phenomenon that you learned as early as you began learning arithmetic but which you might never have used in a difficult question. The phenomenon boils down to this: the number 2943 is the same as $2*1000+9*100+4*10+3*1$. In other words, the digit notation that we are familiar with is, in some sense, a shorthand. Let's see how this can be converted into an SAT problem.

8. Let x be a two-digit number. When the digits of x are reversed, another two-digit number, y, is formed. If $x - y = 54$ and the sum of the digits of x is 12, which of the following is equal to x?

   A. 9
   B. 66
   C. 75
   D. 84
   E. 93

   ANSWER: E. This one is simple enough that you could just plug in the answer choices and check, but let's do it algebraically, since this will be necessary for harder problems. Since x is a two-digit number, the place-value property says that

   $$x = 10T + U,$$

   where U is the units (or ones) digit of x and T is the tens digit. This is the same as saying that as a two-digit number, $x = TU$ (not the product of T and U, but the two-digit number whose first digit is T and whose second digit is U). Thus y is the two-digit number written UT; that is, the number $10U + T$. So

   $$x - y = 9T - 9U = 54.$$

   So $T - U = 6$ and $T + U = 12$, a system of equations which solves to $T = 9, U = 3$.

One family of digits questions asks you to solve an addition, subtraction, multiplication, or division problem with a catch: some digits of the problem are left blank. In this way, the SAT tests your flexibility with and understanding of the familiar methods of adding and subtracting multi-digit numbers. These problems usually don't require the place-value breakdown described above. Here's an example:

9. In the following addition problem, how many different values are possible for N (assume that K, L, and N are digits between 0 and 9)?

$$\begin{array}{r} 5\ K\ 3 \\ +\quad 5\ L\ 7 \\ \hline 1\ N\ 0\ 0 \end{array}$$

   A. 0
   B. 1
   C. 2
   D. 3
   E. 9

ANSWER: B. N can't be greater than 1, because two numbers that are each less than 600 can't add up to 1200. On the other hand, N can't be 0, because two numbers that are each greater than 500 can't add up to 1000. So if N can be any digit, it has to be 1. Indeed, N can be 1, for example, if K=0 and L =9. So there's exactly one possibility. Notice that K and L can be anything so long as K + L = 9 (this is because the sum from the right-most column "carries" to the left).

10. The letters F, G, H, I, J, K, L, M, N, and P all stand for distinct digits in the following subtraction problem. Which of the following can be equal to F?

$$\begin{array}{r} F\ G\ H\ I \\ -\quad\ \ J\ K\ L \\ \hline M\ N\ P \end{array}$$

   A. 1
   B. 3
   C. 5
   D. 7
   E. 8

ANSWER: A. Any subtraction problem can be turned upside down to get an addition problem, in this case: $MNP + JKL = FGHI$. Then, since the addition of $M + G$ can never be more than 19 (if an extra 1 was carried), F can be at most 1 (put another way: two numbers less than 500 can't add up to 1000). Of course, you don't have to turn the problem upside down to get it– you could make the same argument backwards, using "borrowing" instead of carrying.

Practice Problems

1. Let n be a positive integer. Then the function $f(n)$ is the number of different possible ones digits that can occur in a number of the form n^m, where m is a positive integer. For example, $f(5) = 1$. For which of the following numbers is $f(n)$ not equal to 4?

   A. 3
   B. 17
   C. 18
   D. 21
   E. 22

2. An arithmetic sequence 7, 11, 15, . . . is formed by starting at 7 (the first term) and adding 4 to create each successive term. What is the fifteenth term?

   A. 60
   B. 63
   C. 67
   D. 165
   E. 488

3. Sylvia owes Jon $1000. She pays him $1 on January 1st, $2 on January 2nd, and in general pays him 2^{n-1} dollars on January n. On which day will her total payments have exceeded her debt?

   A. January 7
   B. January 8
   C. January 9
   D. January 10
   E. February 13

4. Whenever Yolanda sees a geometric sequence, she erases all the prime numbers. Sheila writes a geometric sequence with common ratio 11 whose first term is 17; then Yolanda sees it. After Yolanda is through with Sheila's sequence, what is the 4th term?

   A. 187
   B. 2057
   C. 22627
   D. 248,897
   E. 2,737,867

5. A sequence is given where the nth term is $n^2 - 1$, starting with the first term $1^2 - 1 = 0$. How many prime numbers are in the sequence? (0 and 1 are not prime numbers).

A. 0

B. 1

C. 2

D. Infinitely many terms of the sequence are prime, and infinitely many are not prime.

E. All the terms in the sequence

6. A three-digit number x isn't divisible by 10. When its digits are reversed, the number y is formed. Suppose $y > x$. Which of these numbers might be $y - x$?

A. 198

B. 251

C. 300

D. 326

E. 524

The following information is used both in question 7 and question 8:

There are fifteen empty buckets arranged in a circle. John pours blue paint into the northmost bucket and then walks clockwise pouring blue paint in every third bucket he passes, continuing around the circle (possibly more than once) until he is pouring paint into the northmost bucket again. Mary starts at the northmost bucket and pours red paint in every fifth bucket, contuing clockwise around the circle until she is pouring paint in the northmost bucket again. Sally pours brown paint in every other bucket, continuing around the circle until she is pouring paint paint in the northmost bucket again.

7. How many buckets have brown paint in them?

A. 2

B. 7

C. 8

D. 9

E. 15

8. In the same set-up as the previous problem, how many of the buckets have both red and blue paint in them?

A. 1

B. 3

C. 5

D. 8

E. 15

9. A sequence is made according to the following rule: $a_1 = 1$, and, when $n > 1$,

$$a_n = na_{n-1}$$

What is a_7?

A. 7

B. 28

C. 42

D. 5040

E. 823543

10. A sequence is made by according to the following rule: $b_1 = 1$, $b_2 = 2$, and when $k > 2$, $b_k = \frac{b_{k-2}}{b_{k-1}}$. Which of the following numbers is the greatest?

A. b_{1021}

B. b_{1022}

C. b_{1023}

D. b_{1024}

E. b_{1025}

11. The symbol $x \simeq y$ means that $x - y$ is an integer. Which statement is true?

A. $\pi \simeq 3\pi$

B. $1 \simeq 3$

C. $\frac{2}{3} \simeq \frac{3}{2}$

D. All of the above

E. None of the above

12. Using the same symbol as in the previous problem, suppose that $x \simeq y$ and $y \simeq z$. Which of the following is NOT necessarily true?

A. $3x \simeq 3y$

B. $x^3 \simeq y^3$

C. $y \simeq x$

D. $x \simeq z$

E. $x \simeq x$

13. Let a_n be a sequence where the first term $a_1 = \frac{1}{2}$ and in general $a_n = \frac{n}{n+1}$. What is the product of the first 100 terms of the sequence?

A. $\frac{1}{10000}$

B. $\frac{1}{101}$

C. $\frac{1}{100}$

D. 100

E. 2360000

14. What is the sum of the first 100 odd positive integers?

   A. 2525
   B. 5050
   C. 10000
   D. 10050
   E. 10100

15. Let E and J be digits between 1 and 9, not equal to one another. Consider the two digit numbers JE and EE (not the products J*E and E*E). The sum JE + EE is NOT divisible by which of the following numbers?

   A. 8
   B. 9
   C. 10
   D. 11
   E. 12

16. Suppose a and b are positive real numbers. If such a triangle exists, $a \clubsuit b$ is the perimeter of a triangle with side-lengths a, b, and ab. If such a triangle exists, $a \heartsuit b$ is the third angle in a triangle which contains angles a and b. Which of the following expressions defines a real number less than 90?

   I. $3 \clubsuit 5$
   II. $90 \heartsuit 90$
   III. $3 \heartsuit 3$

   A. I only
   B. I and II only
   C. I and III only
   D. III only
   E. None defines a real number less than 90.

17. Lisa creates a pattern as follows. She picks two numbers, t_1 and t_2. She lets t_3 be the average of t_1 and t_2, she lets t_4 be the average of t_2 and t_3, and so on. In other words, t_n is the average of t_{n-1} and t_{n-2}. If $t_1 = t_3$, which expression must be equal to $t_{57} - t_{100}$?

   A. $\frac{(t_1 + t_2)}{43}$
   B. 0

    C. $(t_1 + t_2)/(2^{57}) - (t_1 + t_2)/(2^{100})$
    D. 43
    E. $-t_{43}$

18. Now Lisa tries her same pattern with different starting numbers t_1 and t_2. She picks numbers so that $t_1 < t_2$. Which of the following is true of t_{10}?

    I. $t_{10} > t_1$
    II. $t_{10} > t_2$
    III. $t_{10} > (t_1 + t_2)/2$

    A. I only
    B. II only
    C. I and III only
    D. II and III only
    E. All are true

19. The symbols F, I, T, E, and M must represent DISTINCT digits between 1 and 9 (possibly including 1 and/or 9). How many possible values are there for M if the addition below is correct?

$$\begin{array}{cccc} & F & I & T \\ + & F & I & T \\ \hline I & T & E & M \end{array}$$

    A. 0
    B. 1
    C. 2
    D. 3
    E. 4

20. The symbols A, B, and C represent digits from one through ten in the following addition problem. If $C = B+1$, what is A?

$$\begin{array}{ccccc} & A & 1 & 3 & 7 \\ + & A & 8 & 9 & 9 \\ \hline & B & 0 & 3 & C \end{array}$$

    A. 1
    B. 2
    C. 3
    D. 4
    E. 5

21. Let x and y be real numbers. The statement $x \lesssim y$ means that it is both true that $x \leq y$ and that $x^2 \leq y$. For which real numbers x is it true that $-x \lesssim x$?

 A. x, where $-1 \leq x \leq 1$
 B. x, where $x \leq -1$
 C. x, where $x \geq 1$
 D. x, where $0 \leq x \leq 1$
 E. No real numbers.

22. The letters A and B represent DISTINCT digits in the following addition problem. Solve for A:

$$\begin{array}{r} 1\ 0\ A\ 6 \\ +\quad 5\ B\ 3 \\ \hline 1\ 6\ 7\ B \end{array}$$

 A. 5
 B. 6
 C. 7
 D. 8
 E. 9

23. The symbols A, B, and C represent different digits. If B+C = A, what is A?

$$\begin{array}{r} A\ 0\ 0 \\ \times\quad A\ 0\ 0 \\ \hline B\ C\ 0\ 0\ 0\ 0 \end{array}$$

 A. 5
 B. 6
 C. 7
 D. 8
 E. 9

24. In the following subtraction problem, the letters J, K, L, M, and N represent five DISTINCT digits, and L is not 0. Which of the following is equal to M?

$$\begin{array}{r} L\ 1\ M\ N \\ -\quad J\ 1\ K \\ \hline 2\ 1\ 8 \end{array}$$

A. 1
B. 3
C. 4
D. 7
E. 9

25. Suppose that $7^a = b$. Which cannot be the remainder when b is divided by 10?

    A. 1
    B. 3
    C. 5
    D. 7
    E. 9

26. The letter A represents a digit in an addition problem. Solve for A: A2 + 9A= 1A1.

    A. 5
    B. 6
    C. 7
    D. 8
    E. 9

27. The sum of the digits in a certain three-digit positive integer is 13. The hundreds digit is 2, and when the number is added to the same number with its digits reversed, the result is 989. What is the product of the three digits of the number?

    A. 15
    B. 16
    C. 56
    D. 105
    E. 980

28. On January 1, Jon puts one marble in a bowl. The next day, Jon adds three more marbles in the bowl. The next day, he adds five more marbles. Continuing in this pattern, Jon adds an odd number of marbles to his bowl each day, adding two more marbles than he added the day before. After he has added marbles on January 31st, how many total marbles has he added?

    A. 496
    B. 248
    C. 900
    D. 901
    E. 961

29. Lea types a 16-digit integer into her calculator and divides by 7. She gets an infinite decimal expansion, and writes down the first digit after the decimal point. What number does she definitely NOT write down?

    A. 2
    B. 3
    C. 4
    D. 5
    E. 7

30. How many two-digit numbers are equal to the product of their digits?

    A. 0
    B. 1
    C. 5
    D. 9
    E. 10

31. When a and b are positive integers, let $a\|b$ be the remainder when a^b is divided by 9. Which of these numbers CANNOT be $5\|b$ for any positive integer b?

    A. 2
    B. 4
    C. 6
    D. 7
    E. 8

32. 103 is the 16th term in an arithmetic sequence whose 4th term is 7. What is the 12th term?

    A. -17
    B. 8
    C. 71
    D. 79
    E. None of the above

33. Given the addition problem below, which is a possible value for L+M?

$$\begin{array}{cccc} & M & 3 & 7 \\ + & N & 8 & N \\ \hline & 9 & 2 & L \end{array}$$

    A. 5
    B. 6

C. 7

D. All of the above

E. None of the above

The following definition is used in problems 34, 35, and 36: Let $a\heartsuit b$ be the maximum of the two numbers $|a+b|$ and $|a-b|$.

34. What is $-2\heartsuit(-2\heartsuit-2)$?

    A. -6

    B. -4

    C. 0

    D. 4

    E. 6

35. Which of the following is always true for any real number a?

    A. $a\heartsuit a = 2a$

    B. $a\heartsuit a$ is positive

    C. $a\heartsuit a$ is $-a\heartsuit - a$

    D. $a\heartsuit a^2 = a^3$.

    E. $a\heartsuit(-a) = 0$

36. When does $(a\heartsuit b)\heartsuit c = a\heartsuit(b\heartsuit c)$?

    A. Never

    B. Whenever all three numbers are non-negative, but no other time.

    C. Whenever all three numbers are the same sign (or zero), but no other time.

    D. Whenever the product of all three numbers is non-negative, but no other time.

    E. Always

37. How many two digit positive integers are the square of the sums of their digits?

    A. 0

    B. 1

    C. 2

    D. 3

    E. 9

The following definition is used in problems 38 and 39: Suppose m and n are positive integers. Let $m\Delta n = \frac{LCM(m,n)}{GCD(m,n)}$ where $LCM(m,n)$ is the least common multiple of m and n and $GCD(m,n)$ is the greatest common divisor of m and n.

38. What is $(6\Delta10)\Delta15$?

    A. 1
    B. 60
    C. 100
    D. 150
    E. 900

39. Which of the following statements is false?

    A. $m\Delta n$ is always an integer.
    B. $m\Delta n \geq 1$ always.
    C. $m\Delta m = 1$ always.
    D. $m\Delta n = 1$ only when $n = m$.
    E. $GCD(m, m\Delta n) = n$ always.

40. A two-digit positive integer x which is not divisible by 10 is called special if $x + y = 3z$, where y is the number obtained by reversing the digits of x and z is equal to y minus the tens digit of y. (If a number is divisible by 10, it's not special). How many special numbers are there?

    A. 0
    B. 2
    C. 4
    D. 5
    E. 9

41. In each round of the a two-person game, each player chooses one of the words rock paper, or scissors. If a player chooses rock and her opponent chooses scissors, a player chooses scissors and her opponent chooses paper, or a player chooses paper and her opponent chooses rock, she wins a point. Otherwise, she does not. Janet and Jacqui decide to play many rounds of this game. Janet chooses rock, paper, scissors, rock, paper, scissors, over and over in that order. Jacqui chooses rock, paper, rock, paper, rock, paper, over and over in that order. After which number of rounds is their game tied?

    A. 3
    B. 1781
    C. 6315
    D. 67284
    E. 900003

42. Now Janet decides to play her same strategy in a 10,000 round game of rock paper or scissors against Jack. Jack's strategy is to choose rock, paper, rock, paper, scissors,

and then repeat that cycle of five choices over and over. When the game is over, how many points does Janet have?

A. 0

B. 3330

C. 3333

D. 3335

E. 5000

43. The ones-digit of x^2 is equal to the ones-digit of x. What is a possible value of x?

    A. 62248356134

    B. 723082710581

    C. 2234958205847893

    D. 2937496830674907

    E. 2985710849308499

44. A positive two-digit integer x leaves a remainder of 2 when divided by 5. When it is added to the number obtained by reversing its digits, the sum is 88. How many possible values are there for x?

    A. 0

    B. 1

    C. 2

    D. 3

    E. 9

Solutions to Practice Problems

1. **D.** This is a cyclic pattern, although it doesn't look like it. Try experimenting with small numbers to see the pattern. Take a number ending in 2 or 8. Then the ones-digits of its powers cycle through 2, 4, 6, or 8. Similar cycles exist with 3 and 7. But a number ending in 0, 1, or 5 doesn't cycle; all its powers end in the same digit (because $1 * 1 = 1, 5 * 5 = 25$, and $10 * 10 = 100$). As with all other "tricks", you don't have to see this one ahead of time to get the right answer. Just plug the numbers into the calculator and look at the patterns.

2. **B.** If you don't want to memorize the formula for the terms of an arithmetic sequence (or you forget it on test day), just think of it using the definition. The first digit is 7; by the fifteenth term, 4 will have been added on 14 times, so we have 7 + 14*4, which is 63. Make sure you didn't add 4 fifteen times; that gives you the sixteenth term of the sequence! On the SAT, all sequences are numbered so that the first term that you see is the FIRST term of the sequence, not the zeroth term.

3. **D.** The formula for the sum of the first n terms in a geometric series with starting term a and ratio r is given by

$$S = a\frac{r^n - 1}{r - 1}$$

   In the case $n = 2$, as in this problem, that formula is a little nicer; it simplifies to

$$S = 2^n - 1.$$

   A little trial and error (or a good knowledge of logarithms) reveals that $n = 10$ is the first time that

$$2^n - 1 > 1000.$$

   So she will have paid her debt off when she makes the tenth payment, which occurs on January 10.

4. **C.** If you use your calculator, this one will take forever (testing to see if a number is prime is not fast). However, if you think about the definition of geometric series, it should be clear that after the first term of the series, no number can be prime. This is because the common ratio is a factor of any term in the series, but a prime number has no factors other than itself and 1. In this case, the only term Yolanda erases is the first term; the fourth term of Yolanda's sequence is the fifth term of Sheila's; that is, it is $17 * 11^4$, which is choice C..

5. **B.** For each number n, $n^2 - 1$ factors as $(n + 1)(n - 1)$, so no number on the list can be prime UNLESS it happens that $n - 1 = 1$ or $n + 1 = 1$. Since $n > 0$, this leaves

one possibility, namely, when $n = 2, 2^2 - 1 = 3$ is prime. After that, all numbers on the list are composite.

6. **A.** Let H be the hundreds digit of x, T the tens digit of x, and U the units digit. Then $x = 100H + 10T + U$ and $y = 100U + 10T + H$. So

$$y - x = 99U - 99H.$$

Thus $y - x$ must be divisible by 99. Only choice A satisfies this criterion. (And in fact Choice A works: take $x = 254$).

7. **E.** Number the buckets in clockwise order, numbering the northmost bucket 1. Then Sally fills all odd numbers until she gets to 15, then she skips 1 and moves on to 2, filling all the even numbers until she reaches 14. After filling 14, her next bucket is 1, so she stops. In the process, all the buckets were filled with white paint. This cyclic pattern is related to number theory; the reason that Sally fills all the buckets is because the greatest common divisor of 2 and 15 is 1; see the chapter on number theory for more information.

8. **E.** Using the same number as above, John fills buckets 1, 4, 7, 10, and 12, before filling 1 again; Mary fills buckets 1, 6, and 11, before filling 1 again. The only one that got filled with both blue and red paint was number 1.

9. **D.** The rule for a_n shows that a_n is the same as the factorial function $n!$. If you didn't notice this, you could still apply the rule to see that $a_7 = 7a_6 = \ldots = 7 \times 6 \times 5 \times 4 \times 3 \times 2 \times 1 = 5040$.

10. **D.** The sequence alternates between very large numbers growing larger and larger and very small fractions getting closer and closer to 0, with even-index terms corresponding to the large numbers. Choice D is the even-index term with the highest index.

11. **B.** This new symbol is not a function or a binary operation, but is a "relationship" between two numbers. This is a standard example of plugging in the definition and following it.

12. **B.** A is true since $3x - 3y = 3(x - y)$ is an integer whenever $x - y$ is. C is true because $y - x = -(x - y)$ is an integer whenever $x - y$ is. D is true because $x - z = (x - y) + (y - z)$ and the sum of two integers is an integer. E is true because $x - x = 0$, which is an integer. But B is false; for example, let $x = .5$ and $y = -.5$. Then $x - y$ is an integer, but $x^3 - y^3 = .25$, which is not an integer.

13. **B.** Writing the fractions next to each other, you can see that each denominator cancels the neighboring numerator. All we're left with is the numerator of the first term and the denominator of the one hundredth term, which is $\frac{1}{101}$.

14. **C.** You could use the arithmetic sequence formula, or, if you remembered our sum for the first even positive integers, you could subtract that from the sum of the first 200 integers. You could also add 1 to each number, giving you the sum of all the even integers, then subtract 100 for each extra one you added. We'll use the formula. In this case $n = 100$, $a_1 = 1$, and $a_n = 199$. Thus we have $100 * 100 = 10000$.

15. **D.** Since JJ and EE are both divisible by 11, so is their sum JJ + EE. JJ + EE differs from JE + EE by $|J - E|$, which is strictly smaller than 11. So there's no way that JE + EE can be divisible by 11; it either leaves a remainder of $|J - E|$ or 11-$|J - E|$. Checking specific examples should persuade you the other choices are all fine (35 + 55 takes care of B and C; 11 and 61 takes care of A and E).

16. **E.** There is no triangle with side lengths 3, 5, and 15, since $3 + 5 < 15$. Hence I is not defined. There is no triangle containing two different right angles, since the three angles must sum to 180, so II is not defined. III is defined, but it is equal to 174, which is greater than 90.

17. **B.** Since t_3 is the average of t_1 and t_2, but $t_3 = t_1$, we must have that $t_1 = t_2$. But this means $t_2 = t_3$, and so all the averages will just be this same term repeated over and over. So all the terms in the pattern are equal, and the difference between any two of them is 0.

18. **C.** Without using specific numbers, you can imitate Lisa's pattern. Draw a point and label it t_1; move your pen to the right and draw t_2. Then t_3 will lie squarely in the middle, t_4 will lie to the right of t_3 but to the left of t_2, t_5 will fall to the right of t_3 but to the left of t_4, and so on. All the even numbered terms lie to the right of all the odd-numbered terms, so I holds. t_2 is the greatest of all the terms, so II is false. III is true because the expression $\frac{t_1+t_2}{2}$ is just the same as t_3.

19. **D.** The digit I must be 1, because two three-digit numbers can't sum to more than 1998. Now the digit E is either 2 or 3. If E is 2, then $T < 5$, so T is 3 or 4. But T can't be 3, because
$$F + F = 10 + T,$$
and hence T is an even number. So T is 4. Then M is 8. Alternatively, E might be 3. Then T is at least 5. T can't be odd, so T is 8 (and hence F is 9, M is 6) or T is 6 (and hence F is 8, M is 2). These are the three possibilities for M.

20. **B.** From the right-hand column, C = 6, so B = 5. So A = 2. (A 1 is carried into the leftmost column).

21. **D.**. x satisfies two inequalities: $-x \leq x$ and $x^2 \leq x$ (since, of course, $(-x)^2 = x^2$. The first of these inequalities forces x to be non-negative; the latter forces x to be less than or equal to 1. A quick check shows any number in this range works, so the answer is D.

22. **D.** Working from right to left makes this problem much simpler. The right column says $B = 9$. So A must be 8.

23. **E.** The zero digits in the problem are a red herring! This is really a question about square numbers; A is some one-digit number that when squared yields a 2-digit number whose digits sum to A. Trial and error yields that $A = 9$.

24. **B.** Solution: Turn the problem "upside down" to get the addition problem $218 + J1K = L1MN$. L must be 1: it's not 0 by the stipulation of the problem, and the sum of two three-digit numbers will never be bigger than 1998. Since all the digits are different, K must be at least 2. This means that in the units column of the addition performed, we have an extra ten to carry, no matter what N is. So M is equal to $1 + 1 + 1$, which is 3.

25. **C.** Remember that the remainder when a number is divided by 10 is just its ones digit. So the problem is asking what possible ones digits a power of 7 can have. If a number ends in 5, then it is divisible by 5, so it can't be a power of 7 (its prime factorization has a 5 in it, whereas the prime factorization of powers of 7 have only 7s in them). So the answer is C. To see that A, B, D, and E are possible, just experiment with your calculator. In fact, the ones-digits of the powers of 7 rotate in the pattern 7, 9, 3, 1, 7, 9, 3, 1, 7, 9, 3, 1, ...

26. **E.** This digits problem is best viewed as an algebra problem. The equation tells us that
$$10A + 2 + 90 + A = 100 + 10A + 1.$$
Solving for A, we get A = 9.

27. **C.** This is just a system of three equations: let the hundreds digit be H, the tens digit T, and the units digit U. Then we have three equations:
$$H + T + U = 13$$
$$H = 2$$

$$101H + 20T + 101U = 989$$

Solving these gives the answer 247, whose digits multiply to 56.

28. **E.** The general pattern, which should be clear from writing out what happens up till January 7th, is that the total number of marbles on January the Nth is N^2. Why? The sum of the first N odd numbers is an arithmetic series, where $a_1 = 1$ and $a_N = 2N - 1$, so our formula gives

$$N\frac{1 + 2N - 1}{2} = \frac{2N^2}{2} = N^2$$

29. **B.** The number Lea records will be the tenths place in the decimal expansion of $\frac{x}{7}7$, where x is her original 16-digit number. A little experimenting on your calculator will persuade you that A, C, D, and E are all possible, and by elimination the answer must be B. However, it's inconvenient to experiment with 16-digit numbers. Instead, the key to this problem and others about decimal expansions is a knowledge of which types of decimal expansions can appear. For 7ths, if you know $\frac{1}{7}$, $\frac{2}{7}$, $\frac{3}{7}$, $\frac{4}{7}$, $\frac{5}{7}$, and $\frac{6}{7}$, then you know all the possible decimal expansions of an integer over 7. This because you can write a higher number– even a sixteen-digit one– as 7y + remainder, where y is an integer, and the remainder is all that contributes to the decimal. So test only the numbers $\frac{1}{7}$ through $\frac{6}{7}$ in your calculator. By the way, you should notice another pattern: each expansion in decimals contains the pattern "142857142857..." repeatedly. In particular, none of them contain 0, 3, 6, or 9.

30. **A.** If t is the tens digit of x and u is the units digit, the problem is looking for values of x such that $tu = 10t + u$. Solving this equation for t, we get $t = \frac{u}{u-10}$. Since u is between 1 and 9, t must always be negative, but t represents a digit, so this is impossible and there are no solutions.

31. **C.** Translating the symbols to English, $5\|b$ is the remainder when 5b is divided by 9. There's a sloppy solution and a slick solution.

Sloppy solution: if you divide any positive integer by 9, your calculator display will include a decimal termination that looks like .BBBBBBB .... (This only works when the denominator is 9, of course). The remainder is then equal to the digit B. So plug in $\frac{5}{9}$, $\frac{5^2}{9}$, etc. into your calculator; you will eventually see remainders of 2, 4, 7, and 8 appear; therefore, the answer must be C. Slick solution: If 5^b left a remainder of 6 when divided by 9, then we would have an equation of the form $5^b = 9x + 6$. The right side of this equation is divisible by 3, so the left side must be as well. But we already know the prime decomposition of 5^b: it is $5 * 5 * \cdots * 5$, where there are a total of b factors. There's only one prime decomposition of any number, and since 3 isn't in this prime decomposition, the number isn't divisible by 3. On the SAT, it is occasionally best to solve a problem in the sloppy way. If some of the deeper ideas in the number theory chapter are new to you, there is nothing wrong with approaching a problem by making a few calculations. It is only when you must make more than ten or so computations to solve a problem that you should consider searching for a faster solution. Even then, if you finish the section in time, you might come back to a problem that you couldn't find a slick solution for and plug away at your calculator in the hopes of finding a sloppy one.

32. **C.** Whenever it seems like there's too many things you don't know to get started, try a system of equations. In this case, let a_1 be the first term of the sequence and let d be the common difference. Then, since we know the fourth and sixteenth terms, we have

$$7 = a_1 + 3d$$

and

$$103 = a_1 + 15d.$$

Solving this system gives $d = 8$ and $a_1 = -17$. Now use the formula one more time to compute that the 12th term is

$$-17 + 11 * 8 = 71.$$

33. **A.** A one is carried from the middle column to the leftmost, so $M + N = 8$. A one is carried from the rightmost column to the middle, so

$$7 + N = 10 + L.$$

This gives us $L = N - 3$; combining these two equations gives $L + M = 5$.

34. **E.** You can solve it directly, or see the simplification two problems below. We'll show the direct solution here. First, work within the parentheses;

$$-2\heartsuit - 2 = max(|-4|, |0|) = 4.$$

Now, plugging this into the original problem,

$$-2\heartsuit 4 = max(|-6|, |2|) = 6.$$

35. **C.** Choices A, B, D, and E are false respectively when $a = -1, 0, 1, 2$ (remember that 0 is not a positive number, so choice B is wrong). Choice C is a fact about absolute values.

36. **E.** Notice that $a \heartsuit b$ is the maximum of the list $-a-b$, $a+b$, $a-b$, and $b-a$. Of these four, one will always be the same as $|a| + |b|$, and that one will be the largest. So $a \heartsuit b = |a| + |b|$. This operation is associative no matter what a, b, and c are.

37. **B.** The trick is realizing that you only need to look at the two-digit numbers which are perfect squares. Testing them, only 81 meets the criterion, so it is the answer.

38. **A.** Make sure to do the operations in the order provided by the parentheses; taking the LCM and GCD all at once gives the wrong answer. Here is the correct order of operations. Working inside the parentheses first:

$$(6 \triangle 10) = \frac{LCM(6, 10)}{GCD(6, 10)} = \frac{30}{2} = 15.$$

Now, working with the whole problem:

$$15 \triangle 15 = \frac{LCM(15, 15)}{GCD(15, 15)} = \frac{15}{15} = 1.$$

39. **E.** Statement A is true, because the GCD of two numbers is a divisor of both of the numbers, and hence is certainly a divisor of their least common multiple; therefore the division in the definition of $\triangle$ always results in an integer. Since the LCM and GCD of two positive integers are also positive integers, B must be true. Since for any m, $GCD(m, m) = LCM(m, m) = m$, C is true. Finally, if $m < n$, we have that $LCM(m, n) \geq n$ and $GCD(m, n) \leq m$, so $m \triangle n > \frac{n}{m} > 1$. A similar fact holds if $n < m$, so D is true. To see that E is not always true, take m to be 3 and n to be 9.

40. **C.** This problem can only be solved with T and U notation. Setting $x = 10T + U$, we have that $y = 10U + T$ and $z = 9U + T$ (which is $y - U$, since U is the tens digit of y). Then the equation becomes $10T + U + 10U + T = 27U + 3T$, or $2U = T$. So the only four possible choices of U are 1, 2, 3, and 4 (anything bigger makes T to big to be a digit) and the four special numbers are 21, 42, 63, and 84.

41. **D.** Write out what happens in the course of the first few matches. In the first six, the match goes: tie, tie, point for Jacqui, point for Jacqui, point for Janet, point for Janet. This is a cyclic pattern which resets itself after every 6 moves (because 6 is the least common multiple of 2 and 3). After 3 moves, Jacqui is ahead of Janet, and so any number leaving a remainder of 3 when you divide by 6 will have this same problem. Since all the choices but D are divisible by 3 but not by 6, they have this problem. Since the game starts out tied and is tied at the end of each cycle of 6, it will be tied after any number of rounds that's divisible by 6.

42. **C.** This is another cyclic pattern. This time the pattern cycles every 15 rounds. Over the course of fifteen rounds, there are two ties, then Jack wins five rounds, Janet wins five rounds, and the cycle is reset. 10000 isn't divisible by 15 (it needs to be divisible by both 3 and 5), but 9990 is, and $9990/15 = 666$, so $10000 = 666 * 15 + 10$. In each of the first 666 cycles, Janet wins five rounds, but in the course of the first 10 games of the final cycle, Janet wins only 3 games. So she wins a total of $666 * 5 + 3 = 3333$ games.

43. **B.** Think of multiplying numbers out: the last digit of a square depends only on the original number (for example, $17^2 = 289$; the last digit is a 9 because $7^2 = 49$. The only number in the answer choices whose last digit's square ends in itself is choice B, which ends in a 1 (and $1^2 = 1$).

44. **C.** Use T and U notation. The remainder fact tells us $U = 2$ or $U = 7$. The other part is the equation

$$11T + 11U = 88$$

which gives two distinct possible values for T and hence 2 solutions, 62 and 17.

CHAPTER 6

MISCELLANEOUS WORD PROBLEMS

Word problems in the Mathematics portion of the SAT ask you to figure out the underlying mathematics behind a few lines of text and then find the solution. This is perhaps their only universally defining feature; the problems themselves may be structured in a variety of different ways. The key to solving them is to look past the words and translate the problems into a mathematical framework. From there, you just need to figure out the best way to approach the resulting math problem. This often involves manipulating algebraic equations, but can also include guessing-and-checking, dimensional analysis (making sure units and consistent and appropriate), or any number of other techniques you may have learned, including those from other chapters of this book. Don't panic. Word problems don't ask you to do anything new or different from the other SAT math problems. They are simply designed to test your ability to apply your math skills to a real-world scenario.

Note that the outline below is not an exhaustive list of the kinds of word problems you might encounter. It would be impossible to describe all of the different shapes and forms that SAT word problems can come in. There is no fixed formula for how to solve a word problem, however the following approach is recommended:

1. Read the problem carefully.

2. Determine what the problem is asking you to find or do.

3. Determine what information is given.

4. Plan an approach to use the given information to solve the problem. Is it enough or will you need to find an intermediate result first?

5. Implement your plan.

You should be prepared to use any and all of the mathematics you have learned to help you figure things out.

Algebraic Manipulation

The most common type of word problem will ask you to do little more than translate the problem into algebraic equations and then manipulate these equations until you find a solution. Often this involves simply solving two equations with two variables simultaneously, although it may require less or more complicated calculations.

1. If Tom gives Albert $6, Albert will have twice as much money as Tom. Together, they have $20 more than twice what Tom initially has. How much money does Tom initially have?

   A. $20
   B. $24
   C. $32
   D. $36
   E. $38

   ANSWER: E. Let T be the amount of money initially Tom has and A be the amount of money initially Albert has. Together they have $20 more than twice what Tom currently has, so (note that the quantity $T + A$ does not change even when Tom gives Albert some of his money)

   $$T + A = 20 + 2T$$
   $$A - T = 20$$

   If Tom gave Albert $6, Tom would have $T - 6$ dollars and Albert would have $A + 6$ dollars. So

   $$A + 6 = 2(T - 6)$$
   $$A - 2T = -18$$

   So subtracting the second equation from the first gives us $T = \$38$.

2. A cylindrical container is partially filled with water. The depth of the water is two inches less than the height of the remaining unfilled part of the container. If we were to continue to add water to the container until the depth rose another two inches, there would be twice as much water as unfilled space in the container. How tall is the container?

   A. 6 inches
   B. 9 inches
   C. 12 inches
   D. 16 inches

E. 24 inches

ANSWER: A. Let L be the length of the container in inches, and D be the original depth of the water. Then $L - D$ is the length of the remaining unfilled part of the container. So

$$D = L - D - 2$$
$$2D = L - 2$$

Adding two inches of water would mean that there is twice as much water as unfilled space (note that the amount of unfilled space must also go down by two inches for the water to rise two inches), so

$$D + 2 = 2(L - D - 2)$$
$$D + 2 = 2L - 2D - 4$$
$$3D = 2L - 6$$

Multiplying our first equation by 3 and our second equation by 2, we get

$$6D = 3L - 6$$

and

$$6D = 4L - 12$$

Substituting these equations yields

$$3L - 6 = 4L - 12$$
$$L = 6$$

Rate Problems

Another type of word problem tests your ability to work with rates and speeds. For example, the question might provide two different rates and ask how long it would take when the rates are combined somehow. Answering these problems may require you to employ an important and useful trick that involves inverting the rates before combining them. For example, suppose person A takes x hours to complete one unit and person B takes y hours to complete one unit, and we wish to find the time it would take them per unit when working together. We actually need to invert x and y (which are expressed as hours/unit) so that we have each person's rate expressed as units/hour. So person A makes $\frac{1}{x}$ units/hour and person B makes $\frac{1}{y}$ units/hour. Then together, they can make $\frac{1}{x} + \frac{1}{y}$ units per hour, or in other words, it takes $\frac{1}{\frac{1}{x} + \frac{1}{y}}$ hours per unit.

3. If it takes three people six days to build a sailboat, how many people would you need to build five sailboats in nine days?

  A. 6
  B. 7
  C. 9
  D. 10
  E. 12

  ANSWER: D. If it takes 3 people 6 days to build a sailboat, it would take one person 3 times as long, or 18 days to build one boat (a rate of $\frac{1}{18}$ boats per day). So in 9 days, one person could build $\frac{9}{18} = \frac{1}{2}$ of a boat. We wish to build 5 boats, so we would need $\frac{5}{\frac{1}{2}} = 10$ people.

An important tool for these kinds of problems is known as "dimensional analysis." **This simply refers to keeping track of the different units (such as hours, miles, \$, pounds, boats, etc.) and making sure that they cancel with each other properly.** This ensures that you perform the right calculations, which you can double-check by making sure that your final answer is in the correct units. For example, suppose it takes me 40 minutes to travel 50 miles, and I want to know how far I could travel in 2 hours. I would multiply 2 hours by $\frac{60 \text{ minutes}}{1 \text{ hour}}$ (which is the same thing as multiplying by 1). Then the "hours" units would cancel, and I would be left with

$$2 \text{ hours} \cdot \frac{60 \text{ minutes}}{1 \text{ hour}} = 120 \text{ minutes}$$

I know that it takes me $\frac{40 \text{ minutes}}{50 \text{ miles}}$, but multiplying by this would leave me with units of $\frac{\text{minutes}^2}{\text{miles}}$. However, if I invert this quantity to restate my pace as $\frac{50 \text{ miles}}{40 \text{ minutes}}$, I can multiply by 120 minutes and the "minutes" units will cancel, leaving me with

$$120 \text{ minutes} \cdot \frac{50 \text{ miles}}{40 \text{ minutes}} = 150 \text{ miles}$$

This result is in the correct units, so I can be sure that I have found the answer. I will be able to travel 150 miles in two hours.

4. Kelly's car has a fuel efficiency of 20 miles per gallon. She drives for half an hour on local roads at the speed limit of 30 miles per hour, then merges onto the interstate, where she can go twice as fast, and continues for another hour until she reaches her destination. If fuel costs \$2 per gallon, how much did her trip cost?

A. $4.00
B. $5.00
C. $7.50
D. $9.00
E. $12.00

ANSWER: C. We first need to figure out how many miles she traveled. She drives for

$$\frac{1}{2} \text{ hour at } \frac{30 \text{ miles}}{\text{hour}} = 15 \text{ miles}$$

on local roads. She then drives for

$$1 \text{ hour at } \frac{60 \text{ miles}}{\text{hour}} = 60 \text{ miles}$$

on the interstate, for a total of $15 + 60 = 75$ miles. Her car has a fuel efficiency of 20 miles per gallon, meaning that it takes 1 gallon for every 20 miles. So she uses

$$75 \text{ miles} \cdot \frac{1 \text{ gallon}}{20 \text{ miles}} = 3.75 \text{ gallons}$$

Fuel costs $2/gallon, so her trip costs

$$3.75 \text{ gallons} \cdot \frac{\$2}{\text{gallon}} = \$7.50$$

NOT Problems

Sometimes, rather than asking for the answer to a question, a problem will ask you to find which answer would NOT satisfy the conditions described. These problems may require you to think in ways that are different than the thought process for a traditional word problem. It is important to keep in mind (and this holds true not just for NOT problems, but for any SAT question) that there are a limited number of possible answers provided, and you can use this to your advantage. One strategy is to use guess-and-check for each of the four or five candidate solutions to see if they work. If you can come up with a situation where a particular answer WOULD satisfy the conditions described, then you can eliminate it. This may help you narrow down your choices, and you may even be able to find the final answer by elimination.

5. Barry plays golf with five clubs in his bag: with his driver, he hits the ball 200 yards; with his 3-iron, he hits the ball 150 yards; with his 5-iron, he hits the ball 125 yards;

with his 7-iron, he hits the ball 90 yards; and with his 9-iron, he hits the ball 70 yards. On the ninth hole, it takes him 3 shots to cover the 340-yard distance to the green. If he used one club exactly twice and another club exactly once, what club could he NOT have used in getting to the green?

A. driver
B. 3-iron
C. 5-iron
D. 7-iron
E. 9-iron

ANSWER: B. The best way to answer this question is to try out different clubs to see if there is any possible way Barry could have used them to go 340 yards. First, we start with the driver, which he hits 200 yards. He could not have taken two shots with the driver, because that would already be a 400-yard distance, which is more than 340. So he must have hit some other club twice to go the remaining 140 yards. We check and see that indeed, he has a club (the 9-iron) that goes 70 yards on each shot. So both A. and E. can be eliminated, because they both could have been used in a legitimate scenario. Next, we check the 3-iron, which he hits 150 yards. He could not have hit it twice, because this would mean that the other club would have to hit the ball 40 yards, which he doesn't have. If he hit it once (150 yards), he would have to hit some other club twice to make up the remaining 190 yards. However, he doesn't have a club that he hits 95 yards, so this won't work either. So the answer is B.. We can check C. and D. also, just to be sure. If Barry hit his 5-iron twice (125 yards each time) and his 7-iron once (90 yards), he would have hit 340 yards. So C. and D. can also be eliminated.

Percentage/Fraction/Proportion/Ratio

Many word problems will ask you to find a percentage, fraction, proportion, or ratio, so it is important to know exactly what each of these words means. A fraction or proportion refers to the amount in question divided by the total amount. For example, if 2 out of 20 people have curly hair, the fraction of curly-haired people is $\frac{2}{20} = \frac{1}{10}$. A percentage is essentially a fraction, but expressed in percentage terms. To do this, simply multiply the fraction by 100. Using the same example as above, the percentage of people who have curly hair is $\frac{1}{10} \cdot 100 = 10\%$. A ratio is defined as one quantity divided by another. If A = 5 and B = 2, the ratio of A to B is $\frac{5}{2}$.

Problems Involving Lettered Variables

Often, you will be asked to solve a problem that doesn't contain any numbers. These questions will resemble other word problems, but any quantitative material will be written in terms of abstract variables or letters. Don't let this intimidate you - you can solve these problems just as you would any other. The only difference is that you will be doing calculations with letters instead of numbers.

A useful trick if you ever get too confused is to assign a real number (like 2, or 7, etc.) to some or all of the letters or variables before you try to solve the problem. This can help eliminate some of the clutter if you find yourself working with more letters than you can keep track of. It is also a very good trick for double-checking your answer if you are not sure that you got it right. Along the same lines, you can use this technique to help you eliminate answers that don't come out right when you put in real numbers.

6. Allen earns E dollars every year, which he either spends or saves. Of that money, he spends x more dollars than he saves. In terms of E and x, what fraction of his income does he save?

　A. $\frac{E-x}{E}$
　B. $\frac{E-x}{2E}$
　C. $\frac{x}{E-x}$
　D. $\frac{x}{E}$
　E. $\frac{E-x}{E+x}$

ANSWER: B. Let S be the amount of money that he saves. Then he spends $S + x$, and $S + (S + x)$ must equal exactly E (since his earnings are either saved or spent). So

$$E = 2S + x$$
$$S = \frac{E - x}{2}$$

Then the fraction of his income that Allen saves is

$$\frac{S}{E} = \frac{\frac{E-x}{2}}{E}$$
$$= \frac{E - x}{2E}$$

We can check this answer by letting $E = \$1000$ and $x = \$200$. Then Allen would spend \$600 and save \$400 (he spends $x = \$200$ more than he saves out of a total of $E = \$1000$). So the fraction of his income that he saves is

$$\frac{\$400}{\$1000} = \frac{2}{5}$$

Does this agree with our answer B.?

$$\frac{E - x}{2E} = \frac{\$1000 - \$200}{\$2000}$$

$$= \frac{2}{5}$$

So our specific example agrees with (but does not prove) our answer.

Sequences and Series

Some word problems may involve either finite or infinite series or sequences. See the chapter on number theory for some possibly useful properties and formulas. Also, keep in mind that the "brute force method" often works well for these problems, too.

7. Karen opens a bank account with the goal of saving up $2,000. She initially funds the account with $850 and plans to make a deposit every two weeks thereafter, with the deposit amount starting at $500 and increasing $50 each subsequent deposit. She also plans on having to withdraw $600 every three weeks, with that amount decreasing by $50 each time. How long will it take for Karen to reach her goal?

A. 5 weeks
B. 6 weeks
C. 7 weeks
D. 8 weeks
E. 9 weeks

ANSWER: D. In this case, it seems easiest to just use the brute force method - i.e. simply tracking her account balance as we work through all of the deposits and withdrawals until she reaches her goal. It may be a bit tedious and long, but we don't have to invoke any complicated mathematics (which can lead to mistakes) and we know that we will eventually reach the answer.

Week 0: $850 (initial deposit)

Week 1: $850

Week 2: $850 + $500 = $1,350

Week 3: $1,350 - $600 = $750

Week 4: $750 + $550 = $1,300

Week 5: $1,300

Week 6: $1,300 + $600 - $550 = $1350

Week 7: $1,350

Week 8: $1,350 + $650 = $2,000

So our answer is 8 weeks.

Geometry

Some word problems will involve varying amounts of geometry. In these situations, it can be very helpful to draw a picture of the situation. This makes it easier for you to visualize key elements of the problem and apply geometric formulas and identities.

8. Sand drains from the cone-shaped upper chamber of an hourglass, which is 8 inches high and 12 inches in diameter, at a constant rate. The chamber starts out fully filled and it takes exactly one hour for all of the sand to drain from it. How much time is left when the remaining sand in the upper cone is 4 inches deep?

   A. 7.5 minutes
   B. 15 minutes
   C. 30 minutes
   D. 45 minutes
   E. 52.5 minutes

   ANSWER: A. To find the answer, we need to figure out how much sand the upper chamber contains, and how much of that sand will remain when the upper four inches drain out. We need to draw a picture of the hourglass and use the formula for the volume of a cone: $V = \frac{1}{3}\pi r^2 h$. So the full upper chamber (note that the radius is half the diameter) holds $\frac{1}{3}\pi \cdot 36 \cdot 8 = 96\pi$ cubic inches of sand. Now we turn to the remaining 4 inches of sand in the chamber. By properties of similar triangles (since the depth of the sand is half the depth of the full chamber), the radius of the top of the sand must be half the radius of the full chamber: 3 inches. Then the remaining volume of sand is $\frac{1}{3}\pi \cdot 9 \cdot 4 = 12\pi$ cubic inches. So only one-eighth of the sand remains. If the full chamber takes one hour to drain, then the remaining one-eighth of the sand should take one-eighth of an hour, or 7.5 minutes, to drain.

Practice Problems

1. Andrew is taking the bus to his school 8 miles away, but he forgot his homework. If his bus averages a speed of 24 miles per hour, and he left 8 minutes ago, how fast will his mother have to drive so that they arrive at his school at the same time?

    A. 32 miles per hour
    B. 36 miles per hour
    C. 40 miles per hour
    D. 42 miles per hour
    E. 48 miles per hour

2. Three friends collect baseball cards. Bob has 3 more cards than Jim, but half as many as David. If together they have 61 cards, how many cards does Jim have?

    A. 9
    B. 11
    C. 13
    D. 15
    E. 17

3. Two friends work at a deli. Eric can make 3 sandwiches per minute, but Steven can only make 20 less than two-thirds of the number of sandwiches Eric makes every hour. If they work together to fill an order for 210 sandwiches, how long will it take them to finish?

    A. 45 minutes
    B. 48 minutes
    C. 50 minutes
    D. 52 minutes
    E. 60 minutes

4. What is the sum of all the numbers 37 through 181, inclusive?

    A. 14, 986
    B. 15, 805
    C. 15, 982
    D. 16, 120
    E. 18, 543

5. The local high school cafeteria spends $260 on a total of 80 gallons of milk and orange juice. If milk costs $2.80 per gallon, and a gallon of orange juice costs $3.80, how many gallons of orange juice did they buy?

A. 30
B. 33
C. 36
D. 39
E. 42

6. A certain die can only roll a 4 or a 7. Which of the following totals CANNOT be reached within 5 rolls of the die?

    A. 17
    B. 19
    C. 22
    D. 23
    E. 29

7. Mary takes the train from New York to Washington for 4 hours at an average speed of 80 miles per hour. After waiting for an hour, she gets on a plane that flies south to Orlando for an hour and a half at 400 miles per hour. Finally, she spends another three and a half hours driving to Miami at 60 miles per hour. What is Mary's average speed from New York to Miami?

    A. 89 miles per hour
    B. 94 miles per hour
    C. 105 miles per hour
    D. 113 miles per hour
    E. 121 miles per hour

8. Aaron, James, and Walker are swimming together in a lake. Walker is 10 feet away from James, and 6 feet away from Aaron. If James swims 4 feet from his original position, which of the following is NOT a possible distance between Aaron and James?

    A. 1 foot
    B. 3 feet
    C. 8 feet
    D. 15 feet
    E. 21 feet

9. A bakery makes a batch of 53 bagels and has to decide how to sell them. There is an unlimited demand for either packages of 6 bagels, which sell for $5 each, or bags of 16 bagels, which sell for $12 each. Any leftover bagels must be thrown away and have no value. If the bakery wants to maximize revenue from the batch, what is the total combined number of 16-bagel bags and 6-bagel packages they should sell?

A. 4
B. 5
C. 6
D. 7
E. 8

10. The cost of a lift ticket at a certain ski resort consists of a fixed charge for access plus an additional hourly charge. If a two-hour ticket costs $45, and two five-hour tickets cost $150, how much would it cost to buy one ticket that is valid from 10 AM to 5 PM?

A. $90
B. $95
C. $100
D. $105
E. $107.50

11. The senior class at Central High School consists of seven homeroom classes of equal size. If we take a single one of the homeroom classes and split it into groups of eight, we will have five students left over who don't form a full group. How many leftover students would we have if we split the entire senior class into groups of four?

A. 0
B. 1
C. 2
D. 3
E. 5

12. A grocery store sells individual sticks of gum for $0.10 and packs of five sticks of gum for $0.30. Last month they sold 900 total sticks of gum for an average price of $0.07. How many 5-packs of gum did they sell?

A. 135
B. 140
C. 150
D. 156
E. 170

13. Construction of a new power plant requires a cleared rectangular piece of land whose length is three times its width. If a proposal to widen the shorter side of the currently-set-aside plot of land by 100 meters (and lengthen the plot accordingly, so as to maintain the proper rectangular proportions) would yield an additional 90,000 square meters of space, what percentage increase in plot area would this expansion represent?

A. 30 percent
B. 75 percent
C. 200 percent
D. 300 percent
E. 400 percent

14. A certain brand of jellybean comes in 4 colors - red, green, orange, and blue. Ken's bag of beans has some of every color, and he knows that he has exactly 16 green and 12 orange jellybeans. If he were to trade 7 of his red beans for blue beans, the percentage increase in blue beans would be twice the percentage decrease in red beans and the percentage of beans that were blue out of all the beans in the bag would increase by 10%. How many red beans does Ken have?

A. 10
B. 14
C. 18
D. 24
E. 28

15. Caroline is training for a marathon and wants to run every day for a week, starting on the 15th of September. On each even-numbered day, she plans to take a rest and reduce the duration of her run by one third from the previous day. One each odd-numbered day, she plans to double the duration of her run from the previous day. Over the course of the week, she plans to run for 747 minutes. How long does she plan to run the first day of the week?

A. 36 minutes
B. 64 minutes
C. 72 minutes
D. 81 minutes
E. 124 minutes

16. A container truck with cargo bay dimensions 12 feet by 12 feet by 72 feet is packed full with cubic cardboard boxes with sides of length 3 feet. How much of the boxes' outer cardboard surface is not touching the walls, floor, or ceiling of the trucks cargo bay?

A. 3, 744 square feet
B. 12, 448 square feet
C. 16, 992 square feet
D. 24, 296 square feet
E. 33, 754 square feet

17. A stock's P/E ratio is defined as the price of the stock divided by the company's previous year's earnings. If a company's yearly earnings rise by 20%, but the stock price falls 10%, what, to the nearest percentage, is the change in the stock's P/E ratio?

   A. -25%
   B. -13%
   C. no change
   D. +13%
   E. +25%

18. While its running, a leaky lawnmower loses a fraction D of its fuel to drips from a tiny hole in the engine. The tank is currently filled with G gallons, less than its capacity of C gallons of fuel. With no leaking, this would be enough fuel to mow A square feet of grass. In terms of D, C, G, and A, how many square feet of grass could the leaky lawnmower mow if its tank were completely filled?

   A. $GA - D$
   B. $\frac{DC}{GA}$
   C. $\frac{ACD}{G}$
   D. $\frac{AC(1-D)}{G}$
   E. $\frac{A}{1-D}$

19. Starting on the second week of the year, Laura deposits her paycheck for $1,000$ into her bank account every two weeks. Starting the first week of the year, she withdraws 400 for living expenses for her account every week. At the end of the 52-week year, Laura has accumulated $13,400$ in her account. How much did she have in her account after the 5th week?

   A. $6,600$
   B. $8,000$
   C. $8,200$
   D. $8,600$
   E. $9,200$

20. Jamie is three times the age of her younger brother, but in eight years she will only be one year less than twice his age. How old was Jamie when her brother was born?

   A. 3
   B. 6
   C. 10
   D. 12
   E. 14

21. Two parents and their three kids are driving in a car whose frame weighs 1500 pounds. The average weight of the parents is twice the average weight of the children, and the average weight of all the people in the car is 105 pounds. What fraction of the total weight of the car (including passengers) do the parents represent?

    A. $\frac{4}{27}$
    B. $\frac{6}{29}$
    C. $\frac{1}{8}$
    D. $\frac{14}{81}$
    E. $\frac{8}{23}$

22. A school buys electricity at a cost of C dollars per K kilowatts. They prepaid P dollars to the power company this month, and have used U kilowatts so far. In terms of C, K, P, and U, how many more kilowatts can they use before they will need to pay the company more money?

    A. $\frac{P}{C} - U$
    B. $\frac{PC}{K}$
    C. $U + KPC$
    D. $\frac{U-P}{KC}$
    E. $\frac{K}{C(U-P)}$

23. A class of 16 students fills out a teacher-evaluation form and rates their teacher on a scale from 1 to 10. If the average score was 7, what is the highest possible number of students who could have given the teacher a perfect 10?

    A. 7
    B. 8
    C. 9
    D. 10
    E. 11

24. Jon invests his life savings in the stock market. If he loses 20% the first year, what annual return, to the nearest percent, must he earn over the next two years so that his annual return for the whole three year period is 10%?

    A. 6%
    B. 15%
    C. 29%
    D. 36%
    E. 45%

25. Robert surveys 100 of his classmates to see how many hours they sleep each night. If girls average 2 hours more than the boys, and the overall average would rise by half an hour if he surveyed an additional 50 girls, how many girls did Robert originally survey?

   A. 10
   B. 25
   C. 35
   D. 50
   E. 75

26. Maria rides a ski-lift to the top of a mountain at a speed of 5 miles per hour. She then skis straight back down the slope to the bottom of the ski lift at an average speed five times faster than she went up the mountain. If the whole trip took her 30 minutes, how long is the ski slope?

   A. 1 mile
   B. $\frac{15}{7}$ miles
   C. $\frac{17}{6}$ miles
   D. $\frac{25}{6}$ miles
   E. 5 miles

27. General Grocery sells sells only bunches of either five or nine bananas. Which of the following is NOT a possible number of bananas that a customer could buy?

   A. 23
   B. 24
   C. 25
   D. 26
   E. 27

28. It takes Selma five days to read a 250-page book. If she has to read two 300-page books and three 500-page books for a school report, how many days will this take her?

   A. 32
   B. 35
   C. 37
   D. 42
   E. 47

29. A wooden ladder is leaning against a vertical wall, with one end resting 9 feet up the wall and the other end resting on the ground. The ladder slides down the wall 2 feet, so that it is now resting only 7 feet up the wall, but the bottom of the ladder slides no

more than 1 foot along the ground. Which of the following is NOT a possible length for the ladder?

A. 15 feet
B. 20 feet
C. 25 feet
D. 30 feet
E. 35 feet

30. Two brothers work on a farm together. The older brother needs 5 hours to clear an acre of field, but it only takes the younger brother 3 hours. How long would it take them to clear 2 acres of field together?

A. 3 hours and 45 minutes
B. 4 hours
C. 4 hours and 15 minutes
D. 4 hours and 45 minutes
E. 5 hours

31. Alison, Barbara, and Chelsea each start off with A, B, and C (where A, B, and C are whole numbers) candies, respectively. Alison gives Barbara five green candies, Chelsea eats four of her candies, and the new total number of candies is twice the number Alison originally had. In terms of B and C, how many candies does Alison have now?

A. $B + C$
B. $\frac{B-C}{2}$
C. $\frac{B+C-4}{2}$
D. $2B + 2C + 9$
E. $B + C + 1$

32. Phil constructs a rectangle using all of a 40-foot piece of wire. George makes a rectangle from the same piece of wire, but one of the sides is 5 feet shorter and one of the sides is 5 feet longer. As a result, the area of George's rectangle is 25% less than the area of Phil's rectangle. What is the area of Phil's rectangle?

A. 40 square feet
B. 50 square feet
C. 80 square feet
D. 100 square feet
E. 400 square feet

33. The average of four different positive integers is 48. What is the biggest possible of these numbers?

    A. 47

    B. 48

    C. 49

    D. 186

    E. 198

34. Miss Richards' algebra class has N students with an average age of R. Miss Williams' algebra class has M more than twice the number of students in Miss Richards' class and her students' average age is W. Find an expression for the average age of all of the students in both algebra classes.

    A. $\frac{RN+2WN+WM}{3N+M}$

    B. $\frac{RN+WM}{3N+WM}$

    C. $\frac{R+W}{N+M}$

    D. $\frac{NM+RW}{3N+M}$

    E. $\frac{R-M}{N+2M}$

35. Dave is twice as old as Bill was five years ago. Five years from now, Bill will be two-thirds of Dave's age. What is their current combined age?

    A. 28

    B. 30

    C. 35

    D. 47

    E. 65

36. Cara plays basketball for her school and has made 16 of the shots she has taken so far this season. She calculates that in order to double her shooting percentage (the percentage of shots taken that she has made) she would have to make her next 20 baskets in a row. How many shots has she taken so far this season?

    A. 32

    B. 54

    C. 72

    D. 120

    E. 160

37. Ellen is in charge of checking in students in the morning for a day care program and can check in five students per minute. At 8:55, the first student arrives. At 8:56, three more students arrive, and at each subsequent minute two more than the number of students who arrived the previous minute arrive and begin to form a line for checking in. This pattern continues until the student influx peaks with 11 students arriving at

9:00. At this point, the pattern reverses and two less than the number of students who arrived the previous minute arrive until only one last student arrives at 9:05. To the nearest minutes, what time will Ellen be finished checking in all of the students?

A. 9:04
B. 9:05
C. 9:06
D. 9:07
E. 9:08

38. An odometer on a motorcycle measures the number of times the tires rotate, and multiplies by the circumference of the tires to calculate how far it has traveled. In normal conditions, Evan's odometer calculates that it takes 110 miles to get from town A to town B. However, in the winter Evan has to put special treads around his 20-inch tires, and the odometer reads only 100 miles for the journey from town A to town B. How thick are the winter treads?

A. $\frac{1}{2}$ inch
B. 1 inch
C. 2 inches
D. 3 inches
E. 4 inches

39. Abraham can paint 40 feet of fence per hour. If Abraham works together with Benjy to paint a 12,000-foot fence, working 8 hours a day, it will take them 15 days to finish. How long would it take Benjy to do the job alone?

A. 18 days
B. 25 days
C. 30 days
D. 36 days
E. 44 days

40. Sam knows that his friend's phone number is listed within one of three zip codes - 202, 399, or 100. He also knows that the number, when listed either with or without the zip code, always forms a palindrome (a number which is the same read backwards or forwards). How many possible phone numbers could his friend have?

A. 1
B. 2
C. 8
D. 32
E. 148

41. The local library has 12,000 books which are divided into five different categories - nonfiction, adventure, mystery, drama, and romance. The librarian knows that there are the number of romance books and mystery books is equal, and of non-romance books, $\frac{2}{5}$ are nonfiction, and $\frac{3}{10}$ of the books are adventure. Also, he knows that there are twice as many mystery books as drama books. What fraction of the books are mystery or adventure?

   A. $\frac{1}{6}$
   B. $\frac{1}{4}$
   C. $\frac{5}{12}$
   D. $\frac{7}{12}$
   E. $\frac{2}{3}$

42. In four years, the product of two sisters' ages (measured in whole-number years) will be twice the current product of their ages (also measured in whole-number years). Which of the following could be one of their ages in four years?

   A. 7
   B. 11
   C. 12
   D. 14
   E. 15

43. A movie theater with a capacity of 300 people sells out for a Saturday night show. If the theater charges $5 for children and $9 for adults and sells $2,000 in tickets, how many adults went to the show?

   A. 125
   B. 140
   C. 180
   D. 225
   E. 250

44. There are J players on the Junior Varsity football team and V players on the Varsity team. If the average height of the Junior Varsity players is 56 inches, the average height of the Varsity players is 62 inches, and the average height of all the players is 60 inches, what fraction of the football players are on the Varsity team?

   A. $\frac{J+V}{2V}$
   B. $\frac{V-J}{V+J}$
   C. $3J$
   D. $\frac{2}{3}$
   E. $\frac{3J}{2V}$

126

Solutions to Practice Problems

1. **C.** First we need to solve for t, the time in hours it will take for Andrew to get to school. We know that $\frac{24 \text{ miles}}{\text{hour}} \cdot t$ hours has to equal the 8 mile distance to school. So $t = \frac{8}{24} = \frac{1}{3}$ of an hour, or 20 minutes. However, he has already been driving for 8 minutes, so his mother has 12 minutes ($\frac{1}{5}$ of an hour) left to catch up with him before he arrives. So she has to go

$$\frac{8 \text{ miles}}{\frac{1}{5} \text{ hours}} = 40 \text{ miles per hour}$$

2. **C.** We want to translate each of these pieces of information into algebraic statements. First, we know that
$$B = J + 3$$
Also,
$$2B = D$$
Finally,
$$B + J + D = 61$$

Now we can substitute the second equation into the third to get

$$3B + J = 61$$

Finally, we can substitute the first into our new equation to get

$$3(J + 3) + J = 61$$

$$4J + 9 = 61$$

$$J = 13$$

3. **A.** Eric makes 3 sandwiches a minute, or 180 sandwiches per hour, so Steven can make $120 - 20 = 100$ sandwiches per hour. So together they can make 280 sandwiches per hour. This means that their combined rate of sandwich-making is $\frac{1}{280}$ th of an hour per sandwich. So

$$210 \text{ sandwiches} \cdot \frac{\frac{1}{280} \text{ hour}}{\text{sandwich}} = \frac{3}{4} \text{ hour}$$

$$= 45 \text{ minutes}$$

4. **B.** The most direct way to solve this problem is to use the formula for an arithmetic series,

$$S = (X_1 + X_N) \cdot \frac{N}{2}$$

where N is the index on the last term when the first term is indexed to 1. So

$$S = (37 + 181) \cdot \frac{145}{2}$$

$$= 15,805$$

However, if you can't remember or don't feel comfortable with the formula, here is a more intuitive way to think about the problem (which will also get you to the correct answer): Imagine each of the numbers spread out in a line from lowest (37) to highest (181). Now sequentially pair off a series of numbers which all have the same sum. We want to choose $37 + 181 = 218$, $38 + 180 = 218$, $39 + 179 = 218$, ... and so on until we have paired as many numbers as we can (using each number only once). Then we would like to know how many numbers we have to count. Your first instinct might be to subtract 37 from 181, and get 144. But we have to be careful not to conclude from this that we have 144 numbers. There are exactly two numbers were between 1 and 2, inclusive, but $2 - 1$ only equals 1. There are exactly three numbers between 7 and 9, inclusive, but $9 - 7$ only equals 2. So it is pretty clear that to figure out how many numbers we have, we need to add 1 to the difference between 181 and 37. So we are counting $144 + 1 = 145$ numbers. Because 145 is odd, we know that exactly one number will be left over when we finish our pairing. Since we are starting with the outer pair of numbers and moving sequentially inwards at an equal rate from both sides, that last number has to be the exact middle of 37 and 181. We can find this by taking the mean of 37 and 181, which is $\frac{37+181}{2} = 109$. The other 144 numbers have been split into $\frac{144}{2} = 72$ pairs of numbers which sum to 218. So the sum of our entire set of numbers must be $72 \cdot 218 + 109 = 15,696 + 109 = 15,805$.

5. **C.** Let x represent the number of gallons of orange juice. Then $80 - x =$ the number of gallons Since the total was \$260, we know that

$$3.80x + 2.80(80 - x) = 260$$

$$3.8x + 2.8 \cdot 80 - 2.8x = 260$$

$$x = 260 - 2.8(80)$$

$$x = 36$$

6. **A.** Try as we might, we cannot make 17 out of combinations of 4s and 7s. First we try it with zero 7s: When we add multiples of 4 to $7 \cdot 0$, we can get 16 and 20, but not 17. Next we try it with one 7: When we add multiples of 4 to $7 \cdot 1$, we can get 11, 15, and 19, but not 17. Next we try it with two 7s: When we add multiples of 4 to $7 \cdot 2$, we can get 14, and 18, but not 17. If we roll three 7s, we are already at 21, so we cant get 17. We can also solve this by checking the other 4 numbers. Each of them is a possible total. $19 = 1 \cdot 7 + 3 \cdot 4$, $22 = 2 \cdot 7 + 2 \cdot 4$, $23 = 1 \cdot 7 + 4 \cdot 4$, and $29 = 3 \cdot 7 + 2 \cdot 4$.

7. **D.** Average speed $= \frac{\text{total distance traveled}}{\text{total time elapsed}}$. We are not told the distance between New York and Miami, but we can calculate the distance between each of the cities she visits by multiplying her speed (in miles per hour) by the time she spent traveling (in hours). The hours units will cancel, leaving us with the distance in miles. From New York to Washington, we find that she travels

$$4 \text{ hours} \cdot \frac{80 \text{ miles}}{\text{hour}} = 320 \text{ miles}$$

From Washington to Orlando, she travels

$$1.5 \text{ hours} \cdot \frac{400 \text{ miles}}{\text{hour}} = 600 \text{ miles}$$

From Orlando to Miami, she travels

$$3.5 \text{ hours} \cdot \frac{60 \text{ miles}}{\text{hour}} = 210 \text{ miles}$$

So she has traveled a total distance of

$$320 + 600 + 210 = 1130 \text{ miles}$$

in a total time of

$$4 + 1 + 1.5 + 3.5 = 10 \text{ hours}$$

So her average speed is

$$\frac{1130 \text{ miles}}{10 \text{ hours}} = 113 \text{ miles per hour}$$

8. **E.** Since neither Aaron nor Walker move, we know that they remain exactly 6 feet apart. We can imagine them as fixed points on a straight line. We then want to consider the range of positions that James could occupy in relation to these points. To find the farthest distance that James could be from Aaron, we would place James on the other side of Walker along the line (10 feet from Walker and thus 16 feet from

James). Then we assume that James swims 3 feet in the direction away from Aaron so that he is 3 feet further down the line. This would put him 20 feet from James, which is the furthest away he could possibly be. So answer E., 21 feet, is NOT a possible distance. The other four distances are possible (as is any distance between 0 and 20 feet, inclusive).

9. **D.** We want to consider all possible combinations of 16-bagel bags and 6-bagel packages they could sell, and compare the resulting revenue in each case. The bakery could sell either zero, one, two, or three 16-bagel bags, and in each case they would sell as many 6-bagel packages as they can make from the remaining bagels. If they sell zero 16-bagel bags, they will sell eight 6-bagel packages and earn revenue of $0 \cdot \$12 + 8 \cdot \$5 = \$40$. If they sell one 16-bagel bag, they will sell six 6-bagel packages and earn revenue of $1 \cdot \$12 + 6 \cdot \$5 = \$42$. If they sell two 16-bagel bags, they will sell three 6-bagel packages and earn revenue of $2 \cdot \$12 + 3 \cdot \$5 = \$39$. If they sell three 16-bagel bags, they dont have enough bagels left to sell any 6-bagel packages and thus earn revenue of $3 \cdot \$12 + 0 \cdot \$5 = \$36$. So the bakery will choose to sell one 16-bagel bag and six 6-bagel packages (and earn maximum revenue of \$42) for a combined total of 7 bags and packages.

10. **B.** Let us denote the fixed charge as F and the hourly charge as H. Then we know that

$$F + 2H = 45$$

and

$$2(F + 5H) = 150$$

Multiplying the first equation by two and multiplying out the second equation, we get

$$2F + 4H = 90$$

$$2F + 10H = 150$$

Then subtracting the first equation from the second, we find that

$$6H = 60$$

$$H = 10$$

Then we can substitute into any of the equations to find that F = 25. So one seven-hour ticket would cost

$$F + 7H = 25 + 7 \cdot 10$$

$$= \$95$$

11. **D.** Divide each of the homeroom classes into groups of eight, so that there are 5 students leftover for each class. Then to divide the whole senior class into groups of four, we just take the union of each of the already-divided homeroom classes, meaning that we will have seven times as many groups of eight plus 35 leftover students. The groups of eight can simply be divided in half to form groups of four. The other 35 students then form eight more groups of four, leaving only 3 leftover students.

12. **A.** If they sold 900 sticks of gum at an average price of $0.07, then the total amount paid was $900 \cdot \$0.07 = \$63$. Let x be the number of 5-packs of gum sold. Then 5x sticks of gum were sold in 5-packs and $900 - 5x$ sticks of gum were sold individually. Since the total revenue was $63, we need

$$x \cdot \$0.30 + (900 - 5x) \cdot \$0.10 = \$63$$

$$\$90 - \$0.20x = \$63$$

$$\$27 = \$0.20x$$

$$x = 135$$

13. **D.** To calculate a percentage increase, we need to first find out what the original plot area was. Denote its width as some fixed quantity w (in meters). Then its length, by definition, must be 3w, meaning that original area is length $\cdot$ width $= 3w^2$. We also know that if we add 100 meters to this width (forcing us to also add 300 meters to the length to maintain the correct rectangular proportions), our area increases by 90,000 square meters. So the length $\cdot$ width $=$ area formula for the new rectangle tells us that

$$(w + 100)(3w + 300) = 3w^2 + 90,000$$

$$3w^2 + 600w + 30,000 = 3w^2 + 90,000$$

$$600w = 60,000$$

$$w = 100$$

Thus the original area must have been

$$3 \cdot 100^2 = 30,000 \text{ square meters}$$

Percentage increase is defined as

$$100 \cdot \frac{\text{new quantity} - \text{old quantity}}{\text{old quantity}}$$

Thus the percentage increase in area is

$$100 \cdot \frac{120,000 - 30,000}{30,000} = 300 \text{ percent}$$

Note that while the new plot is 4 times larger than the original one, this ratio of sizes (400%) is NOT the same as the percentage increase (300%).

14. **E.** If Ken trades 7 red beans for 7 blue beans, the overall number of beans in his bag does not change. So the fact that the percentage of beans in the bag that are blue would increase by 10% tells us that 7 must be 10% of the total number of beans in the bag. So Ken must have a total of 70 beans. Subtracting out the 16 green and 12 orange jellybeans Ken has leaves 42 beans left over that must be either red or blue. From here, it would be easiest to plug in the possible answers (with the number of red beans being A., B., C., D., or E., and the number of blue beans being 42 minus the number of red beans) to see which satisfies the first condition (the percentage increase in blue beans would be twice the percentage decrease in red beans). We find that for E., the number of red beans, 28, decreases by 25% to 21, while the number of blue beans, 14, increases by 50% (which is twice the percentage decrease in red beans) to 21. For all other answers, this does not hold true.

15. **D.** Let R be the number of minutes she runs on the first day. Then she will run $\frac{2}{3} \cdot R$ on the second day, $\frac{4}{3} \cdot R$ on the third day, $\frac{8}{9} \cdot R$ on the fourth day, $\frac{16}{9} \cdot R$ on the fifth day, $\frac{32}{27} \cdot R$ on the sixth day, and $\frac{64}{27} \cdot R$ on the seventh day. So she runs a total of

$$\frac{27}{27} \cdot R + \frac{18}{27} \cdot R + \frac{36}{27} \cdot R + \frac{24}{27} \cdot R + \frac{48}{27} \cdot R + \frac{32}{27} \cdot R + \frac{64}{27} \cdot R = \frac{249}{27} R$$

minutes for the week. Then we need

$$\frac{249}{27} R = 747$$

$$R = 81$$

16. **C.** Each of the boxes has six sides, each with a surface area of 9 square feet. So each box has a total outer surface area of 54 square feet. The truck is $\frac{12}{3} = 4$ boxes wide and tall, and $\frac{72}{3} = 24$ boxes long. So the truck holds exactly $4 \cdot 4 \cdot 24 = 384$ boxes.

$$384 \text{ boxes} \cdot \frac{54 \text{ square feet}}{\text{box}} = 20,736 \text{ total square feet of surface area (cardboard)}$$

The truck has two walls of dimension 12 feet by 72 feet, two walls of dimension 12 feet by 12 feet, and both a floor and a ceiling of dimension 72 feet by 12 feet, for a total of

$$12 \cdot 72 \cdot 2 + 12 \cdot 12 \cdot 2 + 12 \cdot 72 \cdot 2 = 3,744 \text{ square feet of surface area (truck walls)}$$

So $20,736 - 3,744 = 16,992$ square feet of cardboard is not touching the cargo bay walls, floor, or ceiling.

17. **A.** Let the original stock price be P, and the original earnings be E. Then the original P/E ratio is $\frac{P}{E}$. The stocks price falls 10%, so the new price is $.9P$. The companys earnings rise by 20%, so the new earnings are $1.2E$. So the new P/E ratio is $\frac{.9P}{1.2E} = \frac{3}{4} \cdot \frac{P}{E}$. So the percentage change in P/E ratio is

$$100 \cdot \frac{\text{new P/E - old P/E}}{\text{old P/E}} = 100 \cdot \frac{\frac{3}{4} \cdot \frac{P}{E} - \frac{P}{E}}{\frac{P}{E}}$$

$$= 100 \cdot \frac{-1}{4}$$

$$= -25\%$$

18. **D.** Without leaking, we could mow A square feet with G gallons. We can scale this up to C gallons by multiplying both sides by $\frac{C}{G}$. However, we also lose the fraction D of the fuel to leakage, so we find that we would only be able to mow $A \cdot \frac{C}{G}(1-D) = \frac{AC(1-D)}{G}$ square feet with $G \cdot \frac{C}{G} = C$ gallons. One good way to check this would be to arbitrarily assign realistic values for D, C, G, and A, and see if the answer is correct and/or makes sense. For example, let $G = 10$, $C = 20$, $D = 0.5$, and $A = 1,000$. Then we would be able to mow $\frac{1,000 \cdot 20(1-0.5)}{10} = 1,000$ square feet. This does make sense, because although we have doubled the amount of fuel from 10 to 20 gallons, we are also leaking half the fuel away, so we should only be able to mow $A = 1,000$ square feet with the 10 (= C) gallons that remain in the tank.

19. **C.** The combined effect of the withdrawals and the deposits is a net addition of $200 every two weeks. So if we work backwards from the end of the 52nd week to the end of the 4th week, we would span $\frac{48}{2} = 24$ of these two week periods. Since she added a net of $200 each of these two weeks, she added a total of $24 \cdot \$200 = \$4,800$ during this time. So she must have had $\$13,400 - \$4,800 = \$8,600$ after week 4. Then she would have withdrawn $400 for expenses the 5th week and had a balance of $8,200 after week 5.

20. **E.** Let J be Jamie's age, and B be her younger brother's age. Then

$$J = 3B$$

and

$$J + 8 = 2(B + 8) - 1$$
$$J = 2B + 7$$

Combining this equation with the first yields

$$2B + 7 = 3B$$

$$B = 7$$

Then $J = 21$ and Jamie must have been 14 when her brother was born.

21. **A.** Let w represent the average weight of one of the children. Then the average weight of the parents is 2w, and the average weight of all the passengers is

$$\frac{\text{total weight}}{\text{total number of passengers}} = \frac{2 \cdot 2w + 3 \cdot w}{5} = \frac{7w}{5}$$

$$\frac{7w}{5} = 105$$
$$w = 75$$

Then the passengers add $5 \cdot 105 = 525$ pounds to the cars weight for a net weight of 2025 pounds. The parents in total represent $2 \cdot 2w = 4w = 300$ pounds of that. So the fraction is
$$\frac{300}{2025} = \frac{12}{81} = \frac{4}{27}$$

22. **A.** The price per kilowatt of electricity is $\frac{C}{K}$. (To check this, let $C = \$5$ and $K = 10$. The price per kilowatt would be $\$0.50$, or $\frac{\$5}{10}$.) Since they have used U kilowatts, it has cost them $U \cdot \frac{C}{K}$ dollars, leaving only $P - \frac{UC}{K}$ dollars left. Since the price per kilowatt is $\frac{C}{K}$, you can get $\frac{K \text{ kilowatts}}{C \text{ dollars}}$. Multiplying this by the number of dollars left gives us the number of kilowatts the school can get with the remaining balance,

$$\frac{K}{C} \cdot \frac{P - UC}{K} = \frac{P}{C} - U$$

23. **D.** If the average score was 7, the total number of rating points received from the teacher must have been $7 \cdot 16 = 112$. So it appears that the teacher may have received as many as 11 rating scores of 10. However, if that were the case, 110 of the points would be accounted for by those 11 students, leaving only 2 points received from the remaining 5 students. But since the lowest possible score is 1, this would not be possible. Next we see if 10 students could have given the teacher a perfect score. This would yield 100 points from 10 students, leaving 12 points left over from the remaining 6 students. So each of the other students could have given the teacher a 2 and this would work.

24. **C.** Let M be the amount of money Jon originally invests. If he wants to earn 10% over the three year period, he would want

$$1.1 \cdot 1.1 \cdot 1.1 \cdot M = 1.331M$$

So if x is his annual return over the next two years, we need

$$1.331M = 0.8 \cdot (1+x) \cdot (1+x) \cdot M$$

$$(1+x)^2 = 1.664$$

$$1+x = 1.290$$

$$x \approx 29\%$$

25. **B.** Let g be the number of girls Robert originally surveys and B be the average number of hours the boys sleep each night. Then 100 - g is the number of boys surveyed and B + 2 is the average number of hours the girls sleep. So the original overall average number of hours slept is

$$\frac{g \cdot (B+2) + (100-g) \cdot B}{100}$$

$$= \frac{gB + 2g + 100B - gB}{100}$$

$$= \frac{g + 50B}{50}$$

We also know that if we increased the number of girls by 50, our average would increase by half an hour. This new average would be

$$\frac{(g+50) \cdot (B+2) + (100-g) \cdot B}{150}$$

$$= \frac{gB + 50B + 2g + 100 + 100B - gB}{150}$$

$$= \frac{150B + 2g + 100}{150}$$

$$= \frac{75B + g + 50}{75}$$

So

$$\frac{75B + g + 50}{75} = \frac{g + 50B}{50} + 1/2$$

$$= \frac{g + 50B + 25}{50}$$

Multiplying both sides by 150 yields

$$150B + 2g + 100 = 3g + 150B + 75$$

$$g = 25$$

26. **D.** Let L be the length of the ski slope in miles. She travels up the slope at 5 miles per hour, or $\frac{1 \text{ hour}}{5 \text{ miles}}$. So it takes her

$$L \text{ miles} \cdot \frac{1 \text{ hour}}{5 \text{ miles}} = \frac{L}{5} \text{ hours}$$

to climb the mountain. She skis down five times as fast (25 miles per hour), so it takes her one-fifth of the time to ski back down the mountain, or $\frac{L}{25}$ hours. So the total time she took was

$$\frac{L}{5} + \frac{L}{25} = \frac{6L}{25} \text{ hours}$$

which we need to equal 30 minutes. So

$$\frac{6L}{25} \text{ hours} = \frac{1}{2} \text{ hour}$$

$$L = 25/6 \text{ miles}$$

27. **D.** We can form all of the numbers 23 through 27 by taking nonnegative integer multiples of 5 and 9 except for 26. $23 = 1 \cdot 5 + 2 \cdot 9$, $24 = 3 \cdot 5 + 1 \cdot 9$, $25 = 5 \cdot 5 + 0 \cdot 9$, and $27 = 0 \cdot 5 + 3 \cdot 9$. However, we cannot make a set of 26 bananas out of bunches of only 5 and 9. To double-check this, we can run through all possible combinations of 5 and 9. If we have 0 bunches of 9, 26 is unattainable since it is not a multiple of 5. If we try 1 bunch of 9, we would still need 17 more bananas, which is also not a multiple of 5. If we use 2 bunches of 9, we still need 8 bananas, which is again not a multiple of 5. Finally, we could try 3 or more bunches of 9, but we would have already exceeded 26 bananas (since $3 \cdot 9 = 27$).

28. **D.** She needs to read a total of $2 \cdot 300 + 3 \cdot 500 = 2100$ pages. If she reads 250 pages in 5 days, she can read at a rate of 50 pages per day. So it will take her

$$2100 \text{ pages} \cdot \frac{1 \text{ day}}{50 \text{ pages}} = 42 \text{ days}$$

29. **A.** Draw two right triangles, with the legs of the triangle being the ground and the wall (we assume that the wall is perpendicular to the ground) and the hypotenuse being the ladder. The first triangle represents the original positioning of the ladder. Let X

be the distance along the ground from the wall to where the ladder rests and L be the length of the ladder. By the Pythagorean theorem,

$$X^2 + 9^2 = L^2$$

$$L = \sqrt{X^2 + 81}$$

The second triangle represents the ladder after it slides down the wall. Now the legs of the triangle are of length 7 and (some number between X and X + 1 inclusive). So by the Pythagorean theorem,

$$7^2 + (\text{some number between } X \text{ and } (X+1) \text{ inclusive})^2 = L^2$$

meaning

$$49 + X^2 \leq L^2 \leq 49 + X^2 + 2X + 1$$

Substituting the first equation, we get

$$X^2 + 49 \leq X^2 + 81 \leq X^2 + 2X + 1 + 49$$

Then

$$-1 \leq 31 \leq 2X$$

This tells us that (using the first equation again)

$$X \geq 15.5$$

So

$$L \geq \sqrt{15.5^2 + 81}$$

$$L \geq 17.923$$

So A. is the only answer that will NOT work.

30. **A.** Viewed another way, the older brother clears $\frac{1}{5}$ of an acre of field per hour and the younger brother clears $\frac{1}{3}$ of an acre of field per hour. So together they can clear $\frac{1}{5} + \frac{1}{3} = \frac{8}{15}$ of an acre of field per hour. That means that clearing 2 acres will take them

$$\frac{2 \text{ acres}}{\frac{8 \text{ acres}}{15 \text{ hours}}} = 2 \text{ acres} \cdot \frac{15 \text{ hours}}{8 \text{ acres}}$$

$$= \frac{30}{8} \text{ hours}$$

$$= 3 \text{ hours and } 45 \text{ minutes}$$

31. **E.** Alison now has A - 5 candies, Barbara now has B + 5 candies, and Chelsea now has C - 4 candies. Also, we know that

$$(A - 5) + (B + 5) + (C - 4) = 2(A - 5)$$

$$B + C - 4 = A - 10$$

$$A = B + C + 6$$

But we are interested in the number of candies Alison has now,

$$A - 5 = B + C + 1$$

32. **D.** Let L be the length of Phil's rectangle and W be the width. Then

$$2L + 2W = 40$$

$$L + W = 20$$

$$W = 20 - L$$

and the area of Phil's rectangle is LW. George's rectangle has length L + 5 and width W - 5 (note the perimeter remains that same since $2(L+5)+2(W-5) = 2L+2W = 40$), so its area is $(L + 5)(W - 5)$. We know that this is 25% less than the area of Phil's rectangle, so

$$(L + 5)(W - 5) = .75LW$$

$$LW - 5L + 5W - 25 = .75LW$$

$$\frac{LW}{4} - 5L + 5W - 25 = 0$$

$$LW - 20L + 20W - 100 = 0$$

Substituting the first equation yields

$$L(20 - L) - 20L + 20(20 - L) - 100 = 0$$

$$20L - L^2 - 20L + 400 - 20L - 100 = 0$$

$$L^2 + 20L - 300 = 0$$

The quadratic formula then tells us that

$$L = \frac{-20 \pm \sqrt{400 + 1200}}{2}$$

$$= -10 \pm 20$$

$$= 10 \text{ or } -30$$

We could not have a negative length for the side of a rectangle, so we know

$$L = 10$$

Then

$$W = 20 - L = 10$$

So the area of Phil's rectangle is

$$LW = 100 \text{ square feet}$$

33. **D.** To find the biggest possible number N, let's make the other three as small as possible. However, since they must be positive and distinct integers, these numbers would be 1, 2, and 3. Then

$$\frac{1 + 2 + 3 + N}{4} = 48$$

$$6 + N = 192$$

$$N = 186$$

34. **A.**

$$\text{Average age} = \frac{\text{total number of years}}{\text{total number of students}}$$

$$= \frac{RN + W(2N + M)}{(N + (2N + M))}$$

$$= \frac{RN + 2WN + WM}{3N + M}$$

35. **E.** Let D be Dave's current age and B be Bill's current age. Then

$$D = 2(B - 5)$$

$$= 2B - 10$$

and

$$B + 5 = \frac{2}{3}(D + 5)$$

$$3B + 15 = 2D + 10$$

Substituting the first equation into the second, we get

$$3B + 15 = 4B - 20 + 10$$

$$B = 25$$

Then

$$D = 2B - 10 = 40$$

So their current combined age is

$$B + D = 65$$

36. **E.** Let X be the number of shots she has taken so far this season. Then her shooting percentage is currently

$$100 \cdot \frac{16}{X}$$

If she makes the next 20 baskets in a row, her shooting percentage would be

$$100 \cdot \frac{16 + 20}{X + 20}$$

We know that this would be twice her current shooting percentage, so

$$2 \cdot 100 \cdot \frac{16}{X} = 100 \cdot \frac{16 + 20}{X + 20}$$

$$\frac{32}{X} = \frac{36}{X + 20}$$

$$32(X + 20) = 36X$$

$$32X + 640 = 36X$$

$$4X = 640$$

$$X = 160 \text{ shots}$$

37. **E.** Ellen can check in 5 students per minute, so she takes care of all the students until 8:58, when 7 students arrive. So 2 students are left waiting in line at 8:59, when another 9 students show up. So the line lengthens to 6 at 9:00, when 11 more kids show up. That puts the line at 12 at 9:01, when 9 more students arrive, meaning that the line is up to 16 at 9:02, when 7 more kids arrive. The line peaks at 18 students at 9:03, when 5 more kids arrive, leaving the line at 18 at 9:04, when only 3 students show up. So the line is down to 16 at 9:05, when the last kid shows up. So the line will shrink to 12 by 9:06, 7 by 9:07, 2 by 9:08, and Ellen will finish at 9:08:24, which is closest to 9:08.

38. **C.** Let X be the thickness of the treads. The circumference of the tire without treads is

$$2 \cdot \pi \cdot r = 40\pi \text{ inches}$$

and the circumference of the tire with treads is

$$2 \cdot \pi \cdot (20 + X) = (40 + 2X)\pi \text{ inches}$$

So in normal conditions, the tire rotates $\frac{110 \text{ miles}}{40\pi \text{ inches}}$ times to get from A to B. With treads on, the tire rotates only $\frac{10}{11}$ as many times going from A to B (since the odometer calculates 100 miles instead of 110). So the circumference of the tire without treads on must be $\frac{10}{11}$ times as big as the tire with treads. Then

$$40\pi = \frac{10}{11}(40 + 2X)\pi$$

$$44\pi = (40 + 2X)\pi$$

$$44 = 40 + 2X$$

$$X = 2 \text{ inches}$$

39. **B.** Let B be the number of feet of fence Benjy can paint per hour. Then Abraham and Benjy can paint a combined $40 + B$ feet per hour. So working together, it takes them $\frac{1}{40+B}$ hours to paint each foot. So the 12,000-foot fence will take them $\frac{12,000}{40+B}$ hours working together. We know it will take them 15 days $\cdot \frac{8 \text{ hours}}{\text{day}} = 120$ hours, so

$$120 = \frac{12,000}{40 + B}$$

$$4,800 + 120B = 12,000$$

$$120B = 7,200$$

$$B = 60$$

So it would take Benjy

$$\frac{12,000 \text{ feet}}{\frac{60 \text{ feet}}{\text{hour}}} = 200 \text{ hours}$$

$$= 25 \text{ days}$$

to paint the fence.

40. **B.** Since the full ten-digit number must form a palindrome, the last three digits of the number must mirror the zip code (numbers Z, I, P, respectively) as follows: (ZIP) XXXXPIZ (a slot filled with an "X" could be any number). But we know that the seven-digit number must also form a palindrome. So the number must look like (ZIP) ZIPXPIZ. Then any X in the middle will satisfy the seven-digit palindrome requirement, but now we still have to worry about the 10-digit requirement, which tells us that ZIPZI must equal ZIPXP (the reverse of the remaining five digits PXPIZ). So X must equal Z, and I must equal P in order for the number to be a palindrome. I only equals P for the zip codes 399 and 100. So there are only two numbers that his friend could have: (399) 3993993, or (100) 1001001.

41. **C.** Let R be the number of romance books. Then there are

$$\frac{2}{5}(12,000 - r) = 4,800 - 0.4R \text{ nonfiction books}$$

and

$$\frac{3}{10}(12,000 - r) = 3,600 - 0.3R \text{ adventure books}$$

Also, there are R mystery books, and $\frac{R}{2}$ drama books. Since these are the only five categories, we know that these numbers must add up to the total number of books, 12,000. So

$$4,800 - 0.4R + 3,600 - 0.3R + R + R + 0.5R = 12,000$$

$$8,400 + 1.8R = 12,000$$

$$\frac{9}{5}R = 3,600$$

$$R = 2000$$

So there are 2,000 mystery books and $3,600 - 0.3 \cdot 2000 = 3,000$ adventure books. Then $2,000 + 3,000 = 5,000$ of the 12,000 total books are mystery or adventure. Thus the fraction is $\frac{5}{12}$.

42. **C.** Denote the first sister's current age by A and the second sister's current age by B. Then

$$(A + 4)(B + 4) = 2AB$$

$$AB + 4B + 4A + 16 = 2AB$$

$$AB - 4A = 4B + 16$$

$$A = \frac{4B + 16}{B - 4}$$

Alternately, we could say

$$AB - 4B = 4A + 16$$

$$B = \frac{4A + 16}{A - 4}$$

Either way, it doesn't matter whether we call the sister whose age we are given A or B. It comes down to testing whether $\frac{4A+16}{A-4}$ is a positive whole number. Any number that is either negative or fractional will not work. Also note that since the answers given are the age of one of the sisters four years from now, we have to subtract 4 from from each answer before we can test it (i.e. plug them in for A).

$$\frac{4 \cdot (7 - 4) + 16}{(7 - 4) - 4} = \frac{28}{-1} = -28$$

so A. doesn't work.

$$\frac{4 \cdot (11 - 4) + 16}{(11 - 4) - 4} = \frac{44}{3}$$

so B. doesn't work.

$$\frac{4 \cdot (12 - 4) + 16}{(12 - 4) - 4} = \frac{48}{4} = 12$$

so C. works (Note that the current ages of the sisters would be 8 and 12 and the future ages would be 12 and 16. So $2 \cdot 8 \cdot 12 = 192$ does indeed equal $12 \cdot 16 = 192$.)

$$\frac{4 \cdot (14 - 4) + 16}{(14 - 4) - 4} = \frac{56}{6} = \frac{28}{3}$$

so D. doesn't work, and

$$\frac{4 \cdot (15 - 4) + 16}{(15 - 4) - 4} = \frac{60}{7}$$

so E. doesn't work.

43. **A.** Let C be the number of children and A be the number of adults who went to the show. Then

$$C + A = 300$$

$$C = 300 - A$$

and

$$5C + 9A = 2,000$$

Substituting the first equation into the second,

$$5(300 - A) + 9A = 2,000$$

$$1,500 + 4A = 2,000$$

$$4A = 500$$

$$A = 125$$

44. **D.** We know that

$$\frac{J \cdot 56 + V \cdot 62}{J + V} = 60$$

$$56J + 62V = 60J + 60V$$

$$2V = 4J$$

$$V = 2J$$

So the fraction of total players on the varsity team is

$$\frac{V}{J + V} = \frac{2J}{J + 2J}$$

$$= \frac{2J}{3J}$$

$$= \frac{2}{3}$$

CHAPTER 7

PROBABILITY AND COUNTING POSSIBILITIES

Problems involving probability or counting possibilities are not as common as the other problem types we have reviewed so far. On average, you will see one or two problems like these on a test. They occur closer to the middle or the end of a section: meaning they are considered more difficult by ETS. But mastering these problems is fairly easy and doesn't take that long. It's definitely worth the extra 10 to 40 points on the test to review these types of problems.

Probability

$$Probability = \frac{Desired\ Possibilities}{Total\ Possibilities}$$

Probability questions are as simple as the formula above. There are only two things to determine when solving for a probability. First, find out the total number of possibilities: what are all possible scenarios? Second, pinpoint the number of possibilities that fulfill the desired condition. In how many ways can the condition be met?

1. A drawer has 15 pairs of white socks, 10 pairs of black socks, and 2 pairs of brown socks. If a pair is pulled out of the drawer at random, what is the probability that it is NOT white?

   A. $\frac{2}{27}$

   B. $\frac{10}{20}$

   C. $\frac{12}{27}$

   D. $\frac{5}{9}$

   E. $\frac{4}{5}$

   ANSWER: C. First, what's the total number of possibilities? How many pairs of socks can you pull out? There are a total of $15 + 10 + 2 = 27$ pairs of socks. We only care about the pairs that are not white: brown pairs + black pairs = 12. The probability of not drawing a white pair is simply the ratio of the two: $\frac{12}{27}$.

A problem may give a probability and ask you to calculate the number of desired elements or total possibilities. Just determine the right numbers to plug into the basic probability formula.

2. In a set of cards, there are 12 blue cards. If the probability of drawing a blue card at random is $\frac{1}{3}$, how many cards are in the deck?

A. 4
B. 12
C. 24
D. 36
E. 48

ANSWER: D. Here, we have to solve for the total number of cards. There are 12 blue cards, so desired outcomes = 12. The probability of drawing a blue card is $\frac{1}{3}$. Using the formula, the total number of cards is $\frac{12}{1/3} = 36$.

The trickier problems dealing with probability will require multiple steps to arrive at the answer. Just remember the basic formula, be aware of what the problem is telling you, and figure out what you need to solve for what the problem isn't telling you. Often, the key to multi-step probability questions is finding the total number of possibilities.

R E M E M B E R !

The probability of an event that always happens is 1.

The probability of an event that never happens is 0.

A probability is never greater than 1.

A probability is never less than 0.

Probabilities for all possible scenarios always add up to 1.

Sometimes it is easier to find the probability of an event not happening, and then subtracting it from 1. This is especially true when asked to find the probability of *at least* a certain number (n) events happening. You can use the relation $P(at\ least\ n\ events\ happening) = 1 - P(n\ events\ not\ happening)$.

3. The probability of drawing a red marble from a given bag of marbles is $\frac{2}{5}$, the probability of drawing a green marble is $\frac{3}{10}$, and the probability of drawing a yellow marble is $\frac{1}{4}$. If the remaining three marbles are white, how many red marbles are in the bag?

   A. 60
   B. 24
   C. 18
   D. 15
   E. 8

ANSWER: B. First determine the probability of drawing a white marble. Adding up the probabilities of drawing red, green, and yellow marbles gives $\frac{2}{5} + \frac{3}{10} + \frac{1}{4} = \frac{19}{20}$. All probabilities add up to 1, so the probability of drawing a white marble must be $1 - \frac{19}{20} = \frac{1}{20}$. Using the information we have for white marbles, find the total number of marbles by using the basic equation:

$$Total\ number\ of\ marbles = \frac{Number\ of\ white\ marbles}{Probability\ of\ drawing\ a\ white\ marble} = \frac{3}{1/20} = 60$$

Hence, there are 60 marbles in the bag. Finally, find the number of marbles that are red, again using the basic equation. The number of red marbles is equal to $60 \times \frac{2}{5} = 24$.

Counting Possibilities

Any question that asks how many possible ways there are of arranging a group of things is a "counting possibilities" problem. Drawing the situation out on paper really helps to find the answer quickly. If the problem says 5 things are randomly arranged, then draw 5 lines on your scratch paper. On each line, write the number of possible items that can go in that spot; be aware that each time an item is placed in a spot, there is one less item to place in the next spot. Usually, all you have to do is multiply all the numbers you've written down. Let's walk through an example:

4. Eight contestants are competing in a math tournament. First place will receive a gold medal, second place will receive a silver medal, and third place will receive a bronze medal. No other prizes will be awarded. How many different ways can the three medals be awarded among the eight contestants?

   A. 1
   B. 6

C. 336
D. 512
E. over 1000

ANSWER: C. Since there are three medals to award, there are three positions to draw out:

$$\underline{\hspace{2cm}} \qquad \underline{\hspace{2cm}} \qquad \underline{\hspace{2cm}}$$
$$\textit{gold} \qquad\quad \textit{silver} \qquad \textit{bronze}$$

Now we fill in the positions one at a time: there are 8 contestants, so there are 8 possible people who can win the gold medal—write '8' above the gold position. After the gold medal position is filled, there are 7 contestants left, so there are only 7 people who can receive the silver medal—write '7' above the silver position. Similarly, there are 6 contestants left to fill the bronze position:

$$\frac{8}{\textit{gold}} \qquad\quad \frac{7}{\textit{silver}} \qquad \frac{6}{\textit{bronze}}$$

Thus, the number of ways to award the prizes is $8 \times 7 \times 6 = 336$.

A problem may limit the number of things that can be placed in various positions. The technique used to solve the problem remains the same, just be sure to obey all requirements of the problem.

5. Five books are to be placed on a shelf such that the two tallest books are at the ends of the shelf. In how many different arrangements can the five books be placed?

   A. 1
   B. 2
   C. 6
   D. 12
   E. 120

ANSWER: D. Since all five books are being placed on the shelf, there are five positions to be filled. The problem limits the possible arrangements by stating that the two tallest books must be placed at the ends of the shelf. You should have a diagram that looks like this:

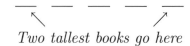

Two tallest books go here

So the first position has 2 possible books that can be placed there: the tallest book or the second tallest book. After we've decided what book to put in position one, there's only one book that can go in position five:

$$\underline{\quad 2 \quad} \ \underline{\quad\quad} \ \underline{\quad\quad} \ \underline{\quad\quad} \ \underline{\quad 1 \quad}$$

Two tallest books go here

After the two tallest books have been placed, the remaining three books must be placed in the three remaining positions:

$$\underline{\quad 2 \quad} \ \underline{\quad 3 \quad} \ \underline{\quad 2 \quad} \ \underline{\quad 1 \quad} \ \underline{\quad 1 \quad}$$

Multiplying all numbers together yields $2 \times 3 \times 2 \times 1 \times 1 = 12$ possible arrangements.

Combinations vs. Permutations

The problems discussed so far involving counting possibilities are of a special type of counting problem called a *permutation*. For permutations, each change in the order of the items, even if the items stay the same, is counted as a new arrangement. This accounts for the large number of arrangements possible. For example, it is significant in a competition who gets first place, who gets second place, and who gets third. Switching the first place and second place winners constitutes a new arrangement.

Unlike permutations, *combinations* are another type of counting problem in which order does not matter. For combinations, a group of selected items can only be counted once; additional arrangements are not counted if their order is switched. It is really groupings that are being counted, not arrangements. This results in a relatively small number of choices compared to permutations of the same number of items. A common example to illustrate this point is ordering pizza toppings. It doesn't really matter whether one orders "pepperoni, sausage, and onion" or "sausage, onion, and pepperoni"—it will be the same pizza either way. Both of these constitute the same grouping.

This chapter has already presented a simple, efficient, and easy to remember method to calculate permutations. The same method can be used to calculate combinations, with one additional step: take the number calculated using the permutation method, and divide by the number of positions *factorial*. If there were 3 positions in the problem, you would divide by 3 factorial (3 factorial is represented as $3! = 3 \times 2 \times 1 = 6$). The symbol $n!$ is used to represent the number of possible ways to arrange n non-repeating items by changing their order. That is why, in combination problems, you divide by $n!$ arrangements, because the order doesn't matter. The number of different arrangements possible must be taken out of the answer. As you will see, the number of combinations will be smaller than the number of permutations for a given size set, since the number of permutations is being divided by a positive integer.

Take the example of choosing pizza toppings:

6. Suppose a pizzeria has 8 pizza toppings to choose from, and a special deal is offered for a large pizza with any 3 toppings. How many combinations of 3 different toppings are available?

A. 3
B. 6
C. 18
D. 24
E. 56

ANSWER: E. There are 3 positions to fill, and 8 topping choices. Using the method shown in example number 4 of this chapter, you would first calculate $8 \times 7 \times 6 = 336$ (that would be the answer if we were calculating permutations). Since there are 3 positions, and the arrangements of the pizza toppings do not need to be counted, the next step is to divide by 3!. Therefore, the number of combinations available is $336 \div 3! = 336 \div (3 \times 2 \times 1) = 336 \div 6 = 56$. One could choose from 56 combinations of 3 different toppings.

Practice Problems

1. A coin flip has an equal probability of turning up heads or tails. If the coin is flipped five times, what is the probability all flips land heads?

   A. $\frac{1}{2}$

   B. $\frac{1}{4}$

   C. $\frac{1}{8}$

   D. $\frac{1}{16}$

   E. $\frac{1}{32}$

2. A piggy bank contains only pennies, nickels, and dimes. The probability of pulling a penny at random is $\frac{1}{2}$, and the probability of drawing a nickel at random is $\frac{2}{5}$. If there are 50 coins in the piggy bank, how many are dimes?

   A. 5

   B. 10

   C. 20

   D. 25

   E. 45

3. Set R contains all of the prime factors of the number 32,040. What is the probability, rounded to the nearest hundredth, that a number chosen at random from set R is a 2?

   A. 0.14

   B. 0.29

   C. 0.43

   D. 0.57

   E. 0.71

4. The ratio of girls to boys in a classroom is 3:4. What is the probability that a student chosen at random is a boy?

   A. $\frac{1}{7}$

   B. $\frac{1}{4}$

   C. $\frac{3}{7}$

   D. $\frac{4}{7}$

   E. $\frac{3}{4}$

5. A set of 100 cards is numbered from 1 to 100. If a card is drawn at random, what is the probability that the number on the card contains the digit 5?

   A. $\frac{1}{20}$

   B. $\frac{9}{100}$

   C. $\frac{1}{10}$

   D. $\frac{11}{100}$

   E. $\frac{19}{100}$

6. How many different ways can a family of four be arranged at a table for four?

   A. 1
   B. 2
   C. 4
   D. 8
   E. 24

7. How many different three-digit numbers can be written using the digits 1 to 5 such that no two digits are the same?

   A. 5
   B. 25
   C. 60
   D. 120
   E. 125

8. A car can fit two people in the front and two people in the back. How many different ways can two adults and two children be placed in the car such that the children ride in the back?

   A. 2
   B. 4
   C. 8
   D. 12
   E. 24

9. A restaurant serves four different types of salads, five different main courses, and two different desserts. How many different dinner combinations are possible if one salad, one main course, and one dessert are chosen?

   A. 40
   B. 20

C. 11

D. 5

E. 3

10. A class has nine boys and seven girls. If one girl and one boy are chosen to represent the class, how many different pairs of class representatives are possible?

A. 9

B. 16

C. 63

D. 72

E. 81

11. Six plants are to be arranged in a line such that the tallest plants are in the center and the shortest plants are on the ends. How many different arrangements of plants can there be?

A. 8

B. 12

C. 30

D. 36

E. 42

12. A group of three girls and three boys are arranged such that the first person in the line is a boy, the second a girl, the third a boy, and so on in an alternating pattern. How many arrangements are possible that fit this pattern?

A. 6

B. 30

C. 36

D. 120

E. 720

13. A three digit number is formed by rolling a six-sided die three times. The result of the first roll is the first digit, the result of the second roll is the second digit, and the result of the third roll is the third digit of the three digit number. How many different three digit numbers can be formed in this way?

A. 6

B. 30

C. 36

D. 120

E. 216

14. Inside a closet are 5 white shirts, 2 of which are striped; there are 7 blue shirts, 3 of which are striped; there are 3 pink shirts, 1 of which is striped. What is the probability of picking at random a shirt that is blue <u>or</u> striped?

   A. $\frac{7}{15}$

   B. $\frac{1}{5}$

   C. $\frac{2}{3}$

   D. $\frac{1}{3}$

   E. $\frac{3}{7}$

15. From a standard deck of 52 playing cards, with two red and two black cards of each number, what is the probability of picking at random a red card <u>or</u> a ten?

   A. $\frac{6}{13}$

   B. $\frac{1}{26}$

   C. $\frac{1}{2}$

   D. $\frac{7}{13}$

   E. $\frac{15}{26}$

16. For problem number 15, if two cards are picked, what is the probability of picking at random both of the red tens?

   A. $\frac{1}{2704}$

   B. $\frac{1}{1352}$

   C. $\frac{1}{1326}$

   D. $\frac{1}{676}$

   E. $\frac{1}{663}$

17. A girl rolls two 6-sided dice, each with the sides numbered 1 through 6. What is the probability that she rolls a sum of 9 <u>or</u> a sum of 7?

   A. $\frac{5}{36}$

   B. $\frac{5}{18}$

   C. $\frac{1}{9}$

   D. $\frac{1}{6}$

   E. $\frac{1}{54}$

18. The girl in problem number 17 makes two rolls of the dice. What is the probability that she will roll a sum of 9 on the first roll <u>and</u> then a sum of 7 on the second roll?

    A. $\frac{5}{36}$

    B. $\frac{5}{18}$

    C. $\frac{1}{9}$

    D. $\frac{1}{6}$

    E. $\frac{1}{54}$

19. Four neighbors get together and decide to paint their houses each a different color, with no two houses being the same color. If they have 6 colors to choose from, how many possible color arrangements are there? (Remember that each change in order using the same colors counts as a new arrangement.)

    A. 360
    B. 120
    C. 60
    D. 24
    E. 6

20. A woman wants to buy four different flavors of coffee grounds, and there are seven to choose from. How many combinations of four flavors are possible?

    A. 28
    B. 35
    C. 112
    D. 210
    E. 840

21. Ten people are getting ready to form 2 teams of five for a game of pick-up basketball. How many different combinations of 2 teams are possible?

    A. 126
    B. 252
    C. 504
    D. 756
    E. 1512

22. A circle is inscribed in an equilateral triangle. What is the probability that a point chosen at random within the triangle will also be inside the circle?

    A. $\frac{\pi}{3\sqrt{3}}$

B. $\frac{\pi}{\sqrt{3}}$

C. $\frac{3\sqrt{3}}{\pi}$

D. $\frac{\sqrt{3}}{\pi}$

E. $\frac{3\pi}{2\sqrt{3}}$

23. Set A={2,4,5,9}, set B={1,3,6,10}, and set C={16,19,23,27}. If a is a number from set A, b is a number from set B, and c is a number from set C, what is the probability that $a \times b > c$?

A. $\frac{7}{12}$

B. $\frac{7}{16}$

C. $\frac{3}{4}$

D. $\frac{9}{16}$

E. $\frac{9}{32}$

24. There are 6 red balls and 6 blue balls in a bag. What is the ratio of the probability of drawing 3 red balls in a row, if they are not replaced, to the probability of drawing 3 blue balls in a row, if they are replaced?

A. $\frac{1}{11}$

B. $\frac{3}{8}$

C. $\frac{4}{3}$

D. $\frac{15}{6}$

E. $\frac{8}{11}$

25. A square is inscribed in a circle. What is the probability that a point chosen at random within the circle will NOT also be inside the square?

A. $\frac{\pi}{\pi-\sqrt{2}}$

B. $\frac{2-\sqrt{2}}{\pi}$

C. $\frac{\pi}{\pi-2}$

D. $\frac{\pi-\sqrt{2}}{\pi}$

E. $\frac{\pi-2}{\pi}$

26. Elaine makes a \$4 purchase and gives the cashier a \$20 bill. If she has an equal probability of receiving any of the possible combinations of bills (out of \$1, \$5, or

$10 bills) for change, what is the probability that she will receive a $5 bill among her change?

A. $\frac{1}{8}$

B. $\frac{1}{4}$

C. $\frac{3}{8}$

D. $\frac{1}{2}$

E. $\frac{5}{8}$

27. A standard deck of 52 playing cards has 4 cards each of 13 different numerical values. What is the probability, rounded to the nearest hundredth, of having <u>exactly</u> one pair of cards of the same numerical value, after drawing 5 cards from a complete deck?

A. 0.16

B. 0.21

C. 0.35

D. 0.42

E. 0.53

28. A standard deck of 52 playing cards has 4 cards each of 13 different numerical values. What is the probability, rounded to the nearest hundredth, of having <u>at least</u> two cards of the same numerical value, after drawing 5 cards from a complete deck?

A. 0.31

B. 0.36

C. 0.42

D. 0.49

E. 0.57

Solutions to Practice Problems

1. **E.** Each time the coin is tossed, there are two possible results: heads or tails. If the coin is tossed five times, there are $2 \times 2 \times 2 \times 2 \times 2 = 32$ total possible results. There's only one case where all tosses land heads. Therefore, the probability of landing all heads is $\frac{1}{32}$.

2. **A.** If the probability of drawing a penny is $\frac{1}{2}$ and the probability of drawing a nickel is $\frac{2}{5}$, then the probability of drawing either a penny or a nickel is $\frac{1}{2} + \frac{2}{5} = \frac{9}{10}$. So the probability of drawing a dime is $1 - \frac{9}{10} = \frac{1}{10}$. Since there are 50 coins in the piggy bank, $\frac{1}{10} \times 50 = 5$ are dimes.

3. **C.** To solve this problem, you must figure out the prime factors of 32,040. The prime factors consist of all the factors of a number that are prime numbers. For this number, they are: $2 \times 2 \times 2 \times 3 \times 3 \times 5 \times 89 = 32,040$. Since there are 7 prime factors, and 3 of them are 2s, the probability that one of them chosen at random is a 2 is: $\frac{3}{7} = 0.43$.

4. **D.** A 3:4 ratio of girls to boys in the classroom is equivalent to saying that for every seven students, three are girls and four are boys. So, the probability of randomly selecting a boy is $\frac{4}{7}$.

5. **E.** With 100 cards, there are 100 total possible cards to draw. The desired possibilities consist of all numbers from 1 to 100 with the digit 5: 5, 15, 25, 35, 45, 50, 51, 52, 53, 54, 55, 56, 57, 58, 59, 65, 75, 85, and 95. There are 19 numbers with at least one digit 5. So, the probability of drawing one of these cards is $\frac{19}{100}$.

6. **E.** There are four positions to fill and four people to place. There are four people to choose from to fill position one, then there are three people left to fill position two, then two people to place in position three, and finally one person left to sit in position four: $4 \times 3 \times 2 \times 1 = 24$.

7. **C.** There are three positions and five digits to choose from: 1, 2, 3, 4, and 5. The first position can be any of the five digits, the second position can be any of the four remaining digits, and the last position must be one of the three final digits: $\underline{5}\,\underline{4}\,\underline{3}$. So, there are $5 \times 4 \times 3 = 60$ different possible numbers.

8. **B.** There are four total positions with limitations. There are two adults and two positions in which to place the adults: $\underline{2}\,\underline{1}$. There are two children and two positions in which to place the children: $\underline{2}\,\underline{1}$. The number of possible arrangements is $2 \times 1 \times 2 \times 1 = 4$.

9. **A.** There are three positions to fill, one for each course of the meal: 4 choices of salad, 5 choices of main course, and 2 choices of dessert. The total number of dinner combinations is $4 \times 5 \times 2 = 40$.

10. **C.** There are two positions to fill: a boy representative and a girl representative. The possible combinations for filling the two positions are $9 \times 7 = 63$.

11. **A.** There are six positions to fill with limitations. The two tallest plants get placed in the two center positions: $\_ \ \_ \ 2 \ 1 \ \_ \ \_$. The two shortest plants go on the two end positions: $2 \ \_ \ 2 \ 1 \ \_ \ 1$. The remaining two plants go in the remaining two positions: $2 \ 2 \ 2 \ 1 \ 1 \ 1$. The total number of possible arrangements is $2 \times 2 \times 2 \times 1 \times 1 \times 1 = 8$.

12. **C.** There are six positions to fill with limitations. The first, third, and fifth positions are boys, while the second, fourth, and sixth positions are girls. Placing one at a time, there are three boys to place in position one, and then three girls to place in position two. Then there are two boys to place in position three and two girls to place in position four. The last two positions are filled with the remaining boy and girl. The number of possible arrangements is $3 \times 3 \times 2 \times 2 \times 1 \times 1 = 36$.

13. **E.** There are three positions to fill: each digit of the three-digit number. Each position can be any of the digits 1 to 6. This problem is different from the others because the digits here can be repeated. The number of three-digit numbers that can be formed by tossing the die is therefore $6 \times 6 \times 6 = 216$.

14. **C.** There are 15 total shirts. Since 7 shirts are blue, and 3 other shirts are also striped (we don't want to count the blue striped shirts twice), there are $7 + 3 = 10$ desired possibilities. Therefore, the probability of picking a shirt that is blue or striped is $\frac{10}{15} = \frac{2}{3}$.

15. **D.** There are 52 cards in the deck, therefore 52 total possibilities. There are 26 red cards, so the probability of picking a red card is $\frac{26}{52}$. In addition, there are 2 black tens that could be picked. (We don't want to count the 2 red tens that have already been counted in the set of 26 red cards.) So, that makes $26 + 2 = 28$ desired possibilities. The probability of picking a red card or a ten is $\frac{28}{52} = \frac{7}{13}$.

16. **C.** Once again, there are 52 cards in the deck, and therefore 52 total possibilities. There are only 2 red tens in the deck, so the probability of picking a red ten as the first card is $\frac{2}{52} = \frac{1}{26}$. The key at this point is that you must assume that the first pick was successfully a red ten. After all, you are trying to calculate the probability that the scenario <u>does</u> happen. Therefore, having picked the first card, there are now 51 cards remaining in the deck, therefore 51 total possibilities. One red ten remains, so the probability of picking it is $\frac{1}{51}$. When you calculate the probability of <u>both</u> one

<u>and</u> another independent events occurring together, you multiply the two probabilities, thus decreasing the total chance over either one of them occurring alone. Therefore, the probability of picking both red tens is $\frac{1}{26} \times \frac{1}{51} = \frac{1}{1326}$.

17. **B.** There are 36 possible outcomes for the roll of 2 dice (since each die has 6 outcomes, that makes $6 \times 6 = 36$ possible outcomes). There are 4 possible ways of rolling a sum of 9: (4,5) (5,4) (6,3) (3,6). So, the probability of rolling a 9 is $\frac{4}{36}$. And there are 6 possible ways of rolling a sum of 7: (1,6) (6,1) (2,5) (5,2) (3,4) (4,3). So, the probability of rolling a 7 is $\frac{6}{36}$. When you calculate the probability of <u>either</u> one <u>or</u> another independent events occurring, you add the two probabilities, thus increasing the total chance over either one of them occurring alone. Therefore, the probability of rolling a sum of 9 <u>or</u> rolling a sum of 7 is $\frac{4}{36} + \frac{6}{36} = \frac{10}{36} = \frac{5}{18}$.

18. **E.** Once again, there are 36 possible outcomes for the roll of 2 dice, which include 4 possible ways of rolling a sum of 9, and 6 possible ways of rolling a sum of 7 (see solution explanation for the previous problem). So, the probability of rolling a 9 is $\frac{4}{36}$, which can also be written as $\frac{1}{9}$ when reduced to lowest terms; and the probability of rolling a 7 is $\frac{6}{36}$, which can also be written as $\frac{1}{6}$ when reduced to lowest terms. When you calculate the probability of <u>both</u> one <u>and</u> another independent events occurring together, you multiply the two probabilities, thus decreasing the total chance over either one of them occurring alone. Therefore, the probability of rolling a sum of 9 on the first roll <u>and</u> then rolling a sum of 7 on the second roll is $\frac{1}{9} \times \frac{1}{6} = \frac{1}{54}$.

19. **A.** There are 4 positions to fill and 6 colors to place: six colors for position one, five colors for position two, four colors for position three, and three colors which remain for position four. This results in $6 \times 5 \times 4 \times 3 = 360$ possible color arrangements.

20. **B.** There are 4 positions to fill and 7 choices of coffee flavors. The first step is similar to the permutation problems: $7 \times 6 \times 5 \times 4 = 840$. However, that's not the answer. Since the order of choices doesn't matter, the answer is much smaller. Divide by the number of positions (4 positions) factorial: $840 \div 4! = 840 \div (4 \times 3 \times 2 \times 1) = 840 \div 24 = 35$. She can choose 35 different combinations of 4 flavors of coffee grounds.

21. **B.** The trick here is to recognize that you only have to solve the problem for one of the teams. For every combination that is counted for team "A," whoever is left will be on team "B," so the process of choosing team A automatically chooses team B. For team A, there are 5 positions to fill and 10 choices of players. The first step is similar to the permutation problems: $10 \times 9 \times 8 \times 7 \times 6 = 30,240$. However, that's not the answer. Since the order of the choices doesn't matter, the answer is much smaller. Divide by the number of positions (5 positions) factorial: $30,240 \div 5! = 30,240 \div (5 \times 4 \times 3 \times 2 \times 1) =$

$30,240 \div 120 = 252$. There are 252 different combinations of players possible for the 2 basketball teams.

22. **A.** Drawing a figure of a circle inscribed in an equilateral triangle will help solve this problem. Then draw the vertical median of the triangle from its top to the midpoint of its base. Use the theorem that the center of the triangle is located at $\frac{1}{3}$ the height of the median—this will also be the center of the circle. For convenience, label the radius of the circle to have a length of 1, and then the upper segment of the median will have a length of 2. Connecting the center of the triangle to the lower right vertex will form a smaller 30-60-90 triangle, as shown in the following diagram:

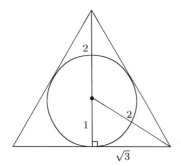

Note the radius of the circle is 1
and the base of the small triangle is $\sqrt{3}$

It is evident that the area of the large equilateral triangle can be calculated:

$$A_T = \frac{1}{2}bh = \frac{1}{2}(2\sqrt{3})(3) = 3\sqrt{3}$$

Since the circle has a radius of 1, the area of the circle is:

$$A_C = \pi r^2 = \pi(1)^2 = \pi$$

This is a geometric probability problem. Therefore, the probability (P) that a point chosen at random within the triangle will also be inside the circle is found using the formula:

$$P = \frac{A_C}{A_T} = \frac{\pi}{3\sqrt{3}}$$

23. **B.** The total number of possible ways that an equation of the form $a \times b > c$ can be written, if there are four choices for each variable, are $4 \times 4 \times 4 = 64$. By plugging in each of the possible values for a and b into the equation, it is quickly determined that 8 combinations are greater than $c = 16$; 8 combinations are greater than $c = 19$; 7 combinations are greater than $c = 23$; and 5 combinations are greater than $c = 27$. The total number of combinations for which $a \times b > c$ is $8 + 8 + 7 + 5 = 28$. Therefore, the probability that the equation will hold true is: $\frac{28}{64} = \frac{7}{16}$.

24. **E.** The probability of drawing 3 red balls, if they are NOT replaced, is: $\frac{6}{12} \times \frac{5}{11} \times \frac{4}{10} = \frac{1}{11}$. The probability of drawing 3 blue balls, if they are replaced, is simply the same for each draw: $\frac{6}{12} \times \frac{6}{12} \times \frac{6}{12} = \frac{1}{8}$. Therefore, the ratio of the two probabilities is:

$$\frac{\frac{1}{11}}{\frac{1}{8}} = \frac{8}{11}$$

25. **E.** Drawing a figure of a square inscribed in a circle will help solve this problem, labeling each side of the square to be length L. Then draw a diagonal of the square of length $L\sqrt{2}$, as shown in the following diagram:

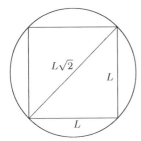

Note the radius of the circle is $\frac{L\sqrt{2}}{2}$

Since each side of the inscribed square has a length L, the area of the square is $A_S = L^2$. The area of the circle can also be calculated:

$$A_C = \pi r^2 = \pi \frac{(L\sqrt{2})^2}{2^2} = \frac{\pi L^2}{2}$$

This is a geometric probability problem. Therefore, the probability (P) that a point chosen at random within the circle will also be inside the square is found using the formula:

$$P = \frac{A_S}{A_C} = \frac{L^2}{\frac{\pi L^2}{2}} = \frac{2}{\pi}$$

However, the problem asks for the probability that the point will NOT be inside the square. Therefore, apply the relation:

$$P(not) = 1 - P = 1 - \frac{2}{\pi} = \frac{\pi - 2}{\pi}$$

26. **C.** She will receive $16 in change from the cashier. The approach to take is to figure out how many combinations of change are possible, and then how many of them involve a $5 bill. Divide and conquer—first consider the first $10: there are 4 possible combinations to make $10 (one $10, two $5s, a $5 and five $1s, or ten $1s), and two of them involve a $5 bill. Then consider the last $6: there are two possible combinations to make $6 (a $5 and a $1, or six $1s), and one of them involves a $5 bill.

Therefore, the total number of combinations to make $16 change is $4 \times 2 = 8$. Three of them involve a $5 bill. Hence, the probability that Elaine will receive a $5 bill is $\frac{3}{8}$.

27. **D.** To solve this problem, calculate the number of ways to draw exactly one pair of cards of the same numerical value, and calculate the total number of possible combinations to draw *any* 5 cards from the deck, and then use the probability formula:

$$Probability = \frac{Number\ of\ desired\ possibilities}{Total\ number\ of\ possibilities}$$

First, figure out the number of ways to get a pair with 2 cards. The first of the two can be any card, so there are 52 possibilities. In order to have a pair, there are only 3 other cards of that same value that could be your second card. After multiplying these two, since the order of the two cards doesn't matter, divide by the number of positions factorial, which is 2!. So far, you have $\frac{52 \times 3}{2 \times 1} = 78$ possibilities.

Next, figure out the number of combinations for your three other cards. The third card could be any of 48 remaining cards, which is the complete deck minus the 4 cards of the numerical value that make up your pair. The fourth card could be any of 44 remaining cards, since you don't want it to match any of the others. And the fifth card could be any of 40 remaining cards, since you don't want it to match any of the others. After multiplying these three, since the order of the three cards doesn't matter, divide by the number of positions factorial, which is 3!. That makes $\frac{48 \times 44 \times 40}{3 \times 2 \times 1} = 14,080$ possibilities.

Multiplying the number of possible first two cards by the last three cards, there are $78 \times 14,080 = 1,098,240$ possibilities for exactly one pair with the five cards.

Calculating the total number of possible combinations to draw any five cards is much simpler. There are 5 positions, and each position has one less possible card than the one before it. After multiplying these five, since the order of the five cards doesn't matter, divide by the number of positions factorial, which is 5!. That makes $\frac{52 \times 51 \times 50 \times 49 \times 48}{5 \times 4 \times 3 \times 2 \times 1} = 2,598,960$.

Finally, the problem can be solved. Using the overall probability formula mentioned in the chapter and in the first paragraph of this solution, plug in the numbers just calculated: $\frac{1,098,240}{2,598,960} = 0.42$. This is the probability of having exactly one pair of cards of the same numerical value.

28. **D.** This problem could be solved the same way as the previous card problem, or you could try a different approach—instead of having to add together the probabilities of every possible number of matches, it would be easier to find the probability of not getting any matches, and then using the formula:

$$P(at\ least\ two\ cards\ matching) = 1 - P(no\ matches)$$

In this case, you have 5 positions. The probability of getting any card on the first draw is $\frac{52}{52} = 1$. The probability of getting a different number on the second draw is $\frac{48}{51}$, because there are 4 of each number and there are 51 cards remaining to draw from. Similarly, the probability of getting a different number than the first two cards on the third draw is $\frac{44}{50}$. The probability of getting a different number from the first three cards on the fourth draw is $\frac{40}{49}$. Finally, the probability of getting a different number from the first four cards on the fifth draw is $\frac{36}{48}$. Multiplying these together, you get: $P(no\ matches) = 1 \times \frac{48}{51} \times \frac{44}{50} \times \frac{40}{49} \times \frac{36}{48} = 0.51$. Therefore, the probability of getting at least two cards of the same numerical value is: $1 - 0.51 = 0.49$.

CHAPTER 8

QUADRILATERALS AND TRIANGLES

There are six types of quadrilaterals to which several theorems and formulas apply: square, rectangle, parallelogram, rhombus, kite, and trapezoid. Some of these shapes are special cases of others; for example, a square is both a rectangle and a rhombus. While it saves time to use existing formulas and theorems that treat the quadrilateral as a whole, these problems usually can be solved by dissecting the figure into triangles. Of special importance are formulas for area and theorems about diagonals of quadrilaterals.

The trapezoid is a special quadrilateral, in the sense that it can be treated as a bottom portion of a triangle that was cut by a line parallel to the base. Therefore, some ratio formulas that are related to similar triangles apply to trapezoids.

Triangles form the foundation for more advanced topics such as circles and solids. It is absolutely essential to know the following axioms and theorems:

- congruence theorems (SSS, SAS, ASA, AAS);

- ratios obtained from similar triangles;

- the properties of angle bisectors in a triangle (inscribed circle);

- the properties of medians in a triangle;

- the properties of altitudes in a triangle;

- Pythagorean theorem;

- special triangles ($30°$-$60°$-$90°$, $45°$-$45°$-$90°$, and $60°$-$60°$-$60°$);

- area formula for a triangle;

- construction of the circumscribing circle.

For example, the solutions to the first two problems below make use of properties of $30°$-$60°$-$90°$ and $45°$-$45°$-$90°$ triangles. The Pythagorean theorem can be used instead, but it saves quite a bit of time to have these properties memorized since many times the triangles involved are one of these two types.

1. What is the length of the diagonal of the rectangle?

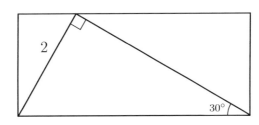

  A. 4

  B. $2\sqrt{3}$

  C. $2\sqrt{6}$

  D. $\sqrt{19}$

  E. $\sqrt{17}$

ANSWER: D. Since the inscribed triangle is 30°-60°-90° with short side of length 2, we have that the long side of the rectangle (which is the hypotenuse of the triangle) is 4. The upper left portion of the rectangle forms another 30°-60°-90° triangle and so the width of the rectangle (which is the long side of that triangle) is $\sqrt{3}$. Now that we have the length and width of the rectangle, the Pythagorean theorem gives the length of the diagonal:

$$\sqrt{4^2 + \sqrt{3}^2} = \sqrt{19}.$$

2. A 45°-45°-90° triangle sits inside of a square as shown. The area of the triangle is 5% of the area of the square. How many times larger is the diagonal of the square than the hypotenuse of the triangle?

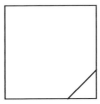

  A. $\sqrt{\frac{2}{5}}$

  B. $3\sqrt{2}$

  C. $2\sqrt{2}$

  D. $\sqrt{10}$

E. $5\sqrt{2}$

ANSWER: D. We may assume (for simplicity) that the base and height of the triangle are 1, making the area of the triangle $\frac{1}{2}$ and the hypotenuse of the triangle $\sqrt{2}$. Since the area of the triangle is .05 times as big as the area A of the square, we have $\frac{1}{2} = .05A$, so $A = 10$. Then the length of the square is $\sqrt{10}$, making the diagonal $\sqrt{10} \times \sqrt{2} = 2\sqrt{5}$. Thus, the length of the diagonal divided by the length of the hypotenuse is $\sqrt{10}$.

Note that choice A. may be eliminated immediately since it is smaller than 1. Note also that ratios of lengths equal ratios of diagonals, so once the length of the square was found to be $\sqrt{10}$ (and hence the ratio of lengths is $\sqrt{10}$ because we assumed the length of the triangle is 1), we could deduce that the ratio of the diagonals is also $\sqrt{10}$.

3. How many quadrilaterals are in the figure shown?

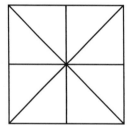

A. 9

B. 8

C. 17

D. 16

E. 12

ANSWER: C. As you can see depicted below, there is one large square, four small squares, four rectangles, and eight trapezoids, for a total of 17 quadrilaterals.

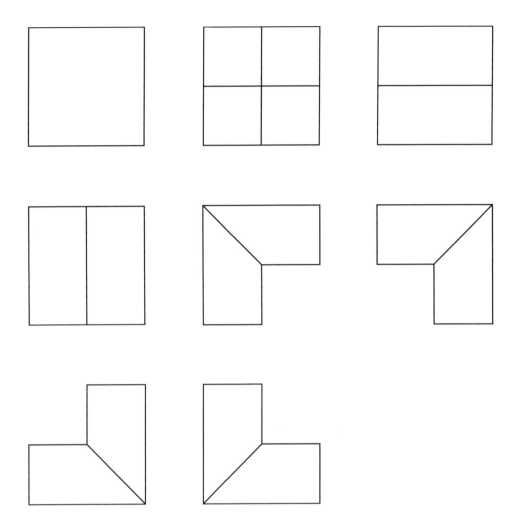

4. Inside triangle I, 80 lines are drawn parallel to the base. Inside triangle II, 81 lines are drawn parallel to the base. How many more trapezoids are in triangle II than triangle I?

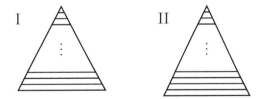

A. 2

B. 9

C. 81

D. 729

E. 6479

ANSWER: C. Using the base of triangle I we can form 80 trapezoids. With the line just above the base, we can form 79 trapezoids. With the line above that we can form 78, etc. Thus, the total number of trapezoids in triangle I is $80 + 79 + 78 + \cdots + 2 + 1$. Similarly, the number of trapezoids in triangle II is $81 + 80 + 79 + 78 + \cdots + 2 + 1$. Thus, triangle II has 81 more.

The solutions to the last two problems required no algebra and very little knowledge of geometry. Rather, they were solved merely by counting. This is a common type of question, but as the reader can appreciate, a fair amount of visualization is required in order to count correctly.

5. A rectangular shed is to be constructed inside a 15 foot by 20 foot rectangular field so that the area of the shed is half the area of the field that remains after construction. What are the dimensions of the shed if the perimeter of the shed is to be as small as possible?

   A. 10×10

   B. 8×12

   C. 4×25

   D. 5×16

   E. 5×20

ANSWER: A. Let the dimensions of the shed be $x \times y$ so that the area of the shed is xy. The area of the plot is 300, and since the area of the shed is half the area of the remaining field, we have $xy = \frac{1}{2}(300 - xy)$. Solving for xy we obtain $xy = 100$. Among the possible choices having area 100, the dimensions 10×10 have the smallest perimeter.

It may also be noted that a square is always a rectangle having minimum perimeter, so we may have started with this information and setup the equation $x^2 = \frac{1}{2}(300 - x^2)$, leading to $x^2 = 100$ and $x = 10$.

Note that the first solution to problem 5 does not yield the answer directly. That is, $xy = 100$ is not sufficient to immediately make the correct choice. Instead, that information must be used in conjunction with the possible choices to decide which one yields the minimum perimeter. If the student finds that s/he has reached a dead end with the algebra, it's wise to try to consolidate whatever progress has been made with the choices given. Notice, for instance, that the information $xy = 100$ is enough to eliminate choices B and D.

6. The area of the trapezoid shown is 12. The top has length 3 and the base has length 5. What is the area of the shaded region?

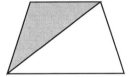

    A. 6

    B. $\frac{15}{2}$

    C. $4\sqrt{2}$

    D. $\frac{9}{2}$

    E. 8

ANSWER: D. The area of the trapezoid is

$$h \times \frac{3+5}{2} = 4h = 12,$$

and so the height is 3. The height of the trapezoid is also the height of the shaded triangle. Thus, the area of the shaded triangle is $\frac{1}{2} \times 3 \times 3 = \frac{9}{2}$.

7. The top of the trapezoid has length 4 and the area of the trapezoid is 21. How long is the base?

    A. $4\sqrt{2}$

    B. 8

    C. $4 + 4\sqrt{2}$

    D. 10

    E. 12

ANSWER: D. The length of the base is the length of the top plus an unknown length x on each side. Since the angles formed with the base are both 45°, the height must also be x. Thus, the area of the trapezoid is

$$\left(\frac{4 + (4 + x + x)}{2}\right) x = \left(\frac{8 + 2x}{2}\right) x = x^2 + 4x.$$

We are told that the area of the trapezoid is 21, so we have $x^2 + 4x = 21$. This can be rewritten as $x^2 + 4x - 21 = (x + 7)(x - 3) = 0$, so we get $x = -7$ or $x = 3$. Since x is positive, $x = 3$ and so the length of the base is $4 + 3 + 3 = 10$.

While formulas for the area of some shapes may be given on the SAT, it saves time to have the basic ones memorized. This includes the area of a trapezoid, as in problems 6 and 7.

8. A *kite* is a quadrilateral in which two sets of sides are of equal length. The diagram below is a kite in which $AB = AD = 2$ and $BC = CD = 1$. If $BD = 1$, what is the length of AC?

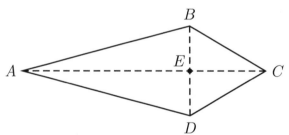

   A. $\sqrt{3} + \sqrt{2}$

   B. $\frac{\sqrt{15} + \sqrt{3}}{2}$

   C. $\frac{5}{2}$

   D. $\sqrt{6}$

   E. $\sqrt{3} + 1$

ANSWER: B. Since the diagram is a kite, AC bisects BD into two segments of length $\frac{1}{2}$. By the Pythagorean theorem, $AE = \sqrt{4 - \frac{1}{4}} = \frac{\sqrt{15}}{2}$ and $EC = \sqrt{1 - \frac{1}{4}} = \frac{\sqrt{3}}{2}$, making $AC = \frac{\sqrt{15} + \sqrt{3}}{2}$.

9. Isosceles triangle $\triangle ABC$ has isosceles right triangle $\triangle ADC$ removed as shown to form an arrow (shaded). The area of the arrow is 15 and the length of BD is 6. What is the length of AC?

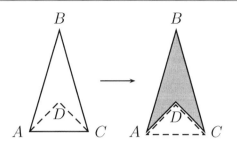

A. 5

B. 4

C. $3\sqrt{2}$

D. $\frac{9}{2}$

E. $2\sqrt{5}$

ANSWER: A. If we label the distance from D to the midpoint of AC x, then the height of the isosceles triangle is $6 + x$. A line drawn from D to the midpoint of AC splits the right triangle into two 45°-45°-90° triangles, each with height x, and so each with base x. Thus, the base of the isosceles triangle is $2x$. The area of the isosceles triangle is

$$\frac{1}{2} \times 2x \times (6 + x) = x^2 + 6x.$$

The area of the right triangle is

$$\frac{1}{2} \times 2x \times x = x^2.$$

Subtracting these gives the area of the arrow: $(x^2 + 6x) - x^2 = 6x = 15$. Thus, $x = \frac{15}{6} = \frac{5}{2}$ and so the length of AC is 5.

10. A rhombus is divided into two parts as shown. In degrees, what is the angle labeled x?

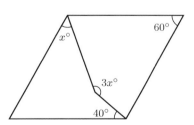

A. 40

B. 45

C. 50

D. 55

E. 60

ANSWER: C.

Opposite corners in a rhombus have equal angles, so two corners are 60° and the other two are 120°. Since part of one corner is 40°, the rest of that corner must be 80°. Thus, we have a quadrilateral with angles 60°, 80°, $3x°$, and $(120 - x)°$. Since these must add to 360°, we have

$$60 + 80 + 3x + (120 - x) = 260 + 2x = 360, \quad \text{so} \quad x = 50°.$$

Problem 10 is a recurring theme among those appearing on the SAT. The fact that all angles of a triangle add to 180° (and so all angles of a quadrilateral add to 360°) is used to deduce the measure of the angle required. The student should become quite comfortable with questions of this type. In the following problems, the reader should take note of other commonalities. These include the use of the Pythagorean theorem, percentages/proportions, basic coordinate geometry, and of course, process of elimination.

Practice Problems

1. A trapezoid is cut into two pieces of equal area by a line segment of length one, forming an equilateral triangle and a smaller trapezoid. The base of the equilateral triangle is what percentage of the base of the large trapezoid?

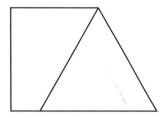

    A. 75%

    B. 80%

    C. 85%

    D. 65%

    E. 70%

2. What is the measure of angle x in the given trapezoid?

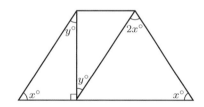

Note: Figure not drawn to scale.

    A. 40°

    B. 45°

    C. 50°

    D. 55°

    E. 60°

3. The parallelogram shown has integer side lengths a and b and an area of 6. Which of the following statements (if any) must be true?

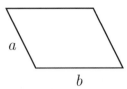

a

b

I. The height is an integer which must be divisible by 2 or 3.

II. The perimeter is an even integer.

III. The product of the diagonals must be 12.

A. I only

B. II only

C. I and II only

D. II and III only

E. none of these

4. The length of AF is 6 and the length of FE is 2. If the ratio of the area of rectangle $ABEF$ to the area of rectangle $ACDF$ is $\frac{1}{5}$, what is the distance between B and D?

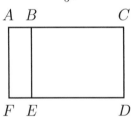

A. 10

B. 8

C. $5\sqrt{2}$

D. $4\sqrt{3}$

E. 12

5. In the figure shown, the parabola $y = x^2 - 2$ intersects the top corners of the rectangle. If the area of the rectangle is $6c$, what is the value of c?

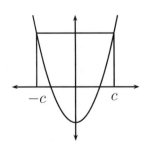

    A. $\sqrt{3}$

    B. 3

    C. $\sqrt{5}$

    D. $2\sqrt{3}$

    E. 5

6. An equilateral triangle is inscribed in a circle of radius 2. What is the area of the triangle?

    A. $3\sqrt{3}$

    B. $3\sqrt{2}$

    C. $3 + \sqrt{3}$

    D. $2 + 2\sqrt{3}$

    E. $\frac{3+\sqrt{3}}{2}$

7. Half the area of a rectangle is removed. The remaining piece then has $\frac{1}{3}$ of its area removed. This remaining rectangle then has $\frac{1}{4}$ of its area removed. This process continues ($\frac{1}{5}$ is removed, etc.) until $\frac{1}{20}$ of the final remaining rectangle is removed. How much of the original rectangle's area remains?

    A. $\frac{1}{4}$

    B. $\frac{4}{9}$

    C. $\frac{1}{20}$

    D. $\frac{19}{20}$

    E. $\frac{3}{5}$

8. Each block in the 6×6 grid is 1 square inch. An unknown number of blocks is shaded. If the ratio of the area of the shaded blocks to the non-shaded blocks is 11, how many blocks are shaded?

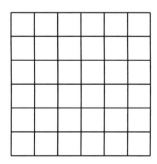

A. 28

B. 30

C. 31

D. 33

E. 34

9. The base of an equilateral triangle has length 10, and is to be tiled with equilateral triangles of base length 4, and equilateral triangles of base length 2. If the total number of triangles used for tiling is 13, how many of each type were used?

   A. 9 small and 4 large

   B. 8 small and 5 large

   C. 7 small and 6 large

   D. 6 small and 7 large

   E. 5 small and 8 large

10. The perimeter of the isosceles triangle is 10. If x is a whole number, which of the following could be the height of the triangle?

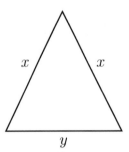

   A. 2

   B. $2\sqrt{3}$

   C. $\sqrt{5}$

   D. 3

   E. $\sqrt{10}$

11. An $m \times n$ grid is to be tiled with the blocks of type I and type II as shown. If the number of type II blocks used is one more than twice the number of type I blocks used, what could be the dimensions of the grid?

A. 6×7

B. 7×7

C. 6×9

D. 5×10

E. 6×8

12. The width of a rectangle is x (where x is an integer greater than 1). The length of the rectangle is one less than twice the width. Inside the rectangle the largest possible square is fitted. In the remaining space, the largest possible square is fitted again. If this process continues, what is the maximum number of squares that can fit inside the rectangle in this way?

    A. $x - 2$

    B. $x - 1$

    C. $2x - 2$

    D. $2x + 1$

    E. $x + 1$

13. The area of square I is 44% larger than the area of square II. The area of square II is 69% larger than the area of square III. What percentage larger is the perimeter of square I than the perimeter of square III?

    A. 47%

    B. 56%

    C. 62%

    D. 68%

    E. 73%

14. The area of the rectangle is equal to the area of the triangle. If the perimeter of the rectangle is twice the height of the triangle, which of the following statements must be true?

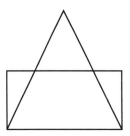

Note: Figure not drawn to scale.

A. The rectangle is a square.

B. The height of the triangle is an integer.

C. The triangle is equilateral.

D. The diagonal of the rectangle is equal to the height of the triangle.

E. The diagonal of the rectangle is an integer.

15. The 7×7 grid shown is to be tiled with tiles of length four and length three (shown to the left of the grid). What is the minimum number of total tiles required to cover the grid?

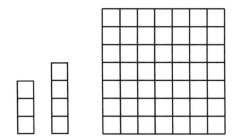

A. 12

B. 13

C. 14

D. 15

E. 16

16. Segment AC is drawn parallel to the base of the large triangle (as shown). The height of the large triangle is 10, and the area of $\triangle ABC$ is $\frac{1}{4}$ of the area of the large triangle. What is the height of $\triangle ABC$?

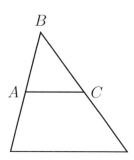

Note: Figure not drawn to scale.

A. 4.5

B. 4.75

C. 5

D. 5.25

E. 5.5

17. The path between the rectangles has uniform width, x. The length of the inner rectangle is 3 times its width, and the perimeter of the outer rectangle is twice the perimeter of the inner rectangle. How many times larger is the area of the outer rectangle than the area of the inner rectangle?

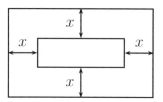

A. 2

B. 3

C. 4

D. 5

E. 6

18. How many triangles are in the trapezoid shown?

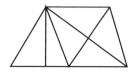

A. 10

B. 12

C. 13

D. 15

E. 16

19. A quadrilateral has endpoints at $(-2, 1)$, $(-1, -2)$, $(5, -3)$, and $(4, 0)$. Which term describes this shape as specifically as possible?

A. Quadrilateral

B. Trapezoid

C. Parallelogram

D. Rectangle

E. Square

20. A building with a square base (shaded dark gray) sits on a rectangular lot. The parking lot (shaded light gray) is seven times the area of the base of the building. If the perimeter of the rectangular lot is 200 and the length of the lot is 80, what is the length of the base of the building?

A. $3\sqrt{6}$

B. $10\sqrt{3}$

C. $2\sqrt{10}$

D. $6\sqrt{2}$

E. $10\sqrt{2}$

Solutions to Practice Problems

1. **B.**

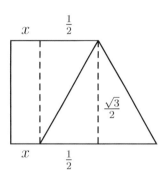

The triangle is equilateral and so the length of the base is 1. We will call the remaining length of the trapezoid's base x. The area of the triangle is $\frac{1}{2} \times 1 \times \frac{\sqrt{3}}{2} = \frac{\sqrt{3}}{4}$, and the area of the smaller trapezoid is $\frac{\sqrt{3}}{2} \times \frac{2x+\frac{1}{2}}{2}$. Since the two parts have equal area, we have

$$\frac{\sqrt{3}}{4} = \frac{\sqrt{3}}{4} \times \left(2x + \frac{1}{2}\right), \quad \text{so} \quad x = \frac{1}{4}.$$

Thus, the length of the trapezoid's base is $\frac{5}{4}$, making the length of the triangle 80% as large.

2. **B.** The missing angle in the triangle on the right is $180-3x$, and so $y = 90-(180-3x) = 3x-90$. From the triangle on the left, $x+y = 90$. Substituting gives $x+(3x-90) = 90$, so $x = 45$.

3. **B.** The area of the parallelogram is given by $bh = 6$ where h is the height. Since b is an integer, h must be 1, 2, 3, or 6. The height can be 1, so statement I is eliminated. The perimeter is $2a+2b$ and so must be an even integer, making statement II necessarily true. The product of the diagonals of a rhombus is equal to twice the area of the rhombus, but the figure shown would only be a rhombus if $a = b$, which is not necessarily true. Thus, statement III can be eliminated.

4. **A.** The area of $ABEF$ is $2 \times 6 = 12$. If we label the length of ED as x, then the area of $ACDF$ is $6 \times (2+x)$. We are told the ratio of the area of $ABEF$ to that of $ACDF$ is $\frac{1}{5}$. That is,

$$\frac{12}{6 \times (2 + x)} = \frac{2}{2 + x} = \frac{1}{5}.$$

Solving, we obtain $x = 8$. The Pythagorean theorem is used to get the length of BD: $\sqrt{6^2 + 8^2} = \sqrt{100} = 10$.

Another approach is as follows: Since the ratio of the areas of these rectangles is $\frac{1}{5}$, the ratio of FE to FD is $\frac{1}{5}$, which means $FD = 10$. Thus, $ED = 8$, and so $BD = 10$. Note: The lengths of the edges of $\triangle DEB$ form a Pythagorean triple.

5. **C.** The length of the rectangle is $2c$ and since the parabola intersects the rectangle at its top corners, the height of the rectangle is the value of the parabola at c, which is $c^2 - 2$. The area of the rectangle is given by $2c(c^2 - 2) = 6c$. Thus,

$$2c^3 - 10c = 2c(c^2 - 5) = 0, \quad \text{so} \quad c = \sqrt{5}.$$

6. **A.** For a triangle inscribed in a circle, the center of the circle is at a point $\frac{2}{3}$ along a median of the triangle; since this circle's radius is 2, and this is $\frac{2}{3}$ the length of a median, a median has length 3. Since the triangle is equilateral, a median is also an altitude and an angle bisector, so drawing one of these divides the original triangle into two smaller 30°-60°-90° triangles whose longer leg has length 3. Therefore, the short leg has length $\frac{3}{\sqrt{3}} = \sqrt{3}$, and the hypotenuse, which is the edge of the original triangle, has length $2\sqrt{3}$. This makes the area $\frac{1}{2} \times 2\sqrt{3} \times 3 = 3\sqrt{3}$.

7. **C.** After the first cut, half of the original rectangle remains. After the second cut, $\frac{2}{3}$ of $\frac{1}{2}$ remains. That is, $\frac{1}{2} \times \frac{2}{3} = \frac{1}{3}$ of the original remains. Then $\frac{3}{4}$ of that rectangle remains, and so $\frac{1}{2} \times \frac{2}{3} \times \frac{3}{4} = \frac{1}{4}$ of the original remains. Continuing in this manner, we see that the last piece is

$$\frac{1}{2} \times \frac{2}{3} \times \frac{3}{4} \times \cdots \times \frac{19}{20} = \frac{1}{20}$$

of the original rectangle.

8. **D.** Labeling the number of shaded blocks x, we have

$$
\begin{aligned}
\frac{x}{36 - x} &= 11 \\
x &= 396 - 11x \\
12x &= 396 \\
x &= 33.
\end{aligned}
$$

This problem could also have been solved by considering each of the choices separately to observe which gives a ratio of 11.

9. **A.** Let x be the number of large equilateral triangles (base length 4) and y be the number of small equilateral triangles (base length 2) needed for the tiling. The area of the equilateral triangle to be tiled is $\frac{1}{2} \times 10 \times 5\sqrt{3} = 25\sqrt{3}$. The area of one of the large tiles is $\frac{1}{2} \times 4 \times 2\sqrt{3} = 4\sqrt{3}$, and the area of one of the small tiles is $\frac{1}{2} \times 2 \times \sqrt{3}$. Thus,

we have the following two equations: $x + y = 13$ and $4\sqrt{3}x + \sqrt{3}y = 25\sqrt{3}$. The latter equation can be simplified by dividing both sides by $\sqrt{3}$, obtaining $4x + y = 25$. All that is left is to solve the system of equations $x + y = 13$ and $4x + y = 25$. Substituting for y in the second equation:

$$4x + (13 - x) = 25, \quad \text{so} \quad 3x = 12 \quad \text{and} \quad x = 4,$$

and so $y = 9$.

10. **C.** The height h is given by the Pythagorean theorem: $h = \sqrt{x^2 - \left(\frac{1}{2}y\right)^2}$. Since the perimeter is 10, we have that $2x + y = 10$, and so $y = 10 - 2x$. Substitution gives $h = \sqrt{x^2 - (5 - x)^2} = \sqrt{x^2 - (25 - 10x + x^2)} = \sqrt{10x - 25}$. Since x is a whole number, it must be 1, 2, 3, or 4. However, x cannot be 1 or 2 since then the height would not exist. Thus, x must be 3 or 4, making the height either $\sqrt{5}$ or $\sqrt{15}$. Only $\sqrt{5}$ is among the given choices.

11. **D.** Let x be the number of type I blocks used for the tiling. Then the number of type II blocks used is $2x + 1$. Type I blocks are composed of 4 individual blocks and type two blocks are composed of two individual blocks. Since the total number of individual blocks tiled is mn, we have

$$4x + 2(2x + 1) = mn, \quad \text{so} \quad 8x + 2 = mn \quad \text{and} \quad 8x = mn - 2.$$

Since x is a whole number, the latter equation says that $mn - 2$ is divisible by 8. Among the given choices, only a 5×10 grid is possible ($5 \times 10 - 2 = 48$ is divisible by 8).

12. **E.** The largest square that can be fit inside the rectangle has length x. The space remaining has width x and length $x - 1$, and so the largest square that can be fit in that space has length $x - 1$. The remaining space has width 1 and length $x - 1$, and so we can fit exactly $x - 1$ squares in it. Thus, the total number of squares is $1 + 1 + (x - 1) = x + 1$.

13. **B.** Labeling the areas of square I, square II, and square III, as x, y, and z, respectively, we have: $x^2 = 1.44y^2 = (1.2y)^2$ and $y^2 = 1.69z^2 = (1.3z)^2$. Thus, $x^2 = (1.2 \times 1.3 \times z)^2$, so $x = 1.56z$. This means x is 56% larger than z, making the perimeter of square I 56% larger than the perimeter of square III.

14. **A.** Labeling the base of the rectangle (which is also the base of the triangle) x, the height of the rectangle y, and the height of the triangle h, we have $xy = \frac{1}{2}xh$, so

$h = 2y$. Since the perimeter of the rectangle is twice the triangle's height, we also have $2x + 2y = 2h$. Simplifying and substituting for h:

$$x + y = h, \quad \text{so} \quad x + y = 2y, \quad \text{and} \quad x = y.$$

Thus, the base of the rectangle is the same as the height of the rectangle, and so it is a square. The other choices might not be true. (In fact, while B., C., or E. can be true, D. is impossible: the rectangle's diagonal is $x\sqrt{2}$, while the triangle's height is $2x$.)

15. **B.** Let x be the number of blocks of length four used, and y be the number of blocks of length 3 used. The grid is 7×7 so 49 squares must be covered, giving the equation $4x + 3y = 49$ which has integer solutions $(10, 3)$, $(7, 7)$, $(4, 11)$, and $(1, 15)$. Thus, the minimum number of blocks needed is $10 + 3 = 13$.

16. **C.** $\triangle ABC$ is similar to the large triangle, so the ratio of their respective heights is the same as the *square root* of the ratio of their respective areas. Since the ratio of their respective areas is $\frac{1}{4}$, the ratio of their respective heights is $\frac{1}{2}$. Thus, $h = 5$.

17. **D.** Labeling the width of the inner rectangle w, its length is then $3w$, and so its perimeter is $8w$. This makes the perimeter of the outer rectangle $16w$. The width of the outer rectangle is $w + 2x$ and the length of the outer rectangle is $3w + 2x$, which means the perimeter of the outer rectangle is also given by $8w + 8x$. Thus, $8w + 8x = 16w$, which means $x = w$, and so the dimensions of the outer rectangle are $3w \times 5w$. Then the area of the inner rectangle is $3w^2$ and the area of the outer rectangle is $15w^2$, making the area of the outer rectangle 5 times as large as the area of the inner rectangle.

18. **C.** It is easiest to remove the vertical segment, count how many triangles there are, then replace the vertical segment, BF, and count how many extra are obtained. Removing BF, we count 10 triangles: $\triangle ACF$, $\triangle ADF$, $\triangle CDE$, $\triangle CDF$, $\triangle CDG$, $\triangle CEF$, $\triangle CFG$, $\triangle DEF$, $\triangle DEG$, and $\triangle EFG$. Replacing BF gives three more: $\triangle ABF$, $\triangle BCF$, and $\triangle BDF$.

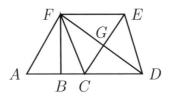

19. **C.** The shape is drawn below, and it is easy to see that it is a parallelogram.

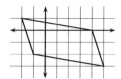

To calculate this, however, requires some work. First, we determine the slopes of the sides: The left edge has a slope of $\frac{-2-1}{-1-(-2)} = -3$; the right edge has a slope of $\frac{0-(-3)}{4-5} = \frac{3}{-1} = -3$, so these two sides are parallel. The top edge has a slope of $\frac{0-1}{4-(-2)} = \frac{-1}{6}$; the bottom edge has a slope of $\frac{-3-(-2)}{5-(-1)} = \frac{-1}{6}$, so these edges are parallel, too.

At this point, the shape must be a parallelogram, but we can check ourselves by verifying that the opposite pairs of edges are also equal in length. The left edge [from $(-2,1)$ to $(-1,-2)$] has length $\sqrt{3^2 + 1^2} = \sqrt{10}$, and the right edge's [from $(4,0)$ to $(5,-3)$] length is $\sqrt{3^2 + 1^2} = \sqrt{10}$, also. Finally, the top edge [$(-2,1)$ to $(4,0)$] has length $\sqrt{1^2 + 6^2} = \sqrt{37}$, and the bottom edge [$(-1,-2)$ to $(5,-3)$] has length $\sqrt{1^2 + 6^2} = \sqrt{37}$.

20. **E.** We label the unknown side of the rectangular lot y and the length of the square base x. Then the perimeter of the lot is given by $160 + 2y = 200$, and so $y = 20$. Since the area of the rectangular lot is seven times that of the base of the building, we have

$$1600 - x^2 = 7x^2, \quad \text{so} \quad 8x^2 = 1600, \quad \text{so} \quad x = \sqrt{200} = 10\sqrt{2}.$$

CHAPTER 9

CIRCLES

Problems that involve circles can be solved with a working knowledge of most circle theorems. These include theorems about inscribed and circumscribed polygons, tangent lines, and chords. The essentials include the Pythagorean theorem, facts about 45°-45°-90° and 30°-60°-90° triangles, formulas for the area and circumference of a circle, and the length of an arc subtended by a given angle.

1. The base and height of the right triangle shown have equal length, and one vertex of the triangle is the center of the semicircle. What is the ratio of the area of the semicircle to the area of the triangle?

A. $\frac{\pi}{2}$

B. 4π

C. $\frac{\pi}{4}$

D. 2π

E. $\frac{3\pi}{2}$

ANSWER: D. Since we are being asked for a ratio and no measurements are given, we may assume (for simplicity) that the base and height of the triangle are both 1. Then the area of the triangle is $\frac{1}{2}$. Since it is a 45°-45°-90° triangle, the hypotenuse (which is the radius of the semicircle) is $\sqrt{2}$. Thus, the area of the semicircle is $\frac{1}{2}\pi(\sqrt{2})^2 = \pi$, making the ratio of the area of the semicircle to the area of the triangle $\pi \div \frac{1}{2} = 2\pi$.

2. One vertex of the triangle is the center of the semicircle, and the right side of the triangle is tangent to the semicircle. What proportion of the triangle's area lies outside the semicircle?

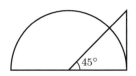

A. $\frac{\pi}{16}$

B. $\frac{\pi}{4}$

C. $\frac{1}{3}$

D. $\frac{\pi}{6}$

E. $1 - \frac{\pi}{4}$

ANSWER: E. The base of the triangle is the radius of the semicircle, and since it is a 45°-45°-90° triangle (because the right edge is tangent, so it forms a 90° angle), the height is also the radius of the semicircle. We may assume the radius of the circle is 1, so the area of the triangle is $\frac{1}{2}$. The area of the triangle that lies inside the semicircle is the area of the sector swept out by 45°. That is, the area of the full circle divided by 8, which is $\frac{\pi}{8}$. We want to know what proportion of the triangle's area lies outside the semicircle. The area outside is $\frac{1}{2} - \frac{\pi}{8} = \frac{4-\pi}{8}$. The proportion of area lying outside is the area outside divided by the total area of the triangle, which is

$$\frac{4-\pi}{8} \div \frac{1}{2} = \frac{4-\pi}{4} = 1 - \frac{\pi}{4}.$$

A common technique has been illustrated in these first problems. Notice that the solutions begin with the assumption that some measurement (the radius or height) is 1, simplifying calculations. Problems of this type may of course be solved without this assumption. For instance, we may label the radius r, but in the process of solving, the rs will cancel out eventually, leaving the desired ratio or proportion.

3. The semicircle pictured has radius 4. If the ratio of the shaded area to the non-shaded area is $\frac{1}{3}$, what is the area of the shaded region?

A. 2π

B. $\frac{8\pi}{3}$

C. $\frac{\pi}{4}$

D. $\frac{4\pi}{9}$

E. $\frac{3\pi}{2}$

ANSWER: A. The area of the semicircle is $\frac{1}{2}\pi \times 4^2 = 8\pi$. The ratio of the shaded to non-shaded area is $\frac{1}{3}$, so the shaded area makes up $\frac{1}{4}$ of the semicircle. Thus, it has an area of 2π.

4. The inner circle is tangent to the outer circle, and the radius of the outer circle is twice the radius of the inner circle. If the shaded region has area 60π, what is the radius of the inner circle?

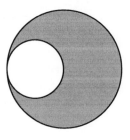

    A. $4\sqrt{5}$

    B. $2\sqrt{3}$

    C. $\sqrt{15}$

    D. $4\sqrt{3}$

    E. $2\sqrt{5}$

ANSWER: E. If the radius of the inner circle is labeled r, then the radius of the outer circle is $2r$, and so the areas of the inner and outer circles are πr^2 and $\pi(2r)^2 = 4\pi r^2$. The difference between these areas is the area of the shaded region. Thus,

$$4\pi r^2 - \pi r^2 = 60\pi, \quad \text{so} \quad r^2 = 20 \quad \text{and} \quad r = 2\sqrt{5}.$$

5. The top edge of the rectangle is tangent to the circle and a vertex of the rectangle is the circle's center. One-third of the rectangle's total area lies inside the circle. As a percentage, how much bigger is the dark-shaded region than the light-shaded region?

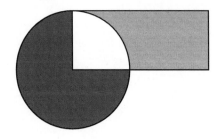

A. 25%

B. 33%

C. 50%

D. 20%

E. 40%

ANSWER: C. Since the area of the overlap is $\frac{1}{3}$ of the total area of the rectangle, the light-shaded area is twice the size of the overlap. Since the dark-shaded area is 3 times the size of the overlap, the dark-shaded area is 50% bigger than the light-shaded area.

The diagrams in problems 3, 4, and 5 all involve shaded regions. Questions involving ratios, proportions, and percentages are often constructed using shading, and the student must learn to contrast various shaded regions visually. Notice, however, that problem 4 also requires a bit of algebra. In the problems that follow, algebra will be needed more frequently, but should be implemented only when necessary. The next two examples use algebra heavily.

6. A circle has center $(4, 2)$ and the line $y = x + 2$ is tangent to the circle. What is the circle's radius? (Hint: first find the equation of the line perpendicular to $y = x + 2$ that passes through the center.)

A. $3\sqrt{3}$

B. 2

C. $2\sqrt{2}$

D. $\sqrt{5}$

E. $2\sqrt{3}$

ANSWER: C. The radius of the circle is the distance between the center and the point of tangency of the line, so we must first find the point of tangency. The line passing through the point $(4, 2)$ and perpendicular to $y = x + 2$ must pass through the center of the circle. This line passes through the point $(4, 2)$ and has slope $m = -1$. Using the point-slope formula we obtain the equation of the perpendicular line: $y - 2 = -1(x - 4)$, or $y = -x + 6$. The point of intersection of these two lines is the point of tangency. Setting the two lines equal to each other: $x + 2 = -x + 6$ gives $x = 2$, so $y = 4$. Thus, the point of tangency is $(2, 4)$. Using the distance formula on the points $(4, 2)$ and $(2, 4)$ yields the radius:

$$\sqrt{(4-2)^2 + (4-2)^2} = \sqrt{8} = 2\sqrt{2}.$$

7. Recall that the equation of a circle of radius r centered at (h, k) is $(x-h)^2+(y-k)^2 = r^2$. A circle centered at the origin with radius $2\sqrt{5}$ intersects the parabola $y = x^2$ at which two points?

    A. $(-\sqrt{3}, 3)$ and $(\sqrt{3}, 3)$

    B. $(-2, 4)$ and $(2, 4)$

    C. $(-2, 5)$ and $(2, 5)$

    D. $(-1, 1)$ and $(1, 1)$

    E. $(\sqrt{2}, 2)$ and $(\sqrt{2}, 2)$

ANSWER: B. Since the equation of a circle centered at (h, k) with radius r is $(x - h)^2 + (y - k)^2 = r^2$, the circle given has equation $x^2 + y^2 = 20$. This problem is solved most easily by plugging each choice into both equations to see which works. Choice C. is eliminated immediately simply by observing that those points are not even on the parabola. However, we can solve the problem directly as follows: Solving for x^2 in the circle equation gives $x^2 = 20 - y^2$. Substituting this for x^2 in the parabola equation gives $y = 20 - y^2$. Re-arranging the last equation into quadratic form yields $y^2 + y - 20 = 0$, and the left side factors: $(y - 4)(y + 5) = 0$, so $y = 4$ or $y = -5$. Since $y = x^2$, y cannot be negative. Thus, $y = 4$ is the only solution, and so the corresponding x values are $x = 2$ and $x = -2$. That is, the points of intersection are $(-2, 4)$ and $(2, 4)$.

8. The two circles shown pass through each other's center and both have radius 3. What is the length of the vertical line segment AB?

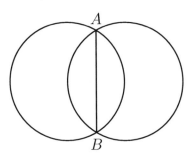

    A. 3

    B. $\frac{\sqrt{2}}{2}$

    C. $3\sqrt{3}$

    D. $2\sqrt{3}$

    E. $\frac{3}{2}$

191

ANSWER: C. Drawing a line from the center of one circle to A and a line from the same center directly to the segment AB, we form a right triangle with a hypotenuse of length 3. The distance between the two centers is 3, so the distance between the center and the segment AB is $\frac{3}{2}$. Thus, the triangle is a 30°-60°-90° triangle, which makes the remaining side $\frac{3\sqrt{3}}{2}$. Doubling this value gives the length of AB.

The solution to problem 8 illustrates the necessity of inserting triangles into some diagrams in order to solve the problem. In addition to the techniques already mentioned, the student should be continuously mindful of when it is appropriate to use process of elimination, or when it is easiest to plug in choices.

Practice Problems

1. A circle of radius $\sqrt{6}$ is inscribed in a regular hexagon. What is the area of the hexagon?

    A. $12\sqrt{3}$

    B. $18\sqrt{2}$

    C. 20

    D. $24\sqrt{3}$

    E. $16\sqrt{6}$

2. The area of the rectangle is equal to the area of the semicircle. If the semicircle has radius 2, what is the perimeter of the rectangle?

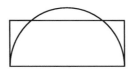

    A. $4 + \pi$

    B. 4π

    C. $8 + \pi$

    D. $4 + 2\pi$

    E. $4\pi + 2$

3. The semicircle has radius 3 and the center is O. What is the area of the shaded region?

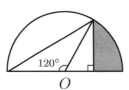

    A. $8\pi - 12\sqrt{3}$

    B. $\frac{12\pi - 9\sqrt{3}}{8}$

    C. $\pi - \frac{\sqrt{3}}{2}$

    D. $\frac{\pi\sqrt{3}}{2}$

    E. $\frac{8\pi - 3\sqrt{3}}{6}$

4. Both circles have radius 2 and intersect each other's center. A triangle is formed using the centers of each circle and a point of intersection of the two circles as shown. What is the area of the shaded region?

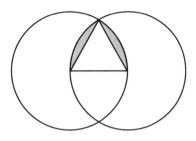

A. $\frac{2\pi}{3} - \sqrt{2}$

B. $\pi - \frac{\sqrt{3}}{2}$

C. $\frac{4\pi - 12}{3}$

D. $\frac{2\pi - 3\sqrt{3}}{3}$

E. $\frac{4\pi}{3} - 2\sqrt{3}$

5. The area of a circle is 9π. One vertex of a quadrilateral is the center of the circle, and the other three vertices lie on the circle. What is the smallest number that the perimeter of the quadrilateral cannot be greater than?

A. 12

B. 14

C. 16

D. 18

E. 20

6. Trapezoid $ABCD$ is inscribed in a semicircle with center E as shown. If $\angle AEB = 60°$ and the distance from B to D is $2\sqrt{6}$, what is the radius of the semicircle?

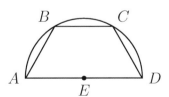

A. 4

B. $\frac{\sqrt{5}}{2}$

C. $\frac{3}{2}$

D. $\sqrt{6}$

E. $2\sqrt{2}$

7. The small circle has radius 2 and is tangent to the large circle. The small circle rolls around the large circle (dotted line) until it returns to its original location. If the small circle made more than 8 revolutions but less than 9, what could be the radius of the large circle?

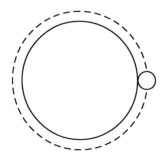

Note: Figure not drawn to scale.

A. 17

B. 19

C. 21

D. 22

E. 23

8. The two large circles shown have radius 3 and the distance between their centers, O and P, is 2. Also, OP is a diameter of the small, light-colored circle in the center of the figure. If the total shaded area (light and dark) is 12π, what is the area of the dark-shaded region?

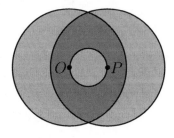

A. $2 + 2\pi$

B. 4π

C. 5π

D. $6 + 2\pi$

E. $\frac{10\pi}{3}$

9. Recall that the equation of a circle of radius r centered at (h, k) is $(x-h)^2+(y-k)^2 = r^2$. Which of the following is **not** the equation of a circle?

A. $\frac{1}{2}x^2 + \frac{1}{2}y^2 - 6 = 0$

B. $x^2 + y^2 - 2x + 6y - 20 = 0$

C. $x^2 + y^2 + 4x - 2y + 8 = 0$

D. $(x + 2y)^2 - 3y^2 - 9 = 4xy$

E. $(x - 1)^2 + (y - 2)^2 = 6 - 4y$

10. The large semicircle has base AC, and D is the midpoint of AC. The small semicircle has base AB, and B is the midpoint of arc AC. If the length of AD is 2, what is the area of the overlap of the two semicircles?

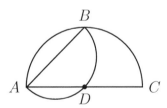

A. $2\pi - 2\sqrt{2}$

B. $\pi\sqrt{2}$

C. $\frac{\pi}{2} + 1$

D. $\frac{2\pi}{3}$

E. $2\pi - 4$

11. The semicircle has radius 2 and the length of the hypotenuse of the right triangle is L. The right triangle and the semicircle have the same area. Which of the following statements about L is true?

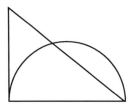

I. $5 < L < 6$.

II. L is a whole number.

III. The exact value of L cannot be determined.

A. I only

B. II only

C. III only

D. I and III only

E. II and III only

12. A rock is dropped into a pond creating a circular ripple that spreads outward. The area of the ripple after 6 seconds was 44% larger than the area of the ripple after 5 seconds. If the radius is increasing at a constant rate, what is the area of the ripple after 7 seconds?

A. 1.96π

B. 2π

C. 2.25π

D. 2.44π

E. 2.56π

13. The diameter of the circle is AD, and the quadrilateral inside the circle is a rhombus. The long diagonal of the rhombus is also a diameter of the circle. If the area of the rhombus is $\frac{1}{3}$ the area of the circle, what is the ratio of BC to AD?

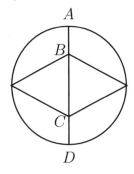

A. $\frac{2\pi}{9}$

B. $\frac{\pi}{6}$

C. $\frac{\pi+2}{8}$

D. $\frac{\pi+3}{10}$

E. $\frac{\pi}{5}$

14. The two chords of the circle are perpendicular and have the same length. Regions I and II total $\frac{1}{3}$ the area of the circle, and the area of region III is five times as large as the area of region I. If the radius of the circle is 2, what is the area of region II?

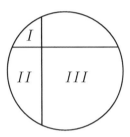

Note: Figure not drawn to scale.

A. $\frac{2\pi}{3}$

B. π

C. $\frac{5\pi}{4}$

D. $\frac{3\pi}{2}$

E. $\frac{7\pi}{4}$

15. Two semicircles of equal area sit inside of a large circle, as shown, so that their diameters are parallel and each semicircle is tangent to the other's diameter. How many times larger is the area of the large circle than the area of one semicircle?

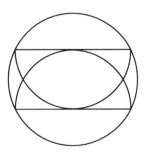

A. 1.5

B. 2

C. 2.5

D. 3

E. 3.5

16. The chord is 20% larger than the radius of the large circle. The center of the small circle lies on the large circle and the small circle is tangent to the chord. The radius of the small circle is what percentage of the radius of the large circle?

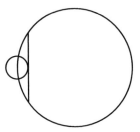

A. 10%

B. 15%

C. 18%

D. 20%

E. 25%

17. Circle A is centered at $(-3, 4)$ and passes through the origin. The diameter of circle B has endpoints $(4, 3)$ and $(10, 11)$. If x is the shortest distance between the two circles, which of the following inequalities is true?

A. $0 < x < .5$

B. $.5 < x < 1$

C. $1 < x < 1.5$

D. $1.5 < x < 2$

E. $2 < x < 2.5$

18. The radius of a circle is enlarged until the area of the circle is 25% bigger. The radius of that circle is enlarged until its area is 80% bigger. The radius of the resulting circle is what percentage bigger than the radius of the original circle?

A. 35

B. 40

C. 20

D. 50

E. E. 105

Solutions to Practice Problems

1. **A.** We can divide the hexagon into six equilateral triangles, so we must use the radius of the circle to calculate the area of one of these triangles and then multiply by 6. Drawing a radius from the center of the circle so that it is perpendicular to one side of the hexagon, we split one of the equilateral triangles into two 30°-60°-90° triangles, each with a long side of length $\sqrt{6}$. Then the base of each 30°-60°-90° triangle has length $\frac{\sqrt{6}}{\sqrt{3}} = \sqrt{\frac{6}{3}} = \sqrt{2}$. Doubling this gives the base of the equilateral triangle. Thus, the area of the equilateral triangle is

$$\frac{1}{2} \times 2\sqrt{2} \times \sqrt{6} = \sqrt{12} = 2\sqrt{3}.$$

   Multiplying by six gives the area of the hexagon.

2. **C.** The area of the semicircle is 2π and so the area of the rectangle is 2π. Since the base of the rectangle is 4, the height must be $\frac{\pi}{2}$. Thus, the perimeter of the rectangle is $8 + \pi$.

3. **B.** The smaller triangle is a 30°-60°-90° triangle and so its base is $\frac{3}{2}$ and its height is $\frac{3\sqrt{3}}{2}$, giving it an area of

$$\frac{1}{2} \times \frac{3}{2} \times \frac{3\sqrt{3}}{2} = \frac{9\sqrt{3}}{8}.$$

   The area of the sector swept out by 60° is $\frac{9\pi}{6} = \frac{3\pi}{2}$. Subtracting the area of the triangle from the area of the sector gives the area of the shaded region:

$$\frac{3\pi}{2} - \frac{9\sqrt{3}}{8} = \frac{12\pi - 9\sqrt{3}}{8}.$$

4. **E.** The triangle is equilateral so all of its angles are 60°. The area of the shaded region on the right is the area of the sector swept out by 60° minus the area of the triangle. The area of the sector is $\frac{\pi \times 2^2}{6} = \frac{2\pi}{3}$. Since the triangle is equilateral with sides of length 2, its height is $\sqrt{3}$. (This is because dropping an altitude would make a 30°-60°-90° triangle with a base of length 1.) So the area of the triangle is $\frac{1}{2} \times 2 \times \sqrt{3}$. Thus, the difference is $\frac{2\pi}{3} - \sqrt{3}$. Doubling this gives the total area of the shaded region.

5. **D.** The two edges of the quadrilateral that are incident on the vertex at the center of the circle have lengths equal to the radius of the circle which, given the area, must be 3. So these two edges together have length 6.

The other two edges of the quadrilateral are chords in the circle. Each one must be shorter than the diameter of the circle, which is 6. So these edges together have length less than 12. The perimeter, therefore, is at most $6 + 12 = 18$.

Notice that the perimeter can be very close to 18. (In particular, it can be greater than 16, so the answer cannot be C..) Consider the very narrow quadrilateral pictured below; the two long edges are each almost 6 units long, so the perimeter is very close to 18.

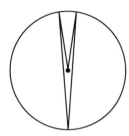

6. **E.** $\triangle AEB$ is isosceles with one angle $60°$, and so it is equilateral. Any triangle inscribed in a semicircle must be a right triangle, so $\triangle ABD$ is a right triangle, having side lengths $2\sqrt{6}$, r, and $2r$. By the Pythagorean theorem, $(2\sqrt{6})^2 + r^2 = (2r)^2$, so $3r^2 = 24$, and $r = 2\sqrt{2}$.

7. **A.** The small circle has radius 2 and so its circumference is 4π. It rolls around the larger circle making more than 8 but less than 9 revolutions, so it traveled more than a distance of 32π but less than 36π. That is, the circumference of the large circle is bigger than 32π but less than 36π, making the radius of the larger circle between 16 and 18.

8. **C.** The area of the dark-shaded region is obtained by subtracting the area of the small center circle from the overlap between the two large circles. Both large circles have area 9π. Adding the area of both large circles gives 18π, but we have counted the overlap twice. Subtracting the overlap once gives the total shaded area (light and dark). That is, $18\pi - x = 12\pi$, so $x = 6\pi$. The distance between the two centers is 2, so the area of the small center circle is $\pi \times 1^2 = \pi$. Thus, the area of the dark-shaded region is 5π.

9. **C.** All the choices can be rewritten in the form $(x - h)^2 + (y - k)^2 = r^2$ except for C.. If we complete the square on both x and y in choice C., we obtain

$$(x^2 + 4x + 4) + (y^2 - 2y + 1) - 4 - 1 + 8 = 0, \quad \text{or} \quad (x + 2)^2 + (y - 1)^2 = -3.$$

Since r^2 cannot be negative, this is not the equation of a circle.

10. **C.** We first draw a line segment from B to D (which must also have length 2). The area of the overlap is obtained by adding the area of $\triangle ABD$ to the area lying between line segment BD and arc BD, which we label x. The area of $\triangle ABD$ is $\frac{1}{2} \times 2 \times 2 = 2$, and since the diameter of the small semicircle is $2\sqrt{2}$, its area is $\frac{1}{2} \times \pi \times \sqrt{2}^2 = \pi$. We can now solve for x: $\pi - 2x = 2$, so $x = \frac{\pi}{2} - 1$. Thus, the area of the overlap is $2 + \frac{\pi}{2} - 1 = \frac{\pi}{2} + 1$.

11. **A.** The base of the right triangle is 4, and since the area of the semicircle is equal to the area of the triangle, we have: $\frac{1}{2} \times 4h = \frac{1}{2} \times \pi \times 2^2$, so $h = \pi$. By the Pythagorean theorem $L = \sqrt{4^2 + \pi^2} = \sqrt{16 + \pi^2}$, and so the exact value of L has been determined, and it lies between 5 and 6.

12. **A.** If the area of the ripple after 5 seconds was πr^2, then the area of the ripple after 6 seconds was $1.44\pi r^2$. This means the radius of the ripple increased by $.2r$. Since the radius of the ripple is increasing at a constant rate, and after 5 seconds it was r, we have that $r = 1$. That is, the radius is increasing at a rate of $.2$ (units/sec). Thus, after 7 seconds the radius is 1.4, making the area after 7 seconds 1.96π.

13. **B.** The area of a rhombus is equal to one-half the product of its diagonals, d_1 and d_2. One diagonal of the rhombus is BC. Since we are told the other diagonal is a diameter of the circle, we know it has length AD. Thus,

$$
\begin{aligned}
\frac{1}{2}d_1 d_2 &= \frac{1}{3}\pi r^2 \\
\frac{1}{2}(BC)(AD) &= \frac{1}{3}\pi \left(\frac{1}{2}AD\right)^2 \\
(BC)(AD) &= \frac{\pi}{6}(AD)^2 \\
\frac{BC}{AD} &= \frac{\pi}{6}.
\end{aligned}
$$

14. **B.** First label the areas of regions I, II, and III as x, y, and z, respectively. Regions I and II total $\frac{1}{3}$ the area of the circle, and the area of region III is five times as large as the area of region I. That is, $x + y = \frac{1}{3}\pi \times 2^2$ (which we will rewrite as $3x + 3y = 4\pi$) and $z = 5x$. Since the chords are the same length and perpendicular, the unlabeled region has the same area as region II. Thus,

$$x + 2y + z = \pi \times 2^2, \quad \text{which is} \quad x + 2y + 5x = 4\pi, \quad \text{so} \quad 3x + y = 2\pi.$$

Solving the equations $3x + 3y = 4\pi$ and $3x + y = 2\pi$ simultaneously for y: $(2\pi - y) + 3y = 4\pi$, so $y = \pi$.

15. **C.** Drawing two vertical chords, we can form an inscribed rectangle having the diameter of one semicircle as its base and the diameter of the other semicircle as its top. Since the semicircles have the same area, the diagonal of the rectangle must pass through the center of the large circle. That is, the diagonal is the diameter of the large circle. We may assume the radius of the semicircle is 1, and so the by the Pythagorean theorem the diagonal is $\sqrt{1^2 + 2^2} = \sqrt{5}$. Thus, the area of the circle is $\pi \left(\frac{\sqrt{5}}{2}\right)^2 = \frac{5\pi}{4}$. Since the area of the semicircle is $\frac{1}{2}\pi \times 1^2 = \frac{\pi}{2}$, the area of the circle is $\frac{5}{2}$ times larger.

16. **D.** We may assume the radius of the large circle is 1. Then the chord has length $\frac{6}{5}$. Forming a right triangle with the center of the large circle, the top of the chord, and the midpoint of the chord, we see that the triangle has height $\frac{3}{5}$ and hypotenuse 1. By the Pythagorean theorem the base is $\sqrt{1^2 - \left(\frac{3}{5}\right)^2} = \frac{4}{5}$. Thus, the radius of the small circle is $1 - \frac{4}{5} = \frac{1}{5}$, making it 20% as large as the radius of the large circle.

17. **A.** The shortest distance between the centers of the circles, minus the radius of each circle, gives the shortest distance between the two circles, labeled x. Thus, we must first find the radius of each circle using the distance formula. Circle A has center $(-3, 4)$ and passes through the origin, so the radius of circle A is $\sqrt{(-3 - 0)^2 + (4 - 0)^2} = \sqrt{25} = 5$. The diameter of circle B has endpoints $(4, 3)$ and $(10, 11)$, making its center $(7, 7)$, and so its radius is the distance between $(4, 3)$ and $(7, 7)$: $\sqrt{(7 - 4)^2 + (7 - 3)^2} = \sqrt{25} = 5$. The distance between the centers is $\sqrt{(7 - -3)^2 + (7 - 4)^2} = \sqrt{109}$, and we can now find x: $\sqrt{109} - 5 - 5 = \sqrt{109} - 10$. Thus, x is between 0 and .5.

18. **D.** We may assume the radius of the original circle is 1. If increased until its area is 25% bigger, then the area of the resulting circle is $\pi + .25\pi = 1.25\pi$. The radius of that circle is increased until its area is 80% bigger, so the resulting area is $1.25\pi + .8 \times 1.25\pi = 2.25\pi$. If we label the radius of the resulting circle r, we have that $2.25\pi = \pi r^2$, so $r = 1.5$. That is, the final radius is 50% bigger than the original.

CHAPTER 10

MULTIPLE FIGURES

Geometry problems that involve multiple figures combine different ideas and concepts in clever ways. Frequently, there is more than one way to solve such problems, but usually only one way is the shortest and most efficient. Solving such problems requires mastery of the basics (axioms and theorems on triangles and circles), as well as creativity and intuition.

Two concepts are worth mentioning because they are sometimes critical in advanced geometry problems, but it may not always obvious when they will be useful; these ideas are similar triangles and angles inscribed in circles. If there doesn't seem to be any clear way of making progress on a problem, try to think about whether either of these ideas can help. Having similar triangles can tell you a lot about ratios of lengths of line segments in a problem; one construction that is favored by many geometry test writers is to form similar triangles using a right triangle with an altitude to its hypotenuse. Angles inscribed in circles are sometimes used, in conjunction with the circle's diameter, to indicate indirectly that a certain angle is a right angle.

Frequently, you can get a deeper insight into the problem by adding your own constructions, such as lines that cut up a shape into smaller triangles; extending lines to intersect with other lines; constructing altitudes, medians, or angle bisectors; constructing circumscribing or inscribed circles; etc. As examples, here are two problems which are made much easier to solve once you add a few lines to the figure.

1. In the figure below, what is the value of x?

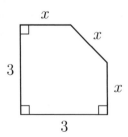

A. $3 - 2\sqrt{3}$

B. $\frac{3\sqrt{2}}{3}$

C. $6 - 3\sqrt{2}$

D. $9 - \sqrt{6}$

E. $\frac{3}{2}$

ANSWER: C. It helps to complete the partial rectangle, as shown below.

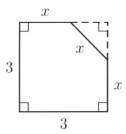

Notice that the dashed lines each have length $3 - x$, so the triangle is isosceles. Since it is also a right triangle, it is 45°-45°-90°, so $x = (3 - x)\sqrt{2}$, which solves to $x = \frac{3\sqrt{2}}{1+\sqrt{2}}$. We can clear the square root from the denominator by multiplying by $\frac{1-\sqrt{2}}{1-\sqrt{2}}$:

$$\frac{3\sqrt{2}}{1+\sqrt{2}} \times \frac{1-\sqrt{2}}{1-\sqrt{2}} = \frac{3\sqrt{2}-6}{1^2 - (\sqrt{2})^2} = \frac{3\sqrt{2}-6}{1-2} = \frac{3\sqrt{2}-6}{-1} = 6 - 3\sqrt{2}.$$

(One can also solve this problem using the Pythagorean theorem: The triangle gives us the equation $(3-x)^2 + (3-x)^2 = x^2$. We can rearrange this to $x^2 - 12x + 18 = 0$. The quadratic equation then gives

$$x = \frac{12 \pm \sqrt{144 - 72}}{2} = \frac{12 \pm \sqrt{72}}{2} = \frac{12 \pm 6\sqrt{2}}{2} = 6 \pm 3\sqrt{2}.$$

$6 + 3\sqrt{2}$ is greater than 3, but x must be smaller than 3, so the answer is $x = 6 - 3\sqrt{2}$.)

2. The circle below has radius r. Square S has a side lying along a diameter of the circle, and its other two vertices lie on the circle. Square T's diagonal is a radius of the circle. If S's area is A_S and T's area is A_T, what is $\frac{A_S}{A_T}$?

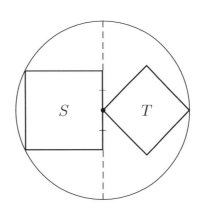

A. $\frac{4\pi}{5}$

B. $\frac{8}{5}$

C. $\frac{3r}{2}$

D. 1

E. $\frac{\pi r^2}{3}$

ANSWER: B. Square T has a diagonal of length r, so its sides each have length $\frac{r}{\sqrt{2}}$. Thus, $A_T = \frac{r^2}{2}$.

To find the length of a side of square S, consider the triangle formed by adding a radius as shown below.

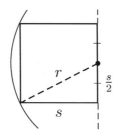

Since the original diagram shows that the circle's center bisects the right side of the square, we can label the lengths as in this diagram. Therefore, we get

$$s^2 + \left(\frac{s}{2}\right)^2 = r^2$$
$$\frac{5s^2}{4} = r^2$$
$$s^2 = \frac{4r^2}{5}.$$

Since $A_S = s^2$, we have determined that $A_S = \frac{4r^2}{5}$.

Now we can find $\frac{A_S}{A_T}$:

$$\frac{A_S}{A_T} = A_S \times \frac{1}{A_T} = \frac{4r^2}{5} \times \frac{2}{r^2} = \frac{8}{5}.$$

This next problem illustrates two points that you should keep in mind: First, don't assume more than the figure tells you. (This is particularly important if the figure is not drawn to scale, as is the case here.) Second, if you can't figure out how to get to the answer using the information given in the problem, it might be useful to try to work backwards, figuring out what information you would need in order to get the answer—you might find that you'll be able to meet in the middle, by working forward and backward, and solve the problem.

3. In the figure below, AC is a diameter of the circle, $\angle BAD = 60°$, and $AB = AD = 2\sqrt{3}$. What is the area of $\triangle BCD$?

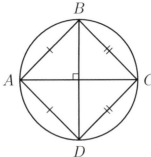

Note: Figure not drawn to scale.

A. 3π

B. $3\pi - \sqrt{3}$

C. 6

D. $\sqrt{3}$

E. $2\sqrt{6}$

ANSWER: D. It is important not to be confused by the figure, which is not drawn to scale. For example, it looks like $\angle BAD$ is a right angle, but we are told it is 60°.

So what do we know? First of all, since $AB = AD$, $\triangle ABD$ is isosceles with $\angle ABD = \angle ADB$. But then, since $\angle BAD = 60°$, $\triangle ABD$ is in fact equilateral, so we know that $BD = 2\sqrt{3}$, also.

Let's name the point where BD intersects AC; we'll call it point E. To find the area of $\triangle BCD$, all we need now is the length of EC. Well, since AC is a diameter of the circle, we know that $\angle ABC$ is a right angle. Therefore, since $\angle ABD = 60°$, we can deduce that $\angle DBC = 30°$. And since BD and AC are perpendicular, $\triangle BCE$ is 30°-60°-90°.

But we still need to know the length of one of the legs of $\triangle BCE$. We know that $\triangle ABE$ is another 30°-60°-90° triangle, so since $AB = 2\sqrt{3}$, we find that $BE = \sqrt{3}$. Therefore, $EC = \frac{\sqrt{3}}{\sqrt{3}} = 1$. This enables us to compute the area of $\triangle BCD$: $\frac{1}{2} \times 2\sqrt{3} \times 1 = \sqrt{3}$.

Another way to approach this problem, after realizing that $\triangle ABD$ is equilateral and so $BD = 2\sqrt{3}$, is to recall that opposite angles of a quadrilateral inscribed in a circle are supplementary. (This is because two opposite angles subtend 2 arcs that total the whole circle, 360°. Since the vertices of the angles are on the circle, together they measure half this amount, or 180°.) This means that $\angle BCD = 120°$. Since $\triangle BCD$ is isosceles, the other two angles must each be 30°. Furthermore, since EC is the perpendicular to the base, it bisects both $\angle BCD$ and the side BD, so $BE = \sqrt{3}$ (since it is half of BD); then $EC = 1$ by the properties of 30°-60°-90° triangles. Now we compute the desired area as before.

Sometimes it may be useful to imagine moving parts of the figure around to get a better grasp of what is being asked. For example, you could solve the next problem without mentally rearranging the pieces, but it becomes much easier when you do so in the right way.

4. The figure below, which consists of 5 squares and 4 quarter circles, has a total area of $180 + 36\pi$. What is its perimeter?

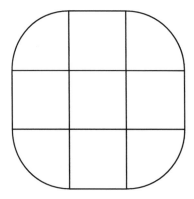

   A. 180

   B. $24 + 12\pi$

   C. $36 + 12\pi$

   D. $36 + 6\pi$

   E. $24 + 6\pi$

ANSWER: B. There are two very important things to notice about this figure. One is that if we were to combine all four corner regions, we would get a single complete circle. The other is that all five squares have sides of the same length, and this is the same as the radius of the pieced-together circle; call this length s. The perimeter of the figure is then $4s$ (s on the top, bottom, left, and right) plus the circumference of the circle, for a total of $4s + 2\pi s$.

The total area of the figure is the sum of the areas of the five squares and the corner sections. Since we are given that the area is $180 + 36\pi$, we have

$$5s^2 + \pi s^2 = 180 + 36\pi.$$

One way to find s is to guess that the coefficients of π must match on both sides of the equation. This gives $s^2 = 36$, so $s = 6$. We can test whether this guess is correct by checking that it satisfies the equation for the area. Once we verify that, we plug $s = 6$ into our formula for the perimeter to get our answer.

We could also solve for s without guessing that the coefficients of π had to match. Here is how: we can rearrange

$$5s^2 + \pi s^2 = 180 + 36\pi$$

to get

$$s^2 = \frac{180 + 36\pi}{5 + \pi}$$

by factoring s^2 out of the left-hand side and dividing by $5+\pi$. Notice that $180 = 36 \times 5$, so we can factor 36 out of the numerator on the right-hand side, leaving $5 + \pi$. This cancels out the denominator, so we get $s^2 = 36$, so $s = 6$.

Some geometry problems you will face are described only in words, without an accompanying figure. For these problems, it is usually helpful to draw yourself a figure so that you can see what is going on and what information will help you solve the problem. Obviously, it is very important to draw a figure that accurately represents the problem as stated, but even if your sketch is very true to the problem, it is still only a sketch. Make sure that you can justify by geometric principles any conclusions you draw; basing your answer only on the way you drew your figure can be dangerous. The next few problems will help you exercise the skills needed to tackle problems without provided figures.

5. The three points $(0,0)$, $(0,10)$, and $(5,0)$ are three vertices of a parallelogram. How many possibilities are there for the position of the fourth vertex?

   A. 0; this situation is impossible

   B. 1

   C. 2

   D. 3

   E. Infinitely many possibilities

ANSWER: D. We are told only the vertices of the parallelogram, not the edges, so let's consider the different ways we might connect those vertices together. Let's call the points $(0,0)$, $(0,10)$, and $(5,0)$ A, B, and C, respectively.

One thing we can do is connect A to B to C. The last vertex (which we'll call D), therefore, has to connect to A and to C to form edges parallel and equal in length to BC and to AB, respectively. AB is vertical and has length 10, so D should be either $(5, 10)$ or $(5, -10)$ in order to make CD match AB. A quick check reveals that only $(5, -10)$ makes AD parallel to BC, so this gives one possibility for D.

Another way we can connect the vertices is B-C-A. Now D has to connect to B and to A. Similarly to the case above, for BD to be parallel to and the same length as AC, D must be either $(-5, 10)$ or $(5, 10)$, but only the former works when comparing AD against BC, so we have one more possibility.

The final way to connect these vertices is C-A-B. These connections mean that we are forming a rectangle, and the final vertex has to be at $(5, 10)$. (Remember that a rectangle is a parallelogram, so this counts in our answer.)

There is no other way to connect A, B, and C together, and since each way of connecting them determines a unique value for the fourth vertex of a parallelogram, these are the only possibilities.

The image below shows the possible parallelograms.

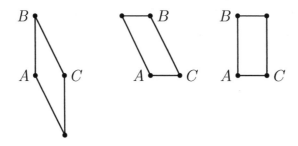

6. A quadrilateral has endpoints at $(-1, -1)$, $(3, 1)$, $(1, 5)$, and $(-3, 3)$. Which term describes this shape as specifically as possible?

   A. Quadrilateral

   B. Parallelogram

   C. Rhombus

   D. Rectangle

   E. Square

ANSWER: E. The shape, a square, is drawn below.

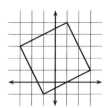

Now let's see how we can reach this conclusion without the picture: First we calculate the slopes of the edges.

- From $(-1, -1)$ to $(3, 1)$ is a slope of $\frac{1-(-1)}{3-(-1)} = \frac{2}{4} = \frac{1}{2}$.
- From $(3, 1)$ to $(1, 5)$ is a slope of $\frac{5-1}{1-3} = \frac{4}{-2} = -2$.
- From $(1, 5)$ to $(-3, 3)$ is a slope of $\frac{3-5}{-3-1} = \frac{-2}{-4} = \frac{1}{2}$.
- Finally, the slope from $(-3, 3)$ to $(-1, -1)$ is $\frac{-1-3}{-1-(-3)} = \frac{-4}{2} = -2$.

We see that opposite sides are parallel and further that adjacent sides form right angles, because the slopes are negative reciprocals of each other. So we have a rectangle.

However, we must also consider the lengths of the sides to see if this rectangle is in fact a square. The lengths are:

- $(-1, -1)$ to $(3, 1)$: $\sqrt{4^2 + 2^2} = \sqrt{20}$;
- $(3, 1)$ to $(1, 5)$: $\sqrt{2^2 + 4^2} = \sqrt{20}$;
- $(1, 5)$ to $(-3, 3)$: $\sqrt{4^2 + 2^2} = \sqrt{20}$;
- $(-3, 3)$ to $(-1, -1)$: $\sqrt{2^2 + 4^2} = \sqrt{20}$.

Since all of these are equal, the rectangle is in fact a square, so the answer is E..

7. A regular hexagon circumscribes a circle of radius 1. What is the radius of a circle which circumscribes this hexagon?

    A. $\frac{2\sqrt{3}}{3}$

    B. $\pi\sqrt{2}$

    C. $\frac{\sqrt{3}}{2}$

    D. $\frac{1}{3\pi}$

    E. $\frac{36\pi}{4}$

ANSWER: A. The problem describes the following picture, but we have added some points and lines:

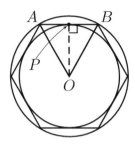

Note that AO and BO are radii of the larger circle, so $\triangle AOB$ is isosceles with angles $\angle OAP$ and $\angle OBP$ congruent. Also, since the hexagon is regular, $\angle AOB = \frac{360°}{6} = 60°$. This tells us that $\triangle AOB$ is in fact equilateral, so $\angle OAP = 60°$, too. Notice that line OP is a radius of the smaller circle, and AB is tangent to the circle; so $\angle OPA$, formed by those lines, is a right angle.

We now know that $\triangle OPA$ is a 30°-60°-90° triangle. The problem tells us that $OP = 1$, so we can determine that $AP = \frac{1}{\sqrt{3}} = \frac{\sqrt{3}}{3}$ and that $AO = \frac{2\sqrt{3}}{3}$.

In many geometry problems, you can solve the problem directly, taking the information you are given and moving step by step toward a solution. Sometimes, though, you will need to solve a problem indirectly, assigning variables to some quantities in your problem and setting up equations which you will solve to find what these values must be. There are, of course, always going to be lots of lengths and areas to choose from; It is important to choose the right ones to get you to the answer in a reasonable way. Here are some problems that require such choices; they should help you get a feel for what parts of the figure are important to focus on.

8. In the figure below, $BC = a$ and $AB = b$. What must x be if the area of trapezoid $BCED$ equals the area of $\triangle ADE$?

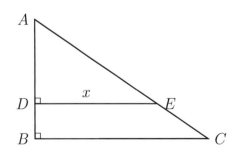

A. $\frac{a+b}{2}$

B. $\frac{a\sqrt{2}}{2}$

C. $b\sqrt{2}$

D. $\frac{ab}{4}$

E. $\frac{a+b}{4a}$

ANSWER: B. If we let $y = AD$, then we can calculate that the area of $\triangle ADE$ is $\frac{xy}{2}$. The problem tells us that this is also the area of trapezoid $BCED$. We can also see that these two areas sum up to the area of $\triangle ABC$. That is, we know that $\frac{xy}{2} + \frac{xy}{2} = \frac{ab}{2}$, so $xy = \frac{ab}{2}$ and $y = \frac{ab}{2x}$.

Notice that $\triangle ABC$ and $\triangle ADE$ are similar. This means that

$$\frac{a}{b} = \frac{x}{y} = \frac{2x^2}{ab}.$$

Isolating x^2 gives $\frac{a^2}{2} = x^2$, so we get

$$x = \frac{a}{\sqrt{2}} = \frac{a\sqrt{2}}{2}.$$

9. The racetrack below consists of two semicircular regions connected by a rectangular region. All angles in the figure are right angles, and the two semicircles on the left are concentric, as are the two on the right. What is the least amount of information you would need to determine how much longer the outer track is than the inner track?

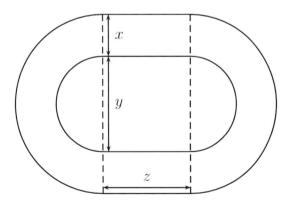

A. The value of x

B. The value of y

C. The value of z

D. The values of x and y

E. The values of y and z

ANSWER: A. Both tracks have the same length in the rectangular region. (This length is $2z$ for each track: z on the top and z again on the bottom. However, since we only care about the difference between the two tracks, this length doesn't matter for this problem.)

The only difference between the two tracks is the circumferences of the semicircles—and since there are two semicircles on each track, we can treat each as one complete circle. (If this is not immediately clear, imagine deleting the rectangular region and bringing the two semicircles of each size together.) Since y is the diameter of the inner track's circle, its circumference is πy. The diameter of the outer circle is $2x + y$, so its circumference is $\pi(2x + y)$. The difference, therefore, is

$$\pi(2x + y) - \pi y = 2\pi x,$$

so the only thing we need to know is x.

10. The figure below is a trapezoid with its top and bottom sides parallel. We can split the trapezoid into three regions—two triangular regions around a central rectangle—as shown below. If the central rectangle accounts for two-thirds of the trapezoid's total area, what is the length of the trapezoid's bottom side, expressed in terms of the length, s, of its left side?

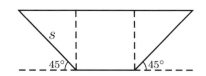

Note: Figure not drawn to scale.

A. s

B. $s\sqrt{2}$

C. $s\sqrt{3}$

D. $2s$

E. s^2

ANSWER: B. Because the top and bottom sides of the trapezoid are parallel, the 45° angles we are told about imply that the two triangular regions in the trapezoids are themselves 45°-45°-90° triangles. This means that the legs of left-hand triangle have length $\frac{s\sqrt{2}}{2}$ and, again since the top and bottom of the trapezoid are parallel, we see that the legs of the right-hand triangle have the same length.

Let's call the length we're looking for—the length of the bottom side—x. We can express the area of the trapezoid as the sum of the areas of the three regions:

$$xs\frac{\sqrt{2}}{2} \quad + \quad \frac{1}{2} \times s\frac{\sqrt{2}}{2} \times s\frac{\sqrt{2}}{2} \quad + \quad \frac{1}{2} \times s\frac{\sqrt{2}}{2} \times s\frac{\sqrt{2}}{2},$$

which can be simplified to $xs\frac{\sqrt{2}}{2} + \frac{s^2}{2}$. We want the area of the rectangle, $xs\frac{\sqrt{2}}{2}$, to be two-thirds of the total area, so we want to find a value for x which satisfies

$$xs\frac{\sqrt{2}}{2} = \frac{2}{3}\left(xs\frac{\sqrt{2}}{2} + \frac{s^2}{2}\right).$$

Distributing and moving the terms with x to the left side, this is

$$xs\frac{\sqrt{2}}{6} = \frac{s^2}{3}, \quad \text{so} \quad x = \frac{2s}{\sqrt{2}} = s\sqrt{2}.$$

Practice Problems

Okay! Now it's time to practice some more problems on your own. Get to it!

1. A rectangle has circles, all of which are congruent, covering its perimeter as shown below. The corner circles are centered on the corners of the rectangle; the other circles are also centered on the rectangle's perimeter; and each circle is tangent to the neighboring ones. If the rectangle's area is 1800, what is the total area of all of the shaded regions?

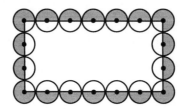

   A. 25π

   B. 72π

   C. 100π

   D. 144π

   E. 250π

2. The curve from A to C is a semicircle, and $\angle B$ is a right angle.

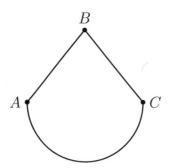

Note: Figure not drawn to scale.

If we were to complete the circle in the figure, which of the following would be possible?

   I. B lies inside the circle.
   II. B lies outside the circle.
   III. B lies on the circle.

    A. I only

    B. III only

    C. I and III only

    D. II and III only

    E. I, II, and III

3. The figure below consists of two semicircular regions connected by a rectangular region. All angles in the figure are right angles, and the two semicircles on the left are concentric, as are the two on the right. If figure's outer boundary (the thin solid loop) has length $16 + 25\pi$, what is the length of the bold loop?

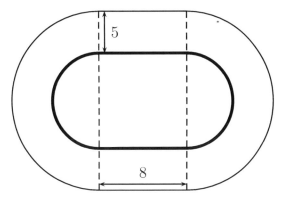

Note: Figure not drawn to scale.

    A. $8 + 7.5\pi$

    B. $8 + 10\pi$

    C. $16 + 15\pi$

    D. $16 + 16\pi$

    E. $32 + 18\pi$

4. The two circles, centered at O and P, each have a radius of 5. If $\angle A$ is a right angle and $AB = AC = 1$, what is the length of DE?

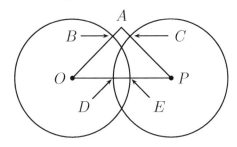

A. $\frac{5\pi}{2}$

B. $\sqrt{2}$

C. 1

D. $10 - 6\sqrt{2}$

E. $5 - 3\sqrt{2}$

5. A circle circumscribes a square with sides of length s. Four squares congruent to the first are tangent to the circle where it touches the inscribed square, as shown. What is the area of the shaded region?

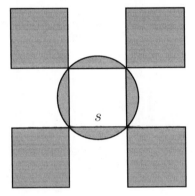

A. $5s + \frac{s^2}{\pi}$

B. $4s^2 + \frac{s}{2}\pi$

C. $3s^2 + \frac{s^2}{2}\pi$

D. $s^2(2 + \pi)$

E. $s + \frac{s^2}{4}\pi$

6. $\triangle ABC$ sits within a regular hexagon with sides of length 1. What is the area of $\triangle ABC$?

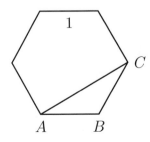

A. $\frac{\sqrt{3}}{8}$

B. $1 + \sqrt{2}$

C. 2

D. $\frac{\sqrt{3}}{4}$

E. $\frac{4\sqrt{3}}{3}$

7. The figure below depicts a square and two triangles. What is the distance between points A and B?

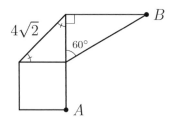

A. $4\sqrt{7}$

B. $5\sqrt{2}$

C. 12

D. 8

E. $4\sqrt{5}$

8. Triangle T has area A and square S has area $2A$. Which of the following *may* be true?

  I.   The perimeter of T is smaller than the perimeter of S.
  II. The perimeter of T is equal to the perimeter of S.
  III. The perimeter of T is greater than the perimeter of S.

A. I only

B. III only

C. I and II only

D. II and III only

E. I, II, and III

9. In the diagram, $ABCD$ is a rectangle, $\angle BGA = 90°$, and $AEFD$ and the shaded region are each squares. Also, $BE = a$ and $EA = b$. What is the area of the shaded square, expressed using only a and b?

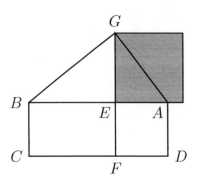

A. $\frac{(a+b)^2}{2}$

B. $2(a-b)^2$

C. $a^2 - b^2$

D. $4b^2 - a^2$

E. ab

10. An eccentric farmer has a parallelogram-shaped pen for his sheep, with a base of length 12 and a height of 3π. One day, he decides that his sheep need more space, so he chooses to enlarge his pen so that it becomes, in total, 81π square meters. He wants to do this using a circular extension, centered at the lower-right corner of the parallelogram, as indicated. What must the radius of this extension be if the farmer's strange desires are to be satisfied?

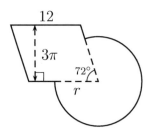

A. 6

B. 2π

C. $3\sqrt{5}$

D. $\frac{15}{2}$

E. $6\sqrt{3}$

11. In the figure, AB is tangent to two congruent circles, which are centered at C and D. Also, the length of FE is 10. What is the circles' radius?

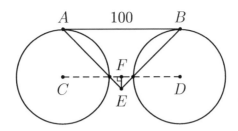

A. $10\sqrt{2}$

B. $25\sqrt{2}$

C. 40

D. $\frac{100\sqrt{3}}{3}$

E. $50\sqrt{2}$

12. An equilateral triangle whose area is $27\sqrt{3}$ is inscribed in a circle. What is the circle's radius?

A. $2\sqrt{2}$

B. 3

C. 6

D. $6\sqrt{3}$

E. $36\sqrt{3}$

13. In the diagram, the larger circles each have radius 3 while the smaller circles each have radius 1. If we were to continue placing circles with radii alternating between 3 and 1 around the entire perimeter of the rectangle, with each circle being tangent to the adjacent circles, how many circles would there be in all?

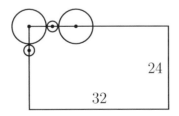

Note: Figure not drawn to scale.

A. 24

B. 28

    C. 32

    D. 36

    E. 40

14. The curve from A to C is a semicircle. If the length of the semicircle is 3π, what is the length of the path from A to C along the upper edges (i.e. what is $AB + BC$)?

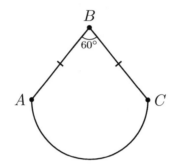

Note: Figure not drawn to scale.

    A. $\frac{4}{3}$

    B. 12

    C. 6π

    D. $\frac{3\pi}{2}$

    E. $\pi\sqrt{3}$

Solutions to Practice Problems

1. **E.** If we call the radius of the circles r, then the rectangle is $6r$ by $12r$. Since its area is 1800, we see that
$$1800 = 6r \times 12r = 72r^2,$$
so $r^2 = 25$ and $r = 5$. This means that each circle's area is 25π.

   Counting up the shaded areas, we find that there are 14 shaded semicircles and 4 circles which are three-quarters shaded. This means there are the equivalent of
$$14 \times \frac{1}{2} + 4 \times \frac{3}{4} = 7 + 3 = 10$$
full circles shaded, so the total shaded area is $10 \times 25\pi = 250\pi$.

2. **B.** First let's consider if B can lie on the circle. An important fact about circles is that, given three points A, B, and C on the circle, $\angle ABC = 90°$ if and only if AC is a diameter of the circle. This is true here, so B lying on the circle is a possibility.

   Can B lie outside the circle? If it did, then there would be a point D on the circle which is inside $\triangle ABC$. Since $\angle B = 90°$, $\angle ADC$ must be greater than $90°$. But this can't be, because of the point just mentioned above — points on the circle always form right angles with diameters of the circle. So B can't lie outside the circle.

   Similarly, if B were inside the circle, we could find a comparable $\angle ADC$ that should be a right angle by the property stated above, but we would have a problem because $\angle B$ is a right angle. This is not possible, either.

   The only possibility, therefore, is III.

3. **C.** Let's call the radius of the inner circle r. Since the circles are concentric, we know that the radius of the outer circle is $5 + r$. The perimeter of the outer loop, which we are told is $16 + 25\pi$, can also be expressed as
$$2 \times 8 + 2\pi \times (5 + r) = 16 + 10\pi + 2\pi r.$$

   (Here, the 2×8 accounts for the straightaways and the $2\pi(5 + r)$ is the length of the circular portion of the loop, a circle with radius $5 + r$.) Equating these gives
$$16 + 10\pi + 2\pi r = 16 + 25\pi,$$
which leads to $r = 7.5$.

   From this, it is straightforward to calculate the answer: 16 for the straightaways and $2\pi \times 7.5 = 15\pi$ for the circular parts.

4. **D.** Notice that $OP = OE + DP - DE$, and we know that $OE = DP = 5$ since both are radii. Rearranging to solve for DE gives $DE = OE + DP - OP = 10 - OP$. Now all we need is the length of OP.

   Since OB and PC are radii of the circles, both have length 5, so $OA = AP = 6$. Therefore, $\triangle AOP$ is isosceles and, since $\angle A$ is a right angle, $\triangle AOP$ is 45°-45°-90°. Using the rule for such triangles, we find that $OP = 6\sqrt{2}$.

   Plugging this in to our equation above, we get $DE = 10 - 6\sqrt{2}$.

5. **C.** Rather than computing the areas of each of the small regions independently, notice that we can "fill in" the hole in the central circle with one of the external squares:

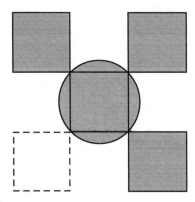

   This shows that the total shaded area is the area of 3 squares plus the area of the circle. Each square's area is clearly s^2. Also, we know that the diameter of the circle is the diagonal of a square, which is $s\sqrt{2}$. Therefore, the radius is $\frac{s\sqrt{2}}{2}$, so the circle's area is $\pi \frac{s^2}{2}$. Adding this to three squares' area gives us $3s^2 + \pi \frac{s^2}{2}$.

   (Of course, without realizing that you can "fill in" the hole in the central circle, you can still solve the problem. You would find the area of the circle, $\pi \frac{s^2}{2}$, and subtract out the area of the *unshaded* square region within the circle, s^2, to find the area of the shaded region in the circle, $\pi \frac{s^2}{2} - s^2$. Then, add to this the areas of the four external squares, $4s^2$, to get the final answer: $(\pi \frac{s^2}{2} - s^2) + 4s^2 = \pi \frac{s^2}{2} + 3s^2$.)

6. **D.** The key facts here are that regular hexagons have angles of 120° and that the altitude to the unequal side of an isosceles triangle bisects both the side and the opposite angle. With these two facts in hand, consider what happens when we draw the altitude of isosceles $\triangle ABC$ from B to AC.

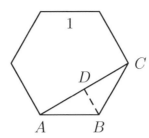

Notice that $\triangle ABD$ is congruent to $\triangle CBD$. This means we can calculate the area for one of the triangles, say $\triangle ABD$, and then double it to get our final answer.

Since the altitude bisects $\angle ABC$, which is $120°$, we can deduce that $\angle ABD = \angle CBD = 60°$. We know that $\angle ADB$ is a right angle because BD is an altitude. So we can use the formula for $30°$-$60°$-$90°$ triangles to find the height, AD, and length of the base, BD, of the triangle:

$$\begin{aligned} AB &= 2 \times BD \quad \text{and} \\ AD &= \sqrt{3} \times BD. \end{aligned}$$

We are given that each side of the hexagon has length 1, so $AB = 1$; this gives us $BD = \frac{1}{2}$ and, therefore, $AD = \frac{\sqrt{3}}{2}$. The area of $\triangle ABD$ is half the product of these two lengths, $\frac{1}{2} \times \frac{\sqrt{3}}{2} \times \frac{1}{2}$. Doubling this to account for $\triangle CBD$'s area as well gives the answer, $\frac{\sqrt{3}}{2} \times \frac{1}{2} = \frac{\sqrt{3}}{4}$.

7. **A.** We can deduce from the two congruent angles that the triangle on the left is isosceles. Also, the square's angles are right angles, so the triangle's third angle must also be $90°$ because together they add up to $180°$, a straight line. So the triangle on the left is a $45°$-$45°$-$90°$ triangle and, given the $4\sqrt{2}$ length of the hypotenuse, we know that the legs have length 4. The other sides of the square must also have length 4, then, so the vertical distance from A to B is 8: a side of the square plus a leg of the triangle.

Since the smallest leg of the $30°$-$60°$-$90°$ triangle has length 4, we know that the side opposite the $60°$ angle has length $4\sqrt{3}$. This is the horizontal distance from A to B.

We can now find the distance from A to B by the Pythagorean theorem:

$$AB = \sqrt{8^2 + (4\sqrt{3})^2} = \sqrt{64 + 16 \times 3}.$$

We can factor out 16 from this sum to get $\sqrt{16 \times (4 + 3)} = 4\sqrt{7}$.

8. **E.** Since the area of a square is s^2, where s is the length of a side, we know that $s = \sqrt{2A}$, so S's perimeter is $4s = 4\sqrt{2A}$. For our purposes, the main thing to note is that the perimeter of S is fixed; that is, given the area, we know the perimeter. This is not the case for T—the perimeter of a triangle is not determined by its area. (That is, there are many triangles with different perimeters that all have the same area.) In fact, it is relatively simple to construct many triangles with area A, some with perimeters smaller than S and some with perimeters larger than S.

For example, consider the figure below, in which the dotted lines depict the square S. The three triangles each have a base of length s and a height of s, so their areas are each $\frac{1}{2}s^2 = A$. Therefore, any of these triangles could be triangle T.

 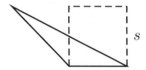 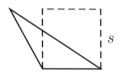

The left most triangle's perimeter is clearly less than S's perimeter, $4s$. (We can even calculate the triangle's perimeter: it is $2s + s\sqrt{2} = (2 + \sqrt{2})s$, which is less than $4s$ because $\sqrt{2} < 2$, so $2 + \sqrt{2} < 2 + 2 = 4$.) Thus, statement I is possible.

If we slide the top point of the triangle far enough to the side (while keeping it on the same horizontal line), we can get the middle triangle, whose perimeter is greater that $4s$. (If it isn't clear that this perimeter is greater than $4s$, imagine sliding the top point even farther to the left; when the point is very far away, the perimeter must be rather large.) This shows that III is possible.

Also, since we can get a smaller perimeter and a larger perimeter, there must be a point at which we get a perimeter of exactly $4s$. The rightmost triangle illustrates this, although it is a bit complicated to calculate this point exactly.

So we see that all three of I, II, and III are possible.

9. **E.** Since $AEFD$ is a square, the lines FG and AB are perpendicular. Also, since $\angle AGB = 90°$, $\triangle AGB$ is a right triangle, and GE is the altitude to its hypotenuse. From this, we can conclude that $\triangle GEB$ and $\triangle AEG$ are similar triangles, which implies

$$\frac{AE}{EG} = \frac{EG}{BE}.$$

Thus we get $(EG)^2 = (BE)(AE) = ab$. Since EG is a side of the shaded square, ab is the area of the shaded region.

10. **D.** First, let's calculate the area of the original pen, i.e., the parallelogram: this is just the length times the height, $12 \times 3\pi = 36\pi$. Since we want the circular extension to bring the total area to 81π, the extension should add $81\pi - 36\pi = 45\pi$ to the area of the pen. The total area of the circle will, of course, be πr^2, but notice that some of that area was already part of the pen. We have to figure out how much of the circle contributes to additional area.

We see that the angle formed by the pen walls was $72°$, so the fraction of the circle that is adding new area to the pen is

$$\frac{360 - 72}{360} = 1 - \frac{1}{5} = \frac{4}{5}.$$

This means that we want the radius to satisfy $\frac{4}{5}\pi r^2 = 45\pi$, so

$$r = \sqrt{\frac{5 \times 45}{4}} = \sqrt{\frac{225}{4}} = \frac{15}{2}.$$

11. **C.** First, let's add some lines and labels to the figure:

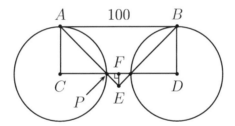

Notice that $ABCD$ is a rectangle: Since AB is tangent to the circles, $\angle CAB = \angle ABD = 90°$. This means that AC and BD are parallel, so $\angle C = \angle D$. The angles in a quadrilateral add up to $360°$, so $\angle C + \angle D = 180°$, so both must be right angles.

$\triangle ACP$ is isosceles because its two legs are radii; since it is also a right triangle, $\angle CAP = 45°$. This means that $\angle BAE = 45°$ as well. Similar reasoning reveals that $\angle ABE = 45°$, too, so $\triangle ABE$ is a $45°$-$45°$-$90°$ triangle.

AB and CD are parallel, so if we extend EF to AB, we get an altitude of $\triangle ABE$. Then, since $\triangle ABE$ is $45°$-$45°$-$90°$, this altitude bisects AB and splits $\triangle ABE$ into two smaller $45°$-$45°$-$90°$ triangles. From this, we can figure out that the height of $\triangle ABE$ is equal to half of the length of AB, so it is 50. AC, a radius, is the height of $\triangle ABE$ minus the length of FE, or $50 - 10 = 40$. So 40 is our answer.

Here is another way we could have solved this problem: After realizing that $\angle CAP = 45°$, we can conclude that $\angle FEP = 45°$, because AC and EF are parallel and both angles are formed by the same line segment, AE. Since $\angle EFP = 90°$, $\triangle EFP$ must be 45°-45°-90°, so $FP = FE = 10$. Then, as above, note that extending EF to AB bisects AB. This shows that $CF = 50$, since it is half as long as AB. Then we get $CP = CF - FP = 50 - 10 = 40$.

12. **C.** The figure below depicts the situation described in the problem.

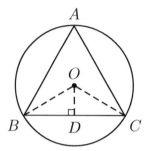

We are told that the area of $\triangle ABC$ is $27\sqrt{3}$. The formula for the area of an equilateral triangle is $\frac{\sqrt{3}}{4}s^2$, where s is the length of a side. (If you are not familiar with this formula, convince yourself that it is correct. It can be seen by dropping an altitude and reasoning about the resulting 30°-60°-90° triangles.) Therefore,

$$\frac{\sqrt{3}}{4}s^2 = 27\sqrt{3}, \quad \text{so} \quad s^2 = 4 \times 27, \quad \text{and} \quad s = \sqrt{4 \times 27} = 2 \times 3\sqrt{3} = 6\sqrt{3}.$$

But this isn't the answer; we need to know more. OB and OC are radii, so $\triangle OBC$ is isosceles. Also notice that $\angle BOC = 120°$ because it encompasses exactly one third of the circle, and angles at the center of the circle have the same measure as the arc they encompass. This means that $\angle OBC = \angle OCB = 30°$, so if we drop an altitude from O to a point D on BC, we know that both $\triangle BOD$ and $\triangle COD$ are 30°-60°-90° triangles. Also, those two triangles are congruent, so $BD = DC$. But BC is a side of the triangle, so $BC = 6\sqrt{3}$, which means that $BD = 3\sqrt{3}$. Then, by the formula for 30°-60°-90° triangles, we know that $OD = 3$ and $OB = 6$, which is our answer.

13. **B.** We can simply move around the perimeter of the rectangle, keeping count. Along the side of length 24, the first circle (whose center is the corner of the rectangle) extends 3 units along the side. The next few circles have their diameters lying along the side of the rectangle; they extend 2 units, then 6, then 2, etc., beyond the last. So the total length covered after the second circle is $3 + 2 = 5$, then $5 + 6 = 11$ after the third, then 13, then 19, then 21. Finally, the next circle, which has radius 3, reaches the corner of the rectangle at a distance of 24 from the previous corner. This is a total of 7 circles.

Continuing the count along the long side of the rectangle shows that there are 9 circles on this side: the first covers 3 units, the next extends 2 more to reach 5, the next reaches 11, then 13, 19, 21, 27, 29, and then the next *radius* of length 3 reaches 32.

The next short side is just like the first one, so it will have another 7 circles. Similarly, the final side, another long side, will have 9 circles. However, it is important to notice that we counted each of the corner circles twice: once when we were looking at the short side of the rectangle and once when looking at the long side. Therefore, our total number of circles is 18 along the long sides, plus 14 along the short sides, minus the 4 corner circles, which we've counted twice, giving us $18 + 14 - 4 = 28$ circles.

14. **B.** The figure shows that $AB = BC$ and, since $\angle B = 60°$, we can deduce that $\triangle ABC$ is equilateral.

    We also know that the semicircle has length 3π, so the entire circle's circumference is 6π and its diameter is 6.

    Since AC is a diameter of the circle, $AC = 6$. Therefore, since $\triangle ABC$ is equilateral, $AB = BC = AC = 6$, so $AB + BC = 12$.

CHAPTER 11

SOLIDS

Solids problems on the SAT include spheres, right cones, cylinders, rectangular prisms, cubes, triangular and square pyramids, and hexagonal or octagonal prisms. Solid geometry generalizes plane geometry to three dimensions, adding the concept of volume, although some problems ask only for surface area. Whereas plane figures have only vertices (corners) and edges (sides), solids have vertices, edges, and faces. Working with solids sometimes requires examining specific cross sections. This simplifies matters by reducing the dimension of the object from a 3-D solid to a 2-D flat cross-section that lies in a plane. This allows us to use familiar concepts and formulas from plane geometry. Sometimes the Pythagorean theorem should be used multiple times in evaluating lengths of diagonals, heights, or lengths and widths.

Mistakes on problems involving solids can often be avoided by carefully reading the question, carefully drawing a diagram if one is not supplied, then labeling the values of the components of the figure such as the length of edges, height of the figure, or any other portion of a figure. Often it is important to recognize a right angle, and if so, the angle should be labeled. Then, it is also helpful to write the formula for the volume or surface area of the solid or portion of the solid in terms of its individual constants, and then inserting the known values of the constant into the formula.

Surface Area and Volume

The surface area and volume of the solids are summarized in a table below:

Note: e = edge of pyramid, s = height of face of pyramid, h = height, r = radius

Solid	Surface Area	Volume
1. Rectangular prism	$2lh + 2lw + 2hw$	lwh
2. Cube	$6s^2$ (s = side)	s^3
3. Cylinder	$2rh\pi + 2r^2\pi$	$\pi r^2 h$
4. Right cone	(lateral) $\pi r \sqrt{r^2 + h^2}$	$\frac{1}{3}\pi r^2 h$
5. Triangular pyramid (tetrahedron)	$3 \times \frac{1}{2}es + e^2$ (e = edge, s = side)	$\frac{1}{3}Bh$
6. Square pyramid	$4 \times \frac{1}{2}es + e^2$	$\frac{1}{3}bh$
7. Sphere	$4\pi r^2$	$\frac{4}{3}\pi r^3$

Below are diagrams of the above solids, labeling the height, edges, and radii.

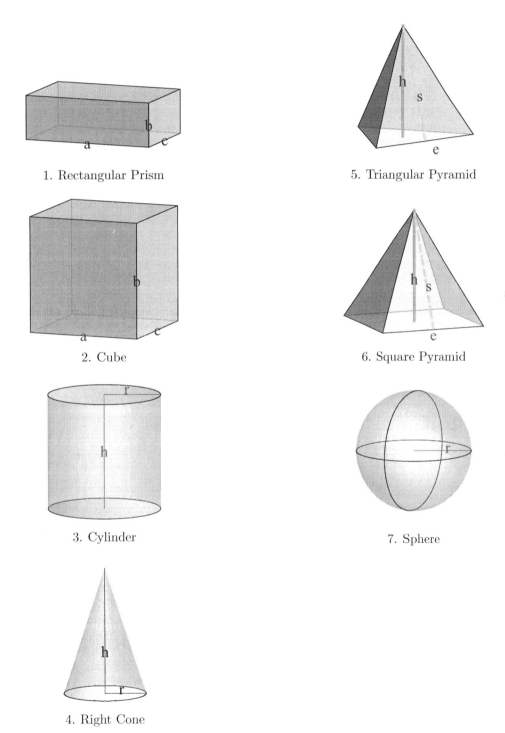

1. Rectangular Prism

5. Triangular Pyramid

2. Cube

6. Square Pyramid

3. Cylinder

7. Sphere

4. Right Cone

Problems with cubes often ask to find a length of a diagonal:

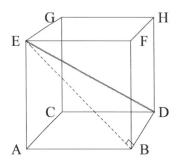

Diagonal ED is shown. To find the length of the diagonal we need the length of two other lines (in this case EB and BD) to produce a triangle, and then use the Pythagorean theorem.

In the above figure, the dashed line EB is drawn. If we can find this length, we can use it together with the length DB to find the hypotenuse ED.

The diagonal EB can be found also by the Pythagorean theorem.

$$ED = \sqrt{(EA)^2 + (AB)^2}.$$

If the length of each side is 5, $EB = 5\sqrt{2}$.

$$\begin{aligned}
(ED)^2 &= \left(5\sqrt{2}\right)^2 + 5^2 = 75 \\
ED &= \sqrt{75} = 5\sqrt{3}
\end{aligned}$$

In a cubic prism, it is always the case that the length of the diagonal adjoining one corner to the opposite top corner is equal to the length of a side of the cube times the square root of 3.

1. Each side of the cube below has length 4 times the square root of 3. What is the length of ED?

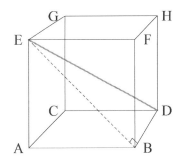

 A. 12

 B. $12\sqrt{3}$

 C. 16

 D. $16\sqrt{2}$

 E. $24\sqrt{3}$

 ANSWER: A. The diagonal is the length times the square root of three: $4*\sqrt{3}*\sqrt{3} = 4*3 = 12$.

2. The figure below is a 4 by 4 by 6 prism with a line that stretches from the midpoint, I, of AB to point H. What is the length of HI?

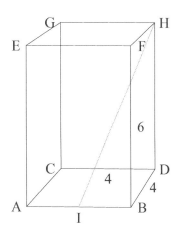

A. $2\sqrt{7}$

B. $3\sqrt{10}$

C. $2\sqrt{14}$

D. $3\sqrt{21}$

E. $4\sqrt{26}$

ANSWER: C.

$$
\begin{aligned}
(DI)^2 &= (IB)^2 + (BD)^2 \\
(DI)^2 &= 2^2 + 4^2 = 20 \\
DI &= \sqrt{20} \\
(HI)^2 &= (DI)^2 + (DH)^2 = 20 + 36 = 56 \\
HI = \sqrt{56} &= 2\sqrt{14}
\end{aligned}
$$

3. The figure below is a 3 by 3 by 3 cube made up of 1 by 1 by 1 cubes. The shaded black represents a hole; the innermost stack of 3 cubes is missing. What is the surface area of the figure?

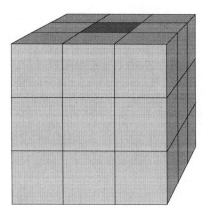

A. 48

B. 54

C. 58

D. 64

E. 68

ANSWER: D. We can use the surface area of a cube and add the surface area of the rectangular prism within, minus its top and bottom.

$$(6 \times 3 \times 3) + (1 \times 3 \times 4) - 1 - 1 = 64.$$

Problems with spheres often combine a sphere and another solid such as a cylinder. Equating the formula for the volume or surface area of a sphere with the volume or surface area of the other solid will yield a solvable equation in terms of a numerical value.

4. A sphere of radius r, and a cylinder whose height is h and whose base is a circle of radius r, have the same volume. What is the area of the base of the cylinder in terms of h? (The volume of a sphere is given by the formula $\frac{4}{3}\pi r^3$).
   A. $\frac{4\pi h^2}{3}$
   B. $\frac{9\pi h^2}{16}$
   C. $\frac{9\pi h^2}{4}$
   D. $\frac{16\pi h^2}{3}$
   E. $\frac{16\pi h^2}{9}$

ANSWER: B. The volume of a sphere is given by $\frac{4}{3}\pi r^3$ and the volume of a cylinder is given by $\pi r^2 h$. This gives rise to the following equation, which we solve for r:

$$\begin{aligned} \frac{4\pi r^3}{3} &= \pi r^2 h \\ r &= \frac{3h}{4} \end{aligned}$$

The area of the base of the cylinder is then

$$\pi r^2 = \pi \left(\frac{3h}{4}\right)^2 = \frac{9\pi h^2}{16}.$$

Square pyramid problems involve at least two steps. The problem is solved by moving steps backwards. You must ask yourself the question: What do we need to know in order to solve the problem? After the last step is determined, go back a step — how can we determine what we need to know?

5. In the square pyramid below, the area of one triangular face BPD is 30 ft^2. The slant height of one triangular face is 12 ft. What is the height of the pyramid?

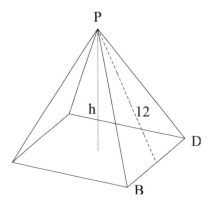

   A. $501\sqrt{3}$

   B. $252\sqrt{5}$

   C. $\frac{\sqrt{551}}{2}$

   D. $\frac{\sqrt{548}}{2}$

   E. None of the above

ANSWER: C.

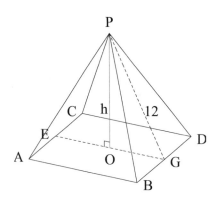

In order to find the height of the pyramid, we need to know the length of line segment GO. If we know that length, we can solve for the height by using the Pythagorean theorem, using length GO and the hypotenuse GP, the latter being the height of the face of the triangle. Going back a step, how do we determine length GO? Length GO is exactly half the distance GE. This is because the base is a square, and length GE is exactly the length of AB. Going back another step, What is the length AB? If the area of the face of the pyramid is 30 and the height is 12, we have $\frac{1}{2}BH =$ area of face of pyramid. Therefore

$$\frac{1}{2}B * 12 = 30$$
$$B = 5$$

So length AB is $\frac{5}{2}$, and therefore length GO is $\frac{5}{2}$ following the argument above. Using the Pythagorean theorem:

$$\left(\frac{5}{2}\right)^2 + h^2 = 12^2$$
$$\frac{25}{4} + h^2 = 144$$
$$h^2 = 144 - \frac{25}{4} = \frac{576}{4} - \frac{25}{4} = \frac{551}{4}.$$

Therefore, $h = \frac{\sqrt{551}}{2}$.

6. What is the height of the square pyramid below?

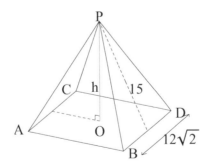

A. $2\sqrt{37}$

B. $2\sqrt{41}$

C. $2\sqrt{67}$

D. $3\sqrt{17}$

E. $3\sqrt{37}$

ANSWER: D.

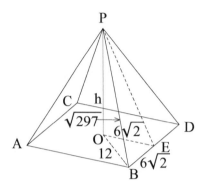

Here is a second way to calculate the height given similar information as in question five, this time using length BP. If we can find length OB and length BP, we can use the Pythagorean theorem to find the height OP. How do we find the length BP? If the base length is $12\sqrt{2}$, length BE is $6\sqrt{2}$. The height of the face of the pyramid is 15. So using the Pythagorean theorem:

$$
\begin{aligned}
BP^2 &= 15^2 + (6\sqrt{2})^2 = 297 \\
BP &= \sqrt{297}
\end{aligned}
$$

If length EB and EO are each $6\sqrt{2}$, using the Pythagorean theorem, length OB is 12. Using the Pythagorean theorem once more:

$$
\begin{aligned}
OB^2 + OP^2 &= \sqrt{297}^2 = 297 \\
12^2 + OP^2 &= 297 \\
OP^2 &= 153 \\
OP &= \text{height } = 3\sqrt{17}.
\end{aligned}
$$

Cone and cylinder problems can greatly vary, and most problems require a different method of solution for each type of problem. However ratios and the Pythagorean theorem are still often involved.

7. In the figure below, if $OE = 4\sqrt{2}$, $BC = 6$, $CD = 3$, $OB = 3$, what is the length of CE?

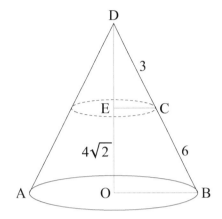

A. $\frac{\sqrt{3}}{4}$

B. $\frac{1}{2}$

C. $\frac{\sqrt{2}}{2}$

D. 1

E. $\sqrt{2}$

ANSWER: D. We can use similar triangles:

$$\frac{EC}{3} = \frac{3}{9}$$
$$EC = 1$$

8. What is the ratio of the area of the base of a cylinder to the volume of the cylinder if $AO = \sqrt{34}$ and the radius is equal to 3?

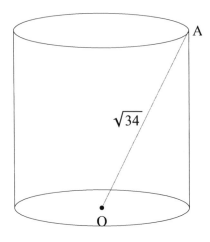

A. $\frac{1}{5}$

B. $\frac{2}{5}$

C. $\frac{3}{10}$

D. $\frac{5}{8}$

E. $\frac{7}{8}$

ANSWER: A. If length $AO = \sqrt{34}$, using the Pythagorean theorem we have:

$$
\begin{aligned}
r^2 + h^2 &= 34 \\
9 + h^2 &= 34 \\
h^2 &= 25 \\
h &= 5
\end{aligned}
$$

The area of a base is given by πr^2 and the volume of the cylinder is given by $V = \pi r^2 h$. Dividing the area of the base by the volume of the cylinder

$$
\frac{\pi r^2}{\pi r^2 h} = \frac{1}{h} = \frac{1}{5}.
$$

9. What is the volume of a cylinder with a hexagonal base with height 20 ft and base-edge length of 15 ft?

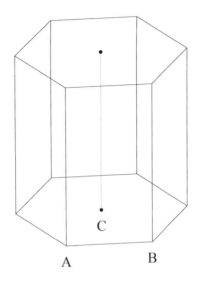

A. $1020\sqrt{2}$

B. $2000\sqrt{2}$

C. $2500\sqrt{2}$

D. $1125\sqrt{3}$

E. $7150\sqrt{3}$

ANSWER: D. Since the area of the base is six times the area of one triangle (shown), we need only find the area of the triangle, multiply that by six, then multiply that by the height, which is given as 20. The question then becomes, what is the area of one triangle? We know the length of the edge of the hexagon, which is also the base of the triangle. If we can find the height of the triangle, we can find the area of the triangle. So now the question becomes, what is the height of the triangle? If AB is 15, then AD is $\frac{15}{2}$. AC is also 15 because the triangles are equilateral. The reason we know that it is an equilateral triangle is because all three angles are sixty degrees The reason the angles are sixty degrees is that $\angle ACB$ is sixty degrees. (One sixth of the 360 degree angle about the center of the hexagon). The remaining angles are also 60 because they are equal, and total 120 degrees.

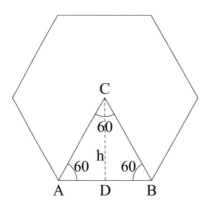

Since $AC = 15$, $h = AC * \frac{\sqrt{3}}{2}$ This is because h is opposite to a sixty degree angle.

Now we have Volume = Area × height = $\frac{1}{2}B \times H \times$ height

$$\frac{1}{2} \times 15 \times \left(\frac{15}{2} \times \sqrt{3}\right) \times 20 = 1125\sqrt{3}$$

10. The surface area of a cubic prism is equal to the volume of a rectangular prism with width and height of 6. What is the ratio of the square of the side of a cube to the length of the rectangular prism?

   A. $1 : 3$

   B. $2 : 3$

   C. $3 : 2$

   D. $6 : 1$

   E. $1 : 6$

ANSWER: D. The surface area of a cube is $6s^2$. The volume of a rectangular prism is Lwh. If $6s^2 = Lwh = 36L$, then

$$\begin{aligned} S^2 &= 6L \\ \frac{S^2}{L} &= 6 \end{aligned}$$

So the ratio is $6 : 1$.

Practice Problems

1. The diagonal AB of the cylinder below is 10, and the diagonal of OB extending from the center of the base is $\sqrt{73}$. What is the radius of the cylinder?

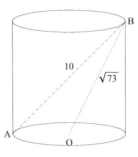

    A. 3
    B. 4
    C. 5
    D. 6
    E. 7

2. In the cylinder of problem 1, what is the ratio of the height to the radius?

    A. $1 : 2$

    B. $2 : 3$

    C. $4 : 7$

    D. $7 : 4$

    E. $8 : 3$

3. In the cube below what is the area of shaded region if the volume of the cube is 27?

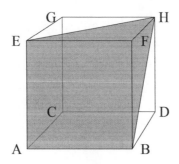

    A. $\frac{20}{3}$

    B. $\frac{21}{5}$

    C. $\frac{27}{2}$

    D. 14

    E. 18

4. In the cubic prism below, diagonal AH is $2\sqrt{6}$. What is the surface area of the prism?

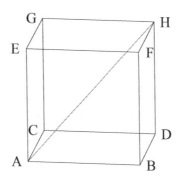

    A. 18

    B. 48

    C. 66

    D. 72

    E. 96

5. The area of the base of a square pyramid is 9, while the height is 3. What is the surface area of the pyramid?

   A. $9 + 2\sqrt{2}$

   B. $9 + 3\sqrt{3}$

   C. $9 + 9\sqrt{5}$

   D. $9 + \sqrt{6}$

   E. $9 + 4\sqrt{7}$

6. The volume of a cylinder is twice the volume of a cone. The height of the cylinder is half the height of the cone. What is the radius of the cone in terms of the radius of the cylinder, r?

   A. $\frac{r\sqrt{3}}{2}$

   B. $\frac{r\sqrt{6}}{2}$

   C. $\frac{r\sqrt{7}}{3}$

   D. $\frac{r\sqrt{11}}{2}$

   E. $\frac{r\sqrt{4}}{3}$

7. The volume of a sphere is given by $\frac{4}{3}\pi r^3$. Which of the following has the same volume as a sphere of radius 3?

   A. A cylinder with height 6 and radius 6

   B. A rectangular prism with height π, length 12, and width 3

   C. A cube with side length 3π

   D. A cylinder with height 2 and radius 4

   E. A rectangular prism with height 2π, length 4, and width 3.

8. Water is drained from a cylindrical tank with radius 4 meters and height 6 meters into a rectangular tank that is 15 meters long, 8 meters wide, and 8 meters high. How many meters high will the water reach in the rectangular tank once the cylindrical tank is empty?

   A. 8

   B. 6

C. $\frac{3\pi}{2}$

D. $\frac{6\pi}{5}$

E. $\frac{4\pi}{5}$

9. The lengths of the sides of a cube were increased so that the surface area of the new cube was 16 times the surface area of the original cube. By what factor did the volume increase?

   A. 4

   B. 16

   C. 32

   D. 64

   E. 96

10. A rectangular prism has dimensions length $= 6$, height $= 3$, width $= 2$. Imagine splitting the prism into two equal prisms by cutting it with a plane parallel to one of the faces. The *total* surface area of the two prisms that result will be greater than the original prism's surface area. However, the amount by which the total surface area increases will depending on how exactly we cut the original prism. If we call the maximum possible increase in surface area A_1 and the minimum possible increase in surface area A_2, what is $A_1 - A_2$?

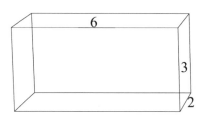

   A. 6
   B. 12
   C. 24
   D. 36
   E. 48

11. The height of a square pyramid is three fourths the height of one triangular surface of the pyramid. What is the area of the base in terms of the height, h?

    A. $\frac{22}{7}h^2$

    B. $\frac{28}{9}h^2$

    C. $\frac{27}{2}h^2$

    D. $\frac{29}{7}h^2$

    E. $\frac{31}{6}h^2$

12. The figure below shows a cone on top of a cylinder. The base of the cone shares the same area as the top of the cylinder. The total volume of the figure is 120π. What is the volume of the cylinder minus the volume of the cone if the height of the cone is equal to the height of the cylinder?

    A. 15π

    B. 30π

    C. 45π

    D. 60π

    E. 75π

13. The volume of a rectangular prism is 12. If each of the 3 integer dimensions of the prism is increased by one unit, the new volume is 36. What is the sum of the dimensions of the new prism?

    A. 7

    B. 10

    C. 13

    D. 14

E. 21

14. What is the length of the diagonal that extends from the center of a base of a cylinder to a point on the edge of the top of the cylinder if the surface area of the cylinder is $24\pi + 16\sqrt{3}\pi$?

A. $2\sqrt{5}$

B. $2\sqrt{6}$

C. $2\sqrt{7}$

D. $4\sqrt{10}$

E. $4\sqrt{11}$

15. What is the volume of a sphere if the surface area of the sphere is 30π?

A. $10\pi\sqrt{\frac{15}{2}}$

B. $12\pi\sqrt{\frac{17}{3}}$

C. $14\pi\sqrt{\frac{19}{4}}$

D. $21\pi\sqrt{\frac{14}{3}}$

E. $28\pi\sqrt{\frac{22}{5}}$

Solutions to Practice Problems

1. **A.**

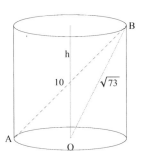

   If r is the radius, the diameter is 2r. We have:

   $$(2r)^2 + h^2 = 10^2$$
   $$r^2 + h^2 = (\sqrt{73})^2$$

   Subtracting the second equation from the first we have:

   $$3r^2 = 27$$
   $$r = 3.$$

2. **E.** We can use the equation $r^2 + h^2 = 73$. Substituting 3 for r, we have:

   $$3^2 + h^2 = 73$$
   $$h^2 = 64$$
   $$h = 8$$

   The ratio then is 8 : 3.

3. **E.** If the volume of the cube is 27, then each side is 3. The area of the shaded region is the area of ABFE plus the area of triangle EHF plus the area of triangle BFH. This is equal to $9 + \frac{9}{2} + \frac{9}{2} = 18$.

4. **B.**

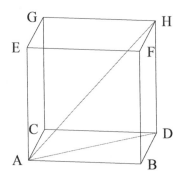

If the diagonal AH is $2\sqrt{6}$ we have using our previous discussion:

$$AH = AB\sqrt{3}$$
$$2\sqrt{6} = AB\sqrt{3}$$
$$AB = 2\sqrt{2}$$

Therefore the dimensions of the cube is $2\sqrt{2} * 2\sqrt{2} * 2\sqrt{2}$, and the surface area is $6 * 2\sqrt{2} * 2\sqrt{2} = 48$

5. **C.**

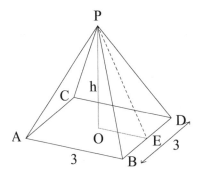

The surface area of the pyramid is the area of the base plus four times the surface area of a face of the pyramid. In order to find the surface area of a face of the pyramid, we need to know only the height of one triangular face and one edge of the base. Since the area of the base is 9 and it is square, we can easily deduce that the length of the edge of the base is 3. Looking at the figure below if the height OP is 3 (given), and OE is $\frac{3}{2}$. Using the Pythagorean theorem:

$$
\begin{aligned}
(PE)^2 &= (OE)^2 + h^2 = \\
&= \left(\frac{3}{2}\right)^2 + 3^2 = \frac{45}{4}. \\
PE &= \frac{3\sqrt{5}}{2}
\end{aligned}
$$

Since the area of a triangle is $\frac{1}{2} \times b \times h$, the area of BPD is $\frac{1}{2} \times 3 \times \frac{3\sqrt{5}}{2}$

The surface area is Base $+ 4 \times$ area of each triangle:

$$
9 + \left(4 \times \frac{9\sqrt{5}}{4}\right) = 9 + 9\sqrt{5}.
$$

6. **A.** If the height of the cone is h, the height of the cylinder is $\frac{h}{2}$. The volume of a cylinder is given by the formula $\pi r^2 h$. The volume of a cone is given by $\frac{1}{3}\pi r^2 h$. If the volume of the cylinder is twice the volume of a cone then, calling the radius of the cone r_2, we have:

$$
\begin{aligned}
\pi r^2 \frac{h}{2} &= 2 \times \frac{1}{3}\pi r_2^2 h. \\
\text{So} \quad \frac{r^2}{2} &= \frac{2}{3}r_2^2.
\end{aligned}
$$

Multiplying both sides of the equation by $\frac{2}{3}$,

$$
\begin{aligned}
\frac{3}{4}r^2 &= r_2^2 \\
r_2 &= \frac{1}{2}\sqrt{3}r.
\end{aligned}
$$

7. **B.** The volume of the sphere is $\frac{4}{3}\pi \times 3^3 = \frac{4}{3}\pi \times 27 = 4\pi \times 9 = 36\pi$. We can test each of the answer choices to see which also gives a volume of 36π:

A. We use $V = \pi r^2 h$, with $r = 6$ and $h = 6$:

$$
V = \pi \times 6^2 \times 6 = \pi \times 36 \times 6 = 196\pi, \text{ which is incorrect}
$$

B. We use $V = lwh$, with $h = \pi$, $l = 12$, and $w = 3$:

$$V = \pi \times 12 \times 3 = 36\pi, \text{ which is the correct value}$$

C. We use $V = s^3$, with $s = 3\pi$:

$$V = (3\pi)^3 = 27\pi^3, \text{ which is incorrect}$$

D. We use $V = \pi r^2 h$, with $r = 4$ and $h = 2$:

$$V = \pi \times 4^2 \times 2 = \pi \times 16 \times 2 = 32\pi, \text{ which is incorrect}$$

E. We use $V = lwh$, with $h = 2\pi$, $l = 4$, and $w = 3$:

$$V = 2\pi \times 4 \times 3 = 24\pi, \text{ which is incorrect}$$

8. **E.** The volume of the cylindrical tank is given by $\pi r^2 h$. Using $r = 4$ and $h = 6$, we then have $V = \pi \times 4^2 \times 6 = \pi \times 16 \times 6 = 96\pi$.

The volume of the water in the rectangular tank is given by lwh, which we set equal to 96π. The height h is the unknown value, so we substitute the values for 15 for l and 8 for w, respectively, and solve for h:

$$
\begin{aligned}
96\pi &= 15 \times 8 \times h \\
96\pi &= 120h \\
\frac{96\pi}{120} &= \frac{120h}{120} \\
\frac{4\pi}{5} &= h
\end{aligned}
$$

9. **D.** The surface area of a cube of side length s is given by $6s^2$. If we let s be the side length of the original cube and x be the side length of the new cube, we have the following:

$$
\begin{aligned}
\text{new surface area} &= 16 \times \text{ (original surface area), which translates into:} \\
6x^2 &= 16 \times 6s^2, \text{ which we solve for } x: \\
x^2 &= 16s^2 \\
x &= 4s.
\end{aligned}
$$

So, the new side length is 4 times the original side length. We use this value, $4s$, to find the new volume. The original volume is given by s^3. We substitute the $4s$ into this equation for s, which gives us the following:

$$(4s)^3 = 64s^3.$$

The volume increased by a factor of 64.

10. **C.**

Cutting the rectangular prism into 2 can be done in 3 ways. The first way will yield 2 equal rectangular prisms of $1 \times 3 \times 6$. There will be an increase in surface area of:

$$(3 \times 6) + (3 \times 6) = 36.$$

The second way will yield 2 equal rectangular prisms of dimension $3 \times 3 \times 2$. The increase in surface area is:

$$(2 \times 3) + (2 \times 3) = 12.$$

The third way will result in two equal rectangular prisms of dimension $6 \times 2 \times 1.5$. The increase in surface area is:

$$(2 \times 6) + (2 \times 6) = 24.$$

Therefore the maximum is 36 and the minimum is 12. The difference is 24.

11. **B.**

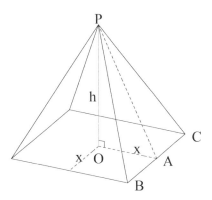

If the height of the pyramid is $\frac{3}{4}$ the height of the triangular surface of the pyramid, the height of the surface is $\frac{4}{3}$ the height of the pyramid. Let x equal the distance between A and O. To find the length AP we have:

$$x^2 + h^2 = (AP)^2 = \left(\frac{4h}{3}\right)^2.$$

Now we have:

$$x = \sqrt{(\frac{4h}{3})^2 - h^2}$$

$$x = \sqrt{\frac{16h^2}{9} - h^2}$$

$$= h * \sqrt{\frac{16}{9} - 1}$$

$$= h * \sqrt{\frac{7}{9}}$$

The area of the base is $(2x)^2$. So:

$$(2x)^2 = (2 * h * \sqrt{\frac{7}{9}})^2$$

$$= 4 * h^2 * \frac{7}{9}$$

$$= \frac{28h^2}{9}$$

12. **D.** There are two ways to solve the problem. Comparing formulas for a cylinder and a cone, the volume of a cone is exactly a third of the volume of a cylinder with the same radius and height. So the ratio of a cone to a cylinder is $1 : 3$. The difference between 1 and 3 is half the total (4). Since the total is 120π, half is 60π.

If this argument did not occur to you, you could also solve it in the following way:

$$\frac{1}{3}\pi r^2 h + \pi r^2 h = 120\pi$$

$$\frac{4}{3}\pi r^2 h = 120\pi$$

$$r^2 h = 90.$$

Therefore the volume of the cylinder is 90π and the volume of the cone is a third of that or 30π. The difference is $90\pi - 30\pi = 60\pi$.

13. **B.** There is an impossible way and an easy way to solve this problem. It is not possible to solve this problem by setting up two simultaneous equations:

$$lwh = 12$$

$$(l+1)(w+1)(h+1) = 36$$

You should immediately see that it is not possible to solve this system of equations because there are three unknowns and only two equations. If you tried to solve it without noticing that problem, you probably grew increasingly frustrated. There must be an easier way!

The easy way is to draw a table:

Possible dimensions before increase:	Possible dimensions after increase:
$1 \times 1 \times 12$	$1 \times 1 \times 36$
$1 \times 2 \times 6$	$1 \times 2 \times 18$
$1 \times 3 \times 4$	$1 \times 3 \times 12$
$2 \times 2 \times 3$ ✓	$1 \times 4 \times 9$
	$1 \times 6 \times 6$
	$2 \times 2 \times 9$
	$2 \times 3 \times 6$
	$3 \times 3 \times 4$ ✓

You can see immediately that the only possible dimensions before the increase are $2 \times 2 \times 3$ as the dimensions after the increase are $3 \times 3 \times 4$, each dimension being one more unit than the initial dimension. The sum then is $3 + 3 + 4 = 10$.

14. **C.** We can tell by the form of the given surface area that the area of the top of the cylinder and base of the cylinder combined is 24π and that the lateral surface area is equal to $16\sqrt{3}\pi$. Since the base and top of the cylinder are equal in area, each has a area of 12π. The area of a the top of the cylinder, being a circle is $\pi * r^2 = 12\pi$. Therefore the radius of the circle is $\sqrt{12}$. The lateral surface area is given by $2\pi * r * h = 16\sqrt{3}\pi$. Therefore $r * h = 8\sqrt{3}$. Since we said that $r = \sqrt{12}$, we have $\sqrt{12}h = 8\sqrt{3}$. So $h = 4$. We can construct a right triangle with its hypotenuse extending from the center of the base of the cylinder to a point on the edge of the top of the cylinder. The distance is $\sqrt{r^2 + h^2}$, where r is the radius of the base of the cylinder and h is the height of the cylinder. This is equal to $\sqrt{12 + 16} = \sqrt{28} = 2\sqrt{7}$.

15. **A.** The volume of a sphere is given by the formula: $\frac{4}{3}\pi r^3$. We need to find r. If the volume of a sphere is 30π, then:

$$\begin{aligned} 4\pi r^2 &= 30\pi \\ r &= \sqrt{\frac{15}{2}} \end{aligned}$$

The volume of the sphere is therefore:

$$\frac{4}{3}\pi \sqrt{\frac{15}{2}}^3 = \frac{4}{3}\pi \times \frac{15}{2}\sqrt{\frac{15}{2}} = 10\pi\sqrt{\frac{15}{2}}.$$

CHAPTER 12

FUNCTIONS AND GRAPHS

Problems that involve coordinate geometry (or analytic geometry) require a solid foundation in both geometry and algebra. In addition, you are expected to know the following concepts and formulas:

Formula of a straight line, $y = mx + b$, where m is the slope of the line and b is the y-intercept;

Formula of a slope, $m = \frac{y1-y0}{x1-x0}$;

Solving a system of equations to find an intersection point;

How the shape of $a * f(x + b) + c$ can be determined knowing only the shape of $f(x)$ without knowing the formula for $f(x)$;

Geometric meaning of inequalities, e.g., $y < x$ represents the set of all points in the plane below the line $y = x$;

To solve the following problem, you need to know how to interpret the effects of each parameter in the general formulas $af(x + b) + c$. The general rules for graphs are:

$|a| > 1$: The graph of $a * f(x)$ is stretched vertically.
$|a| < 1$: The graph of $a * f(x)$ is compressed vertically.
$a > 0$: The graph of $a * f(x)$ has the same vertical orientation as that of $f(x)$.
$a < 0$: The graph of $a * f(x)$ is flipped vertically (reflected about the x-axis).
$b > 0$: The graph of $f(x + b)$ is shifted left b units.
$b < 0$: The graph of $f(x + b)$ is shifted right b units.
$c > 0$: The graph of $f(x) + c$ is shifted up c units.
$c < 0$: The graph of $f(x) + c$ is shifted down c units.

1. The graph of $f(x)$ is shown:

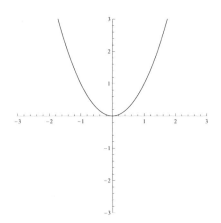

What does the graph of $g(x) = -f(x+1) - 1$ look like?

A.

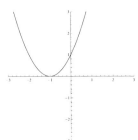

D.

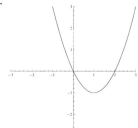

B.

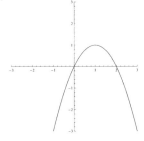

E.

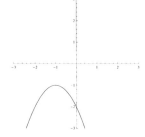

C.

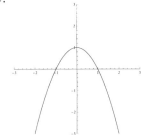

ANSWER: E. The graph is inverted due to the minus sign, shifted left due to $f(x+1)$, and shifted down due to the -1.

2. How does the graph of $-(x-3)^2+4$ compare to x^2?

A. The graph is shifted 3 units to the left and 4 units up.
B. The graph is shifted 3 units to the right, up 4 units, and flipped downwards.
C. The graph is shifted 3 units to the left and flipped downwards.
D. The graph is shifted 4 units to the right and is steeper.
E. The graph is shifted 4 units up and is wider.

ANSWER: B. Looking at the formula for a parabola: $a(x-h)^2+k$, where the vertex is (h,k), the new vertex in our problem is $(3,4)$. The old vertex is $(0,0)$. Thus, the graph shifts every point 3 units to the right and 4 units up. It also flips the graph downwards. The width remains unchanged.

If m is the slope of line AB, then if CD is perpendicular to it, the slope of line CD is $m1 = \frac{-1}{m2}$. To find the equation of a line perpendicular to another line passing through two points, it is necessary to find the slope of the first line, AB, then calculate the slope of the other, CD (by putting a negative sign in front of the slope of the first line and switching the numerator and denominator). After we find the slope of line CD, we use the point-slope method to find the equation of the line. An example is as follows:

3. Find the equation of a line perpendicular to $y = \frac{4}{3}x + \frac{5}{3}$ and passing through $(4,3)$.

A. $y = \frac{3}{4}x + 3$
B. $y = \frac{3}{4}x - 2$
C. $y = \frac{-3}{4}x + 6$
D. $y = \frac{-3}{4}x - 1$
E. $y = \frac{-3}{4}x + 5$

ANSWER: C. If a line has slope m1, the slope of the perpendicular line has slope $\frac{-1}{m1} = m2$. Here the slope of the line is $\frac{4}{3}$, so the slope of the perpendicular line is $\frac{-3}{4}$. We use point $(4,3)$:

$$y = mx + b$$

$$3 = \frac{-3}{4} * 4 + b$$

$$3 = -3 + b$$

$$b = 6$$

So:

$$y = \frac{-3}{4}x + 6$$

4. Which of the following two equations could represent two perpendicular lines:

   A. $y = -2x + 3, y = 4x - 2$
   B. $y = x - 8, y = 8x - 1$
   C. $y = 8x + 1, y = 2x - 8$
   D. $y = -4x + 2, y = \frac{1}{4}x - 1$
   E. $y = 3x - 1, y = 5x + 2$

ANSWER: D. Two lines are perpendicular if the slope of one line, $m1 = \frac{-1}{m2}$, where $m2$ is the slope of the 2nd line. Looking at our answer choices, D is correct since $-4 = \frac{-1}{-1/4}$.

5. Given line AB passing through point A $(1, 1)$ and point B $(3, -3)$, and line CD, $y = 3x + 11$, find the point of intersection of the two lines.

   A. $\left(\frac{4}{5}, \frac{5}{7}\right)$
   B. $\left(\frac{-3}{2}, \frac{6}{7}\right)$
   C. $\left(\frac{14}{5}, \frac{-7}{13}\right)$
   D. $\left(\frac{13}{2}, \frac{29}{5}\right)$
   E. $\left(\frac{-14}{5}, \frac{13}{5}\right)$

ANSWER: E. We find that the slope of line 1 is: $\frac{-3-1}{3-1} = -2$

We use the point $(-3, 3)$:

$$3 = (-2)(-3) + b$$
$$3 = 6 + b$$
$$b = -3$$

Hence the equation of the first line is $y = -2x - 3$

To find the point of intersection we set the two equations equal to each other:

$$-2x - 3 = 3x + 11$$
$$-5x = 14$$
$$x = \frac{-14}{5}$$

We have found the x-coordinate of the point of intersection. To find the y-component, we can use the formula $y = -2x + 3$ to get:

$$y = -2(\frac{-14}{5}) - 3 = \frac{28}{5} - \frac{15}{5} = \frac{13}{5}$$

Therefore the point of intersection is $(\frac{-14}{5}, \frac{13}{5})$.

6. Two points on a line are $(1, 1)$ and $(3, 2)$. Which of the following could also be points on that line?

   A. $(4, 2.5)$
   B. $(9, 8.5)$
   C. $(6, 3.5)$
   D. $(9.5, 11)$

E $(10.5, 12.5)$

ANSWER: A. We find that the slope is $\frac{2-1}{3-1} = \frac{1}{2}$ We use a point on the line, $(1,1)$, then plug in the coordinates of each answer choice that also gives a slope of $\frac{1}{2}$. If we choose the first point $(4, 2.5)$ and $(1, 1)$ We find the slope to be: $\frac{1-2.5}{1-4} = \frac{-1.5}{-3} = \frac{1}{2}$ We can stop here.

Three rules:

1. A function given by $y = \frac{a}{bx+c}$, (for $a, b \neq 0$) has domain of $x \neq \frac{-c}{b}$ and range $y \neq 0$. This is because there is a horizontal asymptote at $y = 0$.

2. A function given by $y = \frac{ax}{bx+c}$, for $a, b \neq 0$ has a domain of $x \neq \frac{-c}{b}$ and a range of $y \neq \frac{a}{b}$ This is because there is a horizontal asymptote at $y = \frac{a}{b}$

3. A function given by $y = \frac{ax^2}{bx+c}$ has no horizontal asymptote, and therefore the range is $(-\infty, \infty)$. The domain is also $x \neq \frac{-c}{b}$.

7. What is the range of $f(x) = \frac{3}{2x+9}$?

A. $(-\infty, \infty)$
B. $(-\infty, 0)$
C. $(0, \infty)$
D. $y \neq 0$
E. $y \neq \frac{3}{2}$

ANSWER: D. From our rules above, $f(x)$ cannot equal zero.

The domain for any function $f(x) = a^{bx+c} + d$ if $a \neq -1, 0, 1$ is $(-\infty, \infty)$. If $a > 0$, the range is (d, ∞). If $a < 0$, the range is $(-\infty, d)$.

8. What is the range of $f(x) = 3^{x-1}$?

A. $(-\infty, \infty)$
B. $(-\infty, 0)$

C. $(0, \infty)$

D. $(-\infty, \frac{1}{3})$

E. $(\frac{-1}{3}, \infty)$

ANSWER: C. From our rules above for exponential functions, the range is $(0, \infty)$ because the constant d is 0.

A function $g(f(x))$ is a function, $g(x)$, of another function, $f(x)$. Two functions $f(x)$ and $g(x)$ are inverse functions if $g(f(x)) = f(g(x)) = x$. To find $g(f(x))$, we can evaluate $f(x)$ for a specific value of x, and then insert the value of $f(x)$ into $g(x)$. For example, if $f(x) = x + 1$ and $g(x)$ is $2x$, and if we are given a point, $x = 2$, then $f(2) = 3$, and $g(f(x)) = g(x = 2) = g(3) = 2 * 3 = 6$. If we do not have a specific value, to find a function in terms of a variable $g(f(x))$, we plug in $(x + 1)$ into $g(x) = g(x + 1) = 2 * (x + 1) = 2x + 2$. To find $f(g(x))$, $f(g(x)) = f(2x) = 2x + 1$. We could also calculate a specific value of a point by first finding the general equation of $g(f(x))$ or $f(g(x))$, and then plugging in a specific value.

9. $g(6) = 21$, $h(x) = g(x + 4) + 3$, $h(2) = $?

A. 15

B. 18

C. 21

D. 24

E. 27

ANSWER: D. To solve this problem, start with $h(x) = g(x + 4) + 3$. If $x = 2$, then we have $h(2) = g(2 + 4) + 3$. $g(2 + 4) = g(6) = 21$ (given). So $h(2) = g(6) + 3$ (given), Therefore $h(2) = 21 + 3 = 24$.

10. $f(x) = x^2 - 1$, $g(x) = \sqrt{x + 1}$. Which of the following is/are true?

I. The functions are inverses of each other.

II. $g(f(x)) = f(g(x))$

III $g(f(x)) = \frac{-1}{x}$

A. I only

B. II only

263

C. I and II only

D. I and III only

E. I, II, and III

ANSWER: C. The functions $f(x)$ and $g(x)$ are inverses because $g(f(x)) = x$ and $f(g(x)) = x$. To prove this,

$$f(g(x)) = f(\sqrt{x+1})$$
$$f(x) = (\sqrt{x+1})^2 - 1$$
$$= x + 1 - 1 = x$$

Similarly,

$$g(f(x)) = \sqrt{x^2 - 1 + 1}$$
$$\sqrt{x^2} = x$$

III is incorrect since $g(f(x)) = x$, not $\frac{-1}{x}$.

Practice Problems

1. One point on a line is $(-16, 1)$. The y-intercept is b. If another point on that line is $(-12, a)$, what is the equation of the line in terms of a and x?

   A. $y = \frac{a-2}{3} + 3a$
   B. $y = \frac{a-1}{4}x + 4a - 3$
   C. $y = 6x - a$
   D. $y = (a+1)x + 16$
   E. $y = \frac{a-1}{a+1} + 2a$

2. A line passes through point $(-3, -10)$. If the slope of the line is m, with b intercept, what is the equation of the line in terms of m and b?

   A. $y = 2mx + 9$
   B. $y = m(x + 3) - 10$
   C. $y = 2m + 11$
   D. $y = m(x - 2) + 4$
   E. $y = (m - 3)x + 3$

3. The inverse of the function of $y = 16x^2 + 1$ is?

   A. $\frac{1-4x}{16x}$
   B. $\frac{1-x}{16x}$
   C. $\frac{1-x^2}{16-x^2}$
   D. $\frac{1}{16x^2} - 1$
   E. $\frac{\sqrt{x-1}}{4}$

4. Which of the following describes the graph of the equation $y = 3x^2 + 6x + 7$?

   I. It is a parabola
   II. It has exactly two real solutions
   III There are no y intercepts

A. I only
B. II only
C. I and II only
D. I and III only
E. I, II, and III

5. In the xy plane, lines AB and CD are perpendicular to each other. Line AB has a slope of 1. The lines intersect at $(-1, -1)$. What is the equation of line CD?

A. $y = -x + 2$
B. $y = -x - 2$
C. $y = -x$
D. $y = x + 1$
E. $y = -x - 1$

6. An absolute value function has a vertex at $(2, 2)$ and intersects the y-axis at $y = 5$. What is the equation of the function in the xy plane?

A. $y = \frac{1}{2}|x + 2| + 2$
B. $y = \frac{-3}{4}|x - 2| + 5$
C. $y = \frac{3}{2}|x - 2| + 2$
D. $y = 5|x + 2| + 2$
E. $y = -4|x - 2| + 2$

7. In the xy-plane, what is the equation of a parabola with a vertex of $(4, -2)$ if it passes through $(7, 13)$?

A. $y = 3x^2 + 18x - 8$
B. $y = 4x^2 - 16x + 9$
C. $y = \frac{5}{3}x^2 - \frac{40}{3}x + \frac{74}{3}$
D. $y = 6x^2 - 17x$
E. $y = 9x^2 + 7$

8. The graph of $f(x)$ is shown:

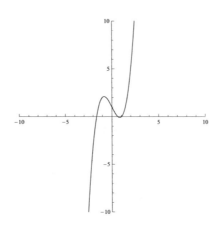

Which of the following is the graph of $-f(x+2) + 3$?

A.

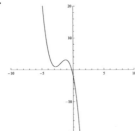

D.

B.

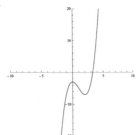

E.

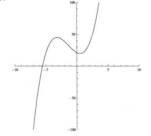

C.

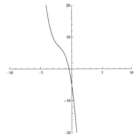

9. The graph of $f(x)$ is shown:

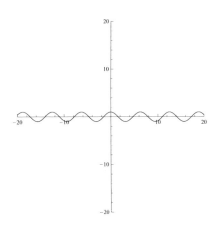

Which of the following represent $-2f(x+2)+1$

A.

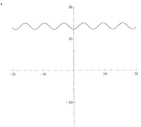

D.

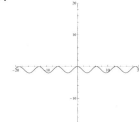

B.

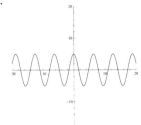

E.

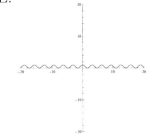

C.

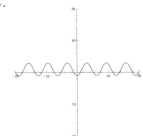

10. A line passes through points $(-4, 0)$ and $(0, 3)$. What is the distance between two points of intersection with the x-axis and the y-axis?

    A. 4
    B. 5
    C. $4\sqrt{2}$
    D. $5\sqrt{2}$
    E. 10

11. The blood level of drug A in a human halves every six hours after it peaks 2 hours after ingestion. After how many hours will only one eighth of the drug remain in the blood stream?

    A. 12 hours
    B. 14 hours
    C. 18 hours
    D. 20 hours
    E. 22 hours

12. Given $f(x) = -2x^2 - 4x - 5$. What is the equation in $ax^2 + bx + c$ format if the graph of $f(x)$ is shifted two units down, left one unit, and flipped downward?

    A. $2x^2 - 3x + 9$
    B. $2x^2 - 4x - 3$
    C. $-2x^2 + 8x - 1$
    D. $2x^2 + 8x + 9$
    E. $4x^2 - 6x + 14$

13. Given $y = -(x - 3)^2 + 2$, what is the distance between the two x-intercepts?

    A. $2\sqrt{2}$
    B. $2\sqrt{2} + 3$
    C. $3\sqrt{2} + 4$
    D. $3\sqrt{3} - 1$
    E. $5\sqrt{3} + 4$

14. A parabola has a vertex of $(2, 4)$ and passes through the point $(3, 0)$. What is the equation of the parabola in the xy plane?

   A. $-4x^2 + 16x - 12$
   B. $4x^2 + 16x - 8$
   C. $6x^2 - 36x + 9$
   D. $-6x^2 + 36x - 2$
   E. $-8x^2 + 41x - 19$

15. Two lines AB and CD are parallel. What is the perpendicular distance between the two lines if line AB intersects the y-axis at -3 and line CD intersects the y-axis at $y = 3$ and the x-axis at -3?

   A. $3\sqrt{2}$
   B. $5\sqrt{2}$
   C. $3\sqrt{3}$
   D. $5\sqrt{3}$
   E. $7\sqrt{3}$

Solutions to Practice Problems

1. **B.** The slope of the line given both points is $\frac{a-1}{-12--16} = \frac{a-1}{4}$. The equation of any line is given by $y = mx + b$. Substituting $\frac{a-1}{4}$ for m, we have:

$$y = \frac{a-1}{4}x + b$$

Using the point $(-16, 1)$, we have:

$$1 = \frac{a-1}{4} * (-16) + b$$
$$1 = \frac{-16a + 16}{4} + b$$
$$1 = -4a + 4 + b$$
$$b = 4a - 3$$

Therefore $y = \frac{a-1}{4}x + 4a - 3$

2. **B.** We have:

$$-10 = m(-3) + b$$
$$-10 + 3m = b$$

Since $y = mx + b$, we have:

$$y = mx + (-10 + 3m)$$
$$y = m(x + 3) - 10$$

3. **E.** To find the inverse of the function, we switch variables to get:

$$x = 16y^2 + 1$$
$$y^2 = \frac{x-1}{16}$$
$$y = \pm\frac{\sqrt{x-1}}{4}$$

Since we are interested in the inverse of the function to be a function, we choose the expression to be positive.

4. **A.** It is a parabolic function since it is a polynomial of degree 2. To find the number of solution a parabolic function has, analyze the determinant $= \sqrt{b^2 - 4ac}$. Here the determinant is $\sqrt{36 - 4*3*7} = \sqrt{-48}$. Since this does not represent a real number, the function has no zeros (x-intercepts), and therefore has no real solutions. There is always a y-intercept for any parabolic function as the domain always includes zero (and every other real value).

5.**B.** We must find the equation of the line CD in the form $y = mx + b$. The slope of line AB is 1, therefore the slope of line CD is $(\frac{-1}{1}) = -1$. Therefore the equation for the line is:

$$y = -x + b$$

Plugging in the point $(-1, -1)$, we have:

$$-1 = -(-1) + b$$
$$b = -2$$

The equation is therefore $y = -x - 2$.

6. **C.** We have $y = a|x - b| + c$, where (b, c) is the vertex. Plugging in $b = 2$ and $c = 2$, we have:

$$y = a|x - 2| + 2$$

We need to find a. Using the point $(0, 5)$ which is the y-intercept, we have:

$$\begin{aligned}
5 = a|0 - 2| + 2 \\
= 2a + 2 \\
2a + 2 = 5 \\
a = \frac{3}{2}
\end{aligned}$$

So the equation is $y = \frac{3}{2}|x - 2| + 2$

7. **C.** First solve for a $y = a(x - h)^2 + k$ form. We have:

$$y = a(x - 4)^2 - 2$$

Plugging in $(7, 13)$:

$$\begin{aligned}
13 = a(7 - 4)^2 - 2 \\
13 = 9a - 2 \\
a = \frac{15}{9} = \frac{5}{3}
\end{aligned}$$

We have:

$$y = \frac{5}{3}(x-4)^2 - 2$$

$$y = \frac{5}{3}(x-4)(x-4) - 2$$

$$y = \frac{5}{3}x^2 - \frac{40}{3}x + \frac{80}{3} - \frac{6}{3}$$

$$y = \frac{5}{3}x^2 - \frac{40}{3}x + \frac{74}{3}$$

The purpose of the solution above it to show you how to find the answer if you didn't have answer choices. For this test, use the quickest method, so plug 7 into each equation and see which one yields 13.

8. **A.** The original graph increases on the interval $(-\infty, -1)$ and $(1, -\infty)$. Since a negative sign is placed in front of the graph of $-f(x+2)+3$, we are looking for a function which decreases on those intervals. Looking at the answer choices, we can eliminate choices B and E. Next, we want the crest at point $(1, 2)$ on the original graph to be a local minimum on the new graph, and specifically shifted 2 to the left. Looking at the graphs, the graph in A has a local minimum at x = -3. Thus A is the correct answer.

9. **C.** Use the process of elimination here. The new graph could not be A because the graph shifts up one unit only, and it is obvious from inspection that the graph in A shifts up by more than one unit. Eliminate D and E because the -2 in front of the $f(x+2)$ amplifies the waves, but the waves are not amplified in D and E. So the choice is between B and C. The original graph has a range of 1 between trough to crest. Since the function is amplified by a factor of 2, we want a function that has a range of 2. Looking at the graphs of B and C, B has a range of 5, while C has a range of 2. Therefore we choose choice C.

10. **B.** The line stretches from $(-4, 0)$ point to $(0, 3)$ on the x-axis. We need simply to find the distance between the two points. Using the Pythagorean Theorem, the distance is $\sqrt{3^2 + (-4)^2} = 5$.

11. **D.** The function of an exponential decay with a half life is: $f(x) = k * \left(\frac{1}{2}\right)^x$, where $x =$ the amount of time passed every time the amount is halved and k is the original amount. Here, $x =$ number of 6-hour periods. When will $k\left(\frac{1}{2}\right)^x = \frac{1}{8}k$? When $x = 3$.

So an eighth remains 18 hours past peak. The peak occurs after 2 hours, so the total time it takes is 20 hours.

12. **D.** Given $-2x^2 - 4x - 5$ We can simply multiply $f(x)$ by -1, substitute $x + 1$ for x and subtract 2:

$$2(x+1)^2 + 4(x+1) + 5 - 2 =$$
$$2(x^2 + 2x + 1) + 4x + 4 + 3 =$$
$$2x^2 + 4x + 2 + 4x + 7 =$$
$$2x^2 + 8x + 9$$

13. **A.** We set $y = 0$ to find the x-intercepts. So we have:

$$0 = -(x-3)^2 + 2$$
$$-2 = -(x-3)^2$$
$$2 = (x-3)^2$$
$$x = \pm\sqrt{2} + 3$$

The distance is $(+\sqrt{2} + 3) - (-\sqrt{2} + 3) = 2\sqrt{2}$

14. **A.** We set $y = a(x-2)^2 + 4$. We need to find a. If we plug in one point $(3, 0)$, we get:

$$0 = a(3-2)^2 + 4$$
$$a = -4$$

Therefore we have:

$$y = -4(x-2)^2 + 4$$
$$y = -4(x-2)(x-2) + 4$$
$$y = -4(x^2 - 4x + 4) + 4$$
$$y = -4x^2 + 16x - 12$$

Again, the quickest solution is to plug in 3 into x and find which equation yields zero.

15. **A.** As you can see from the graph, ONE line perpendicular to both lines AB and CD extends from $(-3, 0)$ to $(0, -3)$. This is because the slope of line CD and AB is 1 (because line CD extends from $(-3, 0)$ to $(0, 3)$., so the slope of the perpendicular line is -1, which extends from $(-3, 0)$ to $(0, -3)$. Using the Pythagorean Theorem, the distance of that line is $\sqrt{3^2 + 3^2} = 3\sqrt{2}$.

CHAPTER 13

FINAL EXAM

1. Given that $|x| > 1$, which of the following is NECESSARILY true?

    I. $x^3 > x^4$
   II. $x^2 - 1 > 0$
  III. $\sqrt[3]{x} > \frac{1}{x}$

A. I only
B. II only
C. I and III
D. II and III
E. I, II, and III

2. If n is an integer not equal to 1 or -1 then all of the following expressions could equal an odd integer EXCEPT

    I. $3n^2 + 6n + 3$
   II. $n^3 - n^2$
  III. $n^4 + n^3$

A. I only
B. I and II
C. I and III
D. II and III
E. I, II and III

3. The angles of a triangle are in the ratio 2x:4x:Kx. What is the largest integer value of K for the triangle to be a right?

A. 2
B. 4
C. 6
D. 8
E. 10

4. For the function g, $g(x)$ is inversely proportional to x, where $x > 0$. If $g(3) = 5$, then what is the value of $g(2)$?

A. $\frac{3}{5}$
B. $\frac{5}{3}$

C. $\frac{3}{10}$

D. $\frac{2}{15}$

E. $\frac{15}{2}$

5. If x and y are real numbers, then $x \odot y$ is the average of $x + y$ and xy. Suppose that $x \odot y = x$. Which of the following is an expression for y in terms of x?

A. $\frac{x}{2}$

B. $\frac{x+y+xy}{2}$

C. $\frac{x}{x+1}$

D. $\frac{x}{2x}$

E. $x - x(2x)$

6. Jamece picks a positive integer, which she names j_1, and writes it down. She multiplies j_1 by 8, then divides by 5, and writes down the REMAINDER, which she names j_2. She continues this pattern (in other words, j_n is the remainder when $8 * j_{n-1}$ is divided by 5) indefinitely. The number 1 is nowhere in her list. What is the 50th number in her list?

A. 0

B. 1

C. 2

D. 3

E. 4

7. Given $x^6 > x^2$ and $n^6 < n^2$, which of the following must be true?

I. $x > n$

II. $x > 1$ or $x < -1$

III. $x^6 > n^6$

A. I only

B. I and II only

C. II and III only

D. I and III only

E. I, II, and III

8. In the figure below, what is the value of x?

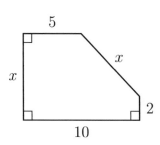

A. $\frac{12}{5}$
B. 5
C. 7
D. $\frac{29}{4}$
E. $\frac{15}{2}$

9. The three inscribed circles are tangent to each other and to the rectangle as shown. If the radius of each of the smaller circles is 1, what is the length of the rectangle?

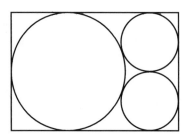

(a) $5 + \sqrt{3}$

(b) $3 + \sqrt{5}$

(c) $6\sqrt{2}$

(d) $3 + 2\sqrt{2}$

(e) $4 + 2\sqrt{2}$

10. The graph of $f(x)$ is shown:

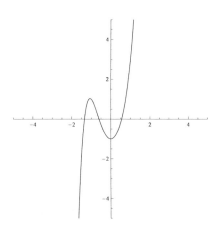

Which of the following is the graph of $-f(x) - 2$?

A.

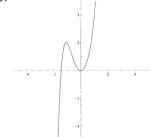

D.

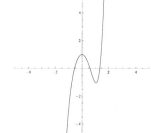

B.

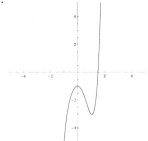

E.

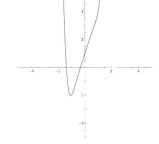

C.

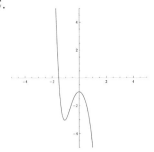

11. In football, you can score by getting a field goal (worth 3 points), a touchdown (worth $6 + 1 = 7$ points if you make the extra point), or a safety (worth 2 points). In a game where there is exactly one safety and an extra point is made after every touchdown, which of the following final scores is NOT possible?

    A. 21 to 14
    B. 14 to 3
    C. 19 to 12
    D. 10 to 3
    E. 14 to 7

12. Ben and Sarah both love to bike. Sarah can ride 12 miles in 45 minutes, but it takes Ben an hour to travel that far. They recently bought a tandem bike which allows them to combine their efforts, with an efficiency loss of one-fourth (so if Sarah rode the tandem with a clone of herself, she could ride $\left(\frac{3}{4}\right)(12 + 12) = 18$ miles in the same 45 minutes). How long would it take Ben and Sarah to travel 42 miles together on the tandem bike?

    A. 40 minutes
    B. 1 hour
    C. 1 hour and 30 minutes
    D. 2 hours
    E. 3 hours and 15 minutes

13. A set of numbers consists of all positive three-digit integers containing at least two digits that are a 1. What is the probability, rounded to the nearest hundredth, that a number chosen at random from this set is a multiple of 3?

    A. 0.09
    B. 0.13
    C. 0.17
    D. 0.26
    E. 0.31

14. If a, b, and c are constants, what is the maximum number of solutions to the system of equations: $x^2 + y^2 = 100$, $y = ax^2 + bx + c$?

    A. 2
    B. 3
    C. 4
    D. 5
    E. 6

15. Joe is 12 miles east of Jack. Joe bikes north at 10 miles per hour. At the same time, Jack bikes south at 8 miles per hour. After half an hour, how many miles apart are Joe and Jack?

    A. 12
    B. 13
    C. 14
    D. 15
    E. 16

16. Rain falls on a cubic block of solid wood (with sides of length 16 inches in each direction) that is left outside, soaking the five out of six faces which are exposed to the air. If this block is cut into 2-inch cubes, what proportion of these cubes will have more than one wet face?

    (A) $\frac{45}{512}$
    (B) $\frac{7}{64}$
    (C) $\frac{49}{256}$
    (D) $\frac{9}{32}$
    (E) $\frac{35}{128}$

17. Arnold and Brian are getting books for their classes. Arnold only needs to get one book for each class he is taking, but Brian, who is taking two fewer classes than Arnold, has to get three books for each of his classes. They end up getting a combined total of 18 books. How many classes is Brian taking?

    (A) 2
    (B) 3
    (C) 4
    (D) 5
    (E) 6

18. In the square pyramid below, the area of the base is 16. The height of the pyramid is 8. What is the surface area of the pyramid?

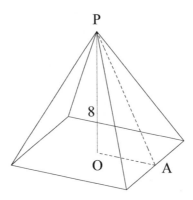

(a) $2\sqrt{15} + 8$

(b) $4\sqrt{17} + 16$

(c) $4\sqrt{19} + 18$

(d) $4\sqrt{23} + 24$

(e) $4\sqrt{23} + 28$

19. A quadrilateral has endpoints at $(1,6)$, $(4,7)$, $(6,1)$, and $(2,0)$. Which term describes this shape as specifically as possible?

   (a) Quadrilateral

   (b) Trapezoid

   (c) Parallelogram

   (d) Rectangle

   (e) Square

20. For what values of x would the below expression be real?

$$\frac{\sqrt{-x+3}+\sqrt{-2x-1}}{2x}$$

   A. $\frac{-1}{2} < x < 3, x \neq 0$

   B. $0 < x < 3, x \neq \frac{-1}{2}$

   C. $0 < x < \frac{-1}{2}$

   D. $x < 3, x \neq \frac{-1}{2}$

   E. $x < \frac{-1}{2}$

FINAL SOLUTIONS

1. **(B)** I is false since $(-2)^3 = 8 \not> 16 = (-2)^4$. II is true because of the following equivalences:

$$|x| > 1 \iff x^2 > 1 \iff x^2 - 1 > 0$$

III is false, since $\sqrt[3]{-27} = -3 \not> \frac{1}{-27}$.

2. **(D)** First note that for any integer n, if n is odd then both $n+1$ and $n-1$ are even, and if n is even then both $n+1$ and $n-1$ are odd. Thus, any product of integers that contains two consecutive integers, i.e. both n and $n+1$ (or $n-1$), must be even for ANY n, since even $\times$ odd $=$ odd $\times$ even $=$ even.

 I. $3n^2 + 6n + 3 = 3(n^2 + 2n + 1) = 3(n+1)^2$ can be either even or odd.

 II. $n^3 - n^2 = n^2(n-1)$ contains both n and $n-1$ so it must be even.

 III. $n^4 + n^3 = n^3(n+1)$ contains both n and $n+1$ so it must be even.

For any integer n, expressions II and III are always even, and can never be odd, whereas expression I can be either odd or even, depending on the value of n, so the answer is II and III.

3. **(C)** For any right triangle, one angle is 90 degrees and the sum of the other two angles is also 90 degrees. Therefore one of the following three cases are possible:

$$\begin{aligned}
Kx &= 2x + 4x = 90 \qquad\qquad (1)\\
Kx &= 6x = 90\\
x &= 15, K = 6
\end{aligned}$$

$$\begin{aligned}
2x &= Kx + 4x = 90 \qquad\qquad (2)\\
2x &= (K+4)x = 90\\
x &= 45\\
K + 4 &= \frac{90}{45} = 2\\
K &= -2
\end{aligned}$$

$$
\begin{aligned}
4x &= Kx + 2x = 90 \\
4x &= (K+2)x = 90 \\
x &= \frac{90}{4} = \frac{45}{2} \\
K+2 &= \frac{90}{x} = \frac{90}{1} \times \frac{2}{45} = 4 \\
K+2 &= 4 \\
K &= 2
\end{aligned}
\tag{3}
$$

The second case is not acceptable since we cannot have negative angles. $K = 6$ is the largest possible integer K value that results in a right triangle.

4. **(E)** $g(x)$ is inversely proportional to x means that $g(x) = \frac{k}{x}$ for some constant k. Since $g(3) = 5$, $g(x)$ is equal to 5 when x is 3. We can substitute these values in the equation above and solve for k:

$$
\begin{aligned}
g(x) &= \frac{k}{x} \\
g(3) &= \frac{k}{3} \\
5 &= \frac{k}{3} \\
k &= 15.
\end{aligned}
$$

Substituting the value of k into the original equation gives us $g(x) = \frac{15}{x}$. We now substitute the 2 into this equation to find $g(2)$. Thus, $g(2) = \frac{15}{2}$.

5. **(C)**
$$
\frac{x+y+xy}{2} = x,
$$
so
$$
y + xy - x = 0.
$$
Thus,
$$
y = \frac{x}{x+1}
$$

6. **(A)** If you picked B, reread the question! As a quick experiment will show, no matter what number j_1 is, the pattern turns into a repeated cycle of the form 1, 3, 4, 2, 1, 3, 4, 2, ... unless j_1 is divisible by 5. So j_1 must be divisible by 5, in which case the pattern goes: j_1, 0, 0, 0, ...

7. **(C)** If $x^6 > x^2$, then x must be greater than 1 or less than -1. If $n^6 < n^2$, $-1 < n < 1$, $n \neq 0$. I is false because x can be smaller than -1 and n is greater than -1. II is true according to the above. x^6 is always greater than 1 but n^6 must be smaller than 1, therefore III is true.

8. **(D)** It helps to complete the partial rectangle, as shown below.

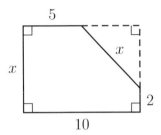

Based on this figure, we can use the Pythagorean theorem to get the equation

$$(x - 2)^2 + 5^2 = x^2.$$

Expanding this yields

$$x^2 - 4x + 4 + 25 = x^2.$$

The x^2 terms cancel, and we can move the x term to the right hand side to get $29 = 4x$, which leads to the answer of $x = \frac{29}{4}$.

9. **(D)** To find the length of the rectangle, we will find the distance d from the center of the large circle to the point where the two smaller circles meet, then add the radius of the big circle and the radius of one of the smaller circles. To find d, we construct an isosceles triangle with corners at the center of each of the three circles, making d the height of the triangle. The two long sides each have length 3, while the short side has length 2. Using the Pythagorean theorem we have: $d^2 + 1^2 = 3^2$, so $d^2 = 8$, and $d = 2\sqrt{2}$. Thus, the length of the base of the rectangle is

$$2 + d + 1 = 2 + 2\sqrt{2} + 1 = 3 + 2\sqrt{2}.$$

10. **(C)** We are looking for a function that decreases on the interval $(-\infty, -2)$ and $(0, \infty)$. This is because the original function increases on those intervals, but our new function has a negative sign placed in front of the $f(x)$. Looking at the graphs, the only choice is (C)

11. **(D)** Try to replicate each of the possible answers:

A. 21 to 14 is possible - (one safety + four field goals + one touchdown with an extra point: $2 + 4 \cdot 3 + 7 = 21$) and (two touchdowns with extra points: $2 \cdot 7 = 14$).

B. 14 to 3 is possible - (one safety + four field goals: $2 + 4 \cdot 3 = 14$) and (one field goal: 3).

C. 19 to 12 is possible - (one safety + one field goal + two touchdowns with extra points: $2 + 3 + 2 \cdot 7 = 19$) and (four field goals: $4 \cdot 3 = 12$).

D. 10 to 3 is not possible because the only way for the losing team to end up with 3 points is to score one field goal. So the winning team must have been the one to score the safety. This means that they would need to score the other 8 points with some combination of field goals and touchdowns. Two or more touchdown wouldn't work because there would be too many points. One touchdown wouldn't work because there would be 1 point left over. Also, zero touchdowns wouldn't work because you can't score exactly 8 points with just field goals.

E. 14 to 7 is possible - (one safety + four field goals: $2 + 4 \cdot 3 = 14$) and (one touchdown with an extra point: 7).

12. **(D)** Ben can ride at a pace of 12 miles per hour, but Sarah can ride at 12 miles per 45 minutes, or 16 miles per hour. So their combined rate, with a $\frac{1}{4}$ efficiency loss, is $\left(\frac{3}{4}\right)(12 + 16) = 21$ miles per hour, or $\frac{1}{21}$ of an hour per mile. Then 42 miles would take them $\frac{42}{21} = 2$ hours.

13. **(D)** If you write out all of the positive three-digit integers that contain at least two digits that are a 1, you will see that there are 27 of them (including 111, which contains three ones). To figure out which of those numbers are divisible by 3, use a quick trick you may already know—any integer is divisible by 3 if the sum of its digits is also divisible by 3. You can quickly determine that 7 of the numbers are divisible by 3: {111, 114, 117, 141, 171, 411, 711}. Therefore, the probability that one of those 27 numbers is divisible by 3 is: $\frac{7}{27} = 0.26$.

14. **(C)** The first equation is a circle of radius 10 centered at the origin. The second equation is the standard form of a parabola. A parabola can intersect a circle at most four times, so there are at most four solutions to the system of equations.

    One can also solve this problem thinking algebraically, rather than geometrically. To use this algebraic approach, plug the value of y from the second equation into the first: $x^2 + y^2 = x^2 + (ax^2 + bx + c)^2 = 100$. This gives a *quartic* (that is, fourth-degree) polynomial, which can have as many as four solutions. Each solution for x in this polynomial will lead to a corresponding value of y, given by $y = ax^2 + bx + c$.

15. **(D)** The distance between them after a period of time is the length of the hypotenuse of the triangle whose sides are the vertical and horizontal distance between them. After half an hour Joe has traveled $\frac{10}{2} = 5$ miles north and Jack has traveled $\frac{8}{2} = 4$ miles south, making the vertical distance between them 9 miles. The horizontal distance between them is still 12 miles. By the Pythagorean theorem, the hypotenuse is 15 miles.

16. **(B)** Cutting up the block will yield $8^3 = 512$ smaller cubes. Of these, only the ones that were originally along the edges or corners of two wet faces will have more than one wet face (to visualize this, draw a picture). On the top, there are 4 corner cubes with three wet faces and $4 \cdot 6 = 24$ cubes with two wet faces along the edges formed by the upper face and the side faces of the block. In addition, there are $4 \cdot 7 = 28$ more cubes with two wet faces along the edges where the side faces of the block meet. This yields a total of $4 + 24 + 28 = 56$ out of the 512 cubes having more than one wet face. $\frac{56}{512}$ reduces to $\frac{7}{64}$.

17. **(C)** Let A be the number of classes Arnold is taking and B be the number of classes Brian is taking. Then
$$A - B = 2$$
and
$$A + 3B = 18$$
Subtracting the first equation from the second yields
$$4B = 16$$
$$B = 4$$

18. **(B)** If the area of the base is 16, each length is 4, and the length of AO is 2. Using the Pythagorean theorem:
$$\begin{aligned} (AC)^2 &= 8^2 + 2^2 = 68 \\ AC &= \sqrt{68}. \end{aligned}$$

This is the height of one triangular surface of a pyramid. Since the length of the base is 4, we have the area of the surface of the pyramid as:

$$\frac{1}{2} \times \sqrt{68} \times 4 + 16 = 4\sqrt{17} + 16.$$

19. **(A)** The shape is drawn below:

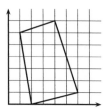

It may be clear from the picture that none of the sides are parallel, and so the answer must be (A), but let's see how to determine the answer without having a figure.

The first thing to determine is the slopes of the sides. The line from $(1,6)$ to $(4,7)$ has a slope of $\frac{7-6}{4-1} = \frac{1}{3}$. The line from $(4,7)$ to $(6,1)$ has a slope of $\frac{1-7}{6-4} = \frac{-6}{2} = -3$. Continuing around, the next two slopes are $\frac{0-1}{2-6} = \frac{-1}{-4} = \frac{1}{4}$ and $\frac{6-0}{1-2} = -6$.

Since none of the slopes are equal, none of the sides are parallel, so the shape is nothing more specific than a quadrilateral.

(If we had found that some of the slopes were equal, then we would have to see which sides' lengths were equal and which angles were right angles in order to determine what kind of quadrilateral we were dealing with.)

20. **(E)** Because of the first square root expression, x must be smaller than 3. Because of the second square root expression, x must be smaller than $-1/2$. The denominator must not equal zero, thus x cannot equal zero. Therefore, x must be smaller than $-1/2$.

Made in the USA